# Microsoft Dynamics AX 2009 Development Cookbook

Solve real-world Dynamics AX development problems with over 60 simple but incredibly effective recipes

**Mindaugas Pocius**

BIRMINGHAM - MUMBAI

# Microsoft Dynamics AX 2009 Development Cookbook

First published: December 2009

Production Reference: 1111209

Published by Packt Publishing Ltd.
32 Lincoln Road
Olton
Birmingham, B27 6PA, UK.

ISBN 978-1-847199-42-3

www.packtpub.com

Cover Image by Parag Kadam (paragvkadam@gmail.com)

# Credits

**Author**

Mindaugas Pocius

**Reviewers**

David Probst

Fred Shen

**Acquisition Editor**

Douglas Paterson

**Development Editor**

Ved Prakash Jha

**Technical Editor**

Pallavi Kachare

**Copy Editor**

Leonard D'Silva

**Editorial Team Leader**

Akshara Aware

**Project Team Leader**

Lata Basantani

**Project Coordinator**

Srimoyee Ghoshal

**Proofreader**

Chris Smith

**Indexer**

Rekha Nair

**Production Coordinator**

Dolly Dasilva

**Cover Work**

Dolly Dasilva

# About the Author

**Mindaugas Pocius** is currently a freelance Dynamics AX technical and functional consultant and trainer at DynamicsLab Limited (www.dynamicslab.com). The company specializes in providing development, consulting, and training services for Microsoft Dynamics AX resellers and customers.

Mindaugas started his IT consultant career back in 2001 while still in his Information Technology Master Studies in Lithuanian university. Since then he has become a recognized Microsoft Certified Professional for AX in all major areas: Development (including Enterprise Portal), Configuration & Installation, Financials, Project, Trade & Logistics. He is also a Certified Microsoft Trainer for Dynamics AX and has delivered numerous Dynamics AX Development and Financial trainings across the Europe.

From 2001 till 2009, Mindaugas participated in over 15 Dynamics AX implementations, ranging from small 10-15 to international 100-500 user projects. He has had a wide range of development, consulting, and leading roles while always maintaining a significant role as a business application developer.

I would like to thank my family for their support during the writing of this book, for their understanding of my long hours spent on this work. I would also like to thank all the people who made this book possible.

# About the Reviewers

**David Probst** has a background in Economics and Computer Science and has been working professionally on Microsoft Dynamics AX since 2001, focusing on specific modules including CRM, Service Management, Shop Floor Control, and Environmental Sustainability.

**Fred Shen** started to work with Dynamics AX in 2004. He was a team member on the very first AX project localizing AX for the Chinese market. After that, he worked for a leading service provider of business, information technology, and communications solutions—Fujitsu Australia. In 2008, he joined Epartners Australia as a senior technical consultant.

Fred Shen is also one of the webmasters in MBSCN.NET, the Chinese Microsoft Dynamics user group. He was recognized as a Dynamics AX Most Valuable Professional for the contribution he has made to the Chinese Dynamics AX communities.

# Table of Contents

# Preface

As a Dynamics AX developer, your responsibility is to deliver all kinds of application customizations, whether they are small adjustments or bespoke modules. Dynamics AX is a highly customizable system and requires a significant amount of knowledge and experience to deliver quality solutions. A single goal can be achieved in multiple ways, and there is always a question—which way is the best?

This book takes you through numerous practically proven recipes to help you with the daily development tasks. Each recipe contains detailed step-by-step instructions along with application screenshots and in-depth explanations. The recipes cover multiple Dynamics AX modules, and as a result, the book gives a developer an overview of the functional aspects of the system too.

## What this book covers

The book's content is presented in six chapters covering the following areas:

Chapter 1, *Processing Data* focuses on data manipulation. It explains how to build data queries, how to check and modify existing data, and how to read or write comma-separated and XML files.

Chapter 2, *Working with Forms* covers the various aspects of using Dynamics AX forms. In this chapter, dialogs and their events are explained. Various useful features like splitters, saving last values, changing form appearance, dynamic controls, and others are also explained.

Chapter 3, *Working with Data in Forms* basically supplements the previous chapter and explains about data organization in forms. The examples in this chapter include instructions on how to build form data filters, process multiple records at a time, create data wizards, checklists, and the use of colors and images.

Chapter 4, *Building Lookups* covers all kinds of lookups in the system. The chapter starts with a simple automatically generated lookup, continues with more advanced ones, and finishes with standard Windows lookups like the file selection dialog or the color picker.

Chapter 5, *Processing Business Tasks* explains the usage of Dynamics AX business logic API. This chapter discusses topics on processing journals, purchase, and sales orders. Other features like posting financial vouchers directly, modifying transaction texts and creating electronic payment formats are included too.

Chapter 6, *Integration with Microsoft Office* shows how MS Word, Excel, Outlook, and Project can be used with Dynamics AX.

## Who this book is for

This book is for Dynamics AX developers primarily focused on delivering time-proven application modifications. Although new X++ developers could use this book along with their beginner's guides, this book is more focused on people who are willing to raise their programming skills above the beginner's level and at the same time learn the functional aspects of Dynamics AX. So, some Dynamics AX coding experience is expected.

## What you need for this book

All the coding examples were done in virtual Microsoft Dynamics AX 2009 Image from Microsoft Learning Download Centre. The following list of software from the virtual image was used in this book:

- Microsoft Windows Server 2003 Enterprise Edition (Service Pack 2)
- Dynamics AX 2009 RTM (kernel version: 5.0.593.0, application version: 5.0.593.0)
- Microsoft Office Excel 2007
- Microsoft Office Word 2007
- Microsoft Office Outlook 2007
- Microsoft Office Project 2007 (installed manually as an additional component)
- Notepad
- Internet Explorer 7

The mentioned software does not necessary have to be in a virtual image. The recipes could be implemented in any Dynamics AX 2009 RTM environment with no previous modifications.

Although all recipes were tested on the mentioned software, they might work on older or newer software versions without any implications or with minor code adjustments.

# Conventions

In this book, you will find a number of styles of text that distinguish between different kinds of information. Here are some examples of these styles, and an explanation of their meaning.

Code words in text are shown as follows: "We call the table's `renamePrimaryKey()`, which does the actual renaming."

A block of code will be set as follows:

```
numRef.DataTypeId = typeId2ExtendedTypeId(typeid(EmplId));
numRef.ReferenceHelp = literalstr("Employee identification");
numRef.WizardContinuous      = false;
numRef.WizardManual          = NoYes::No;
numRef.WizardAllowChangeDown = NoYes::Yes;
```

When we wish to draw your attention to a particular part of a code block, the relevant lines or items will be shown in bold:

```
public server static NumberSequenceReference numRefEmplId()
{
    return NumberSeqReference::findReference(
        typeid2extendedtypeid(typeid(EmplId)));
}
```

The code in this book generally follows the best practice guidelines provided by Microsoft, but there are some exceptions:

▶ No text labels were used to make the code clear.

▶ No three letter codes in front of each new AOT object were used.

▶ No configuration or security keys were used.

▶ Object properties that are not relevant to the topic being discussed are not set.

Some other considerations:

▶ Each recipe demonstrates the principle and is not a complete solution.

▶ The assumption is that no other modifications are present in the system.

▶ The code might not have all possible validations that are not relevant to the principle being explained.

▶ To demonstrate the principle and simplify the demonstration, the code in some recipes is placed in a job or in the `main()` of a newly created class to make sure it can be executed from AOT.

▶ The code might have more variables than required to make sure it is clear for all audiences.

▶ Sometimes unnecessary code wrapping is used to make sure the code fits into the page width of this book and is easily readable.

New terms and important words are shown in bold. Words that you see on the screen, in menus or dialog boxes for example, appear in our text like this: "Click **Transactions** to note the existing transactions:"

# Reader feedback

Feedback from our readers is always welcome. Let us know what you think about this book—what you liked or may have disliked. Reader feedback is important for us to develop titles that you really get the most out of.

To send us general feedback, simply drop an email to feedback@packtpub.com, and mention the book title in the subject of your message.

If there is a book that you need and would like to see us publish, please send us a note in the SUGGEST A TITLE form on www.packtpub.com or email suggest@packtpub.com.

If there is a topic that you have expertise in and you are interested in either writing or contributing to a book, see our author guide on www.packtpub.com/authors.

# Customer support

Now that you are the proud owner of a Packt book, we have a number of things to help you to get the most from your purchase.

## Downloading the example code for the book

Visit http://www.packtpub.com/files/code/9423_Code.zip to directly download the example code.

The downloadable files contain instructions on how to use them.

## Errata

Although we have taken every care to ensure the accuracy of our contents, mistakes do happen. If you find a mistake in one of our books—maybe a mistake in text or code—we would be grateful if you would report this to us. By doing so, you can save other readers from frustration, and help us to improve subsequent versions of this book. If you find any errata, please report them by visiting http://www.packtpub.com/support, selecting your book, clicking on the **let us know** link, and entering the details of your errata. Once your errata are verified, your submission will be accepted and the errata added to any list of existing errata. Any existing errata can be viewed by selecting your title from http://www.packtpub.com/support.

# Piracy

Piracy of copyright material on the Internet is an ongoing problem across all media. At Packt, we take the protection of our copyright and licenses very seriously. If you come across any illegal copies of our works in any form on the Internet, please provide us with the location address or web site name immediately so that we can pursue a remedy.

Please contact us at copyright@packtpub.com with a link to the suspected pirated material.

We appreciate your help in protecting our authors, and our ability to bring you valuable content.

# Questions

You can contact us at questions@packtpub.com if you are having a problem with any aspect of the book, and we will do our best to address it.

# 1
# Processing Data

In this chapter, we will cover the following topics:

- ▶ Creating a new number sequence
- ▶ Renaming the primary key
- ▶ Merging two records
- ▶ Adding document handling notes
- ▶ Using a normal table as temporary table
- ▶ Copying a record
- ▶ Building a query object
- ▶ Using a macro in a SQL statement
- ▶ Executing a direct SQL statement
- ▶ Enhancing the data consistency check
- ▶ Exporting to an XML file
- ▶ Importing from an XML file
- ▶ Creating a comma-separated value file
- ▶ Reading a comma-separated value file
- ▶ Deleting all company transactional data

# Introduction

This chapter focuses on data manipulation exercises. Here, we will discuss how to work with query objects from X++ code. We will also discuss how to reuse macros in X++ SQL statements and how to send SQL statements directly to the database. This chapter will explain how to rename primary keys, how to merge and copy records, how to add document handling notes to selected records, and how to clean up the testing system by deleting all transactional data.

# Creating a new number sequence

Number sequences in Dynamics AX are used to generate a specifically formatted number for record identification. Numbers could be anything from voucher numbers or transaction identification numbers to customer or vendor accounts.

When developing custom functionality, very often one of the tasks is to add a new number sequence to the system to support newly created tables. Dynamics AX contains a list of **NumberSeqReference** derivative classes, which hold the number sequence data for the specific module.

These classes are read by the number sequence wizard which detects existing number sequences and proposes to create the missing or newly created ones. The wizard is normally run as a part of the application initialization, but it can be rerun at any time later when expanding Dynamics AX functionality and new standard number sequences are required. The wizard also has to be rerun if new custom number sequences are added to the system.

In this recipe, we will add a new number sequence to the system. In a standard application, employee number is not driven by any number sequence, so we will enhance this by creating an employee number sequence functionality.

## How to do it...

1. Open the **NumberSeqReference_General** class in AOT, and add the following code to the bottom of `loadModule()`:

```
numRef.DataTypeId = typeId2ExtendedTypeId(typeid(EmplId));
numRef.ReferenceHelp = literalstr("Employee identification");
numRef.WizardContinuous        = false;
numRef.WizardManual            = NoYes::No;
numRef.WizardAllowChangeDown   = NoYes::Yes;
numRef.WizardAllowChangeUp     = NoYes::Yes;
numRef.WizardHighest           = 9999;
numRef.SortField               = 7;
this.create(numRef);
```

2. Run the number sequence wizard by clicking on the **Wizard** button in **Basic | Setup | Number sequences | Number sequences**, and click **Next**:

3. Delete everything apart from the line where **Module** is **Basic** and **Reference** is **Employee** (use keyboard shortcut *ALT+F9* to delete lines). Note the number sequence code **Basi_202**, and click **Next**:

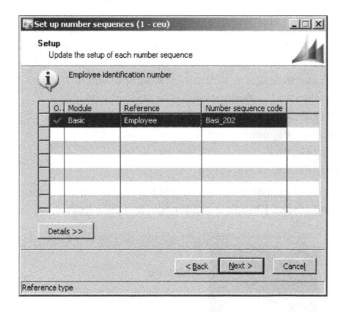

4. On the last page, click **Finish** to complete the wizard:

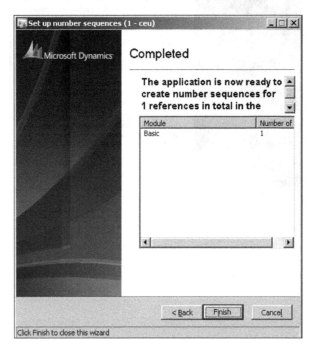

5. Find the newly created number sequence in **Number sequences** form:

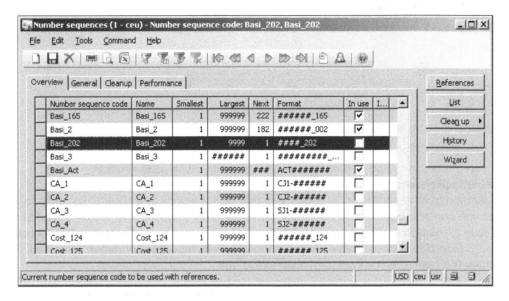

6. Open **Basic | Setup | Company information** and go to the **Number sequences** tab page. Here, we should see the new number sequence code along with the existing ones:

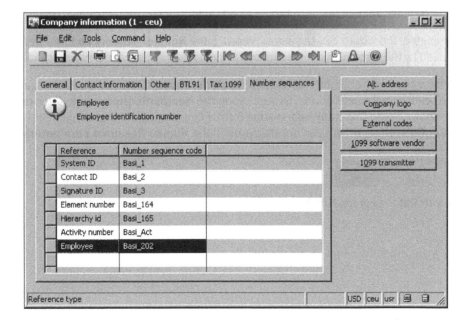

7. The last thing to do is to create a helper method for this sequence. Locate **CompanyInfo** table in AOT and add the following method:

```
public server static NumberSequenceReference numRefEmplId()
{
    return NumberSeqReference::findReference(
        typeid2extendedtypeid(typeid(EmplId)));
}
```

## How it works...

We start the recipe by adding a number sequence initialization code into the **NumberSeqReference_General** class. As we can understand from its name, it holds initialization of all general number sequences that do not belong to any particular module. Employee number sequence partially matches this criterion, although we could have added the code to the **NumberSeqReference_HRM** class, which is used in the **Human Resources** module. Moreover, we could have created a totally new **NumberSeqReference** class. This is normally the case when new custom modules are built.

The code in `loadModule()` defines default number sequence settings to be used in the wizard like data type, description, highest possible number, etc. Additional options like starting sequence number, number format, and others could also be added here. All mentioned options could be changed while running the wizard. On the second step of the wizard, the **Details >>** button can be used to display more options. The options could also be changed later in the **Number sequences** form before or after the number sequence is actually used.

Once completed, the wizard creates a new record in the **Number sequences** form, which can then be used by the system.

The number sequences added to the **NumberSeqReference** classes are also automatically shown on relevant parameter forms. Sequences in the **NumberSeqReference_General** class are shown in the **Company information** form. For example, number sequences in the **NumberSeqReference_HRM** class are displayed in the **Human Resource parameters** form.

## See also

Working with Data in Forms, Handling number sequences

# Renaming the primary key

Most of you who are familiar with the application probably used the standard **Rename** function. This function allows us to rename the primary key of almost any record. It is irreplaceable if a record was saved by mistake or simply needs renaming. The function ensures data consistency, that is, all related records are renamed too. It can be accessed from the **Record information** form, which can be opened by selecting **Record info** from the right-click menu on any record:

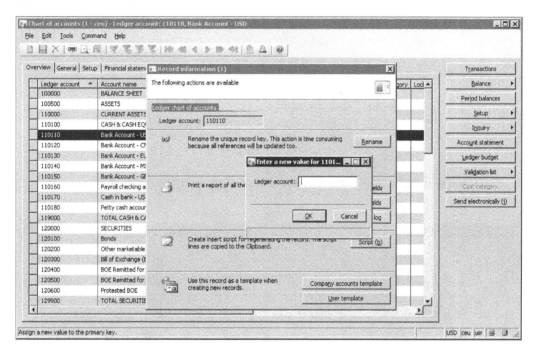

When it comes to mass renaming, this function might be very time consuming as it would need to be run on every record. An alternative is to create a job that automatically runs through all required records and calls this function.

This recipe will explain how the record primary key can be renamed through code.

As an example, we will create a job that renames general ledger account **110110** by adding the letter **C** in front of it. You can use any other ledger account in this example.

## How to do it...

1.  Open AOT to create a new job called **LedgerAccountRename**, and enter the following code:

```
static void LedgerAccountRename(Args _args)
{
    LedgerTable ledgerTable;
    ;

    select firstonly ledgerTable
        where ledgerTable.AccountNum == '110110';

    if (ledgerTable.RecId)
    {
        ledgerTable.AccountNum = 'C' + ledgerTable.AccountNum;
        ledgerTable.renamePrimaryKey();
    }

}
```

2.  Open **General ledger | Chart of Accounts Details** and find the account to be renamed:

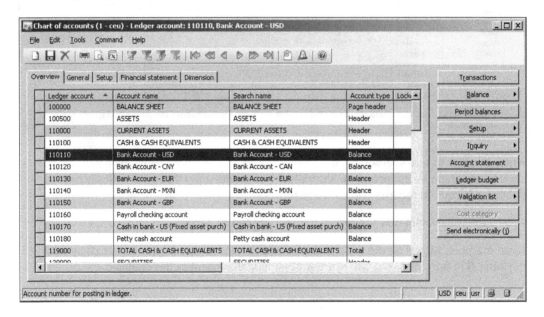

3. Click **Transactions** to note existing transactions:

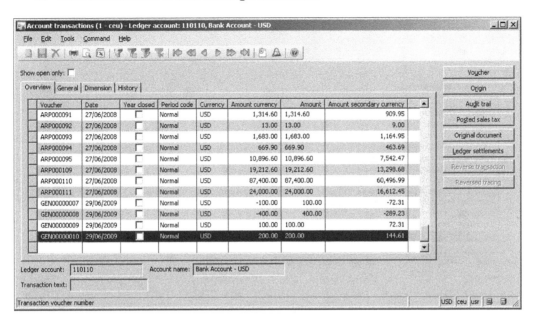

4. Now, run the job. To check if the renaming was successful and the account retained all its transactions and other related records, open **General ledger | Chart of Accounts Details**, and find the new account:

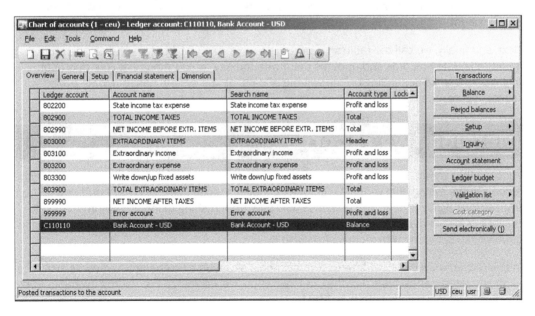

5. Click **Transactions** to see that existing transactions are still in place:

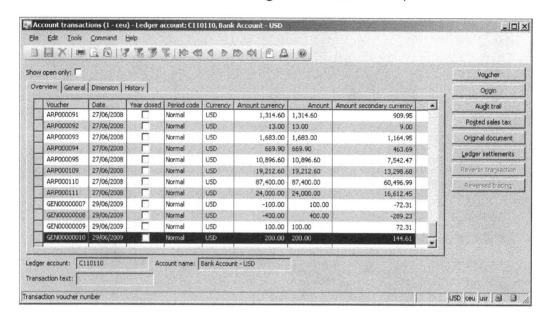

## How it works...

In this recipe, first we select the desired ledger account, that is, **110110**. If the `where` clause is removed, then in such a case, all ledger accounts would be updated to have **C** in front of each account.

Next, and finally, we call the table's `renamePrimaryKey()`, which does the actual renaming. It finds all related records and updates them with the new account number. The operation might take a while depending on the volume of data, as the system has to update every related record.

# Merging two records

I noticed that sometimes for various operational reasons, people by accident create duplicate records in the system like vendors, customers, ledger accounts, etc and start entering transactions against them. The reasons could vary from rushing to input new information to the lack of knowledge of how to use the system. But regardless of why this happened, they will always need someone with technical skills to fix it.

In this recipe, we will explore how to correct such a situation by merging two records including all their related transactions. For the demonstration, we will merge two vendor accounts **5001** and **5002** into a single one, that is, **5001**.

## How to do it...

1. Open AOT, create a new job called **VendAccountMerge**, and enter the following code:

```
static void VendAccountMerge(Args _args)
{
    VendTable                  vendTable;
    VendTable                  vendTableDelete;
    PurchJournalAutoSummary jourSummary;
    #define.vend('5001')
    #define.vendDelete('5002')
    ;

    ttsbegin;
    delete_from jourSummary
        where jourSummary.VendAccount == #vendDelete;
    select firstonly forupdate vendTableDelete
        where vendTableDelete.AccountNum == #vendDelete;
    select firstonly forupdate vendTable
        where vendTable.AccountNum == #vend;
    vendTableDelete.merge(vendTable);
    vendTable.doUpdate();
    vendTableDelete.doDelete();
    ttscommit;
}
```

2. Open **Account payable | Vendor Details** to check the vendors to be merged:

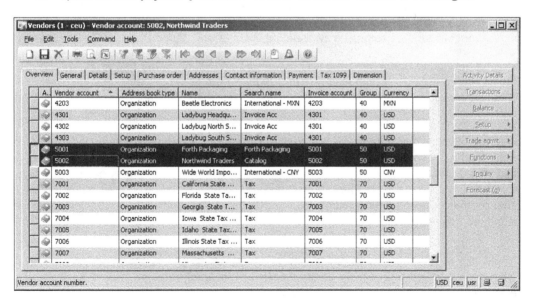

3.  Run the job to merge the vendor accounts.

4.  Open **Account payable | Vendor Details** to see the results:

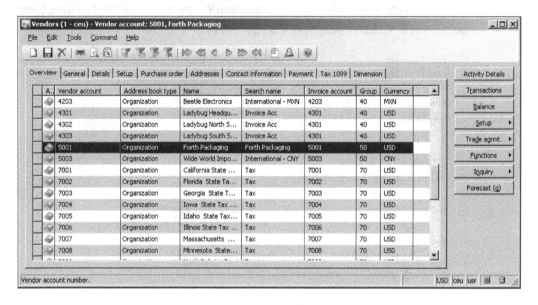

## How it works...

Once vendor accounts are merged, all their related records are going to be merged too, that is, all transactions, contacts, addresses, configuration settings, and so on from both vendors will be moved to a single one. Normally, there are no issues with merged transactional data, but vendor configuration settings may issue duplicate errors.

For example, vendor **5001** has bank account **Bank1** and vendor **5002** has bank account **Bank2**. After merging both vendors, vendor **5001** will have both bank accounts attached. If both bank accounts were named the same, then the system would issue a duplicate record error.

So before we start merging records, we need to either manually or programmatically delete or rename settings that might issue duplicate errors. In this example, in the first block of code, right after the variable declaration, we delete only the default auto-summary posting settings, which are stored in the **PurchJournalAutoSummary** table. Depending on the circumstances, other settings like vendor bank accounts, requests for quotes, and so on, have to be corrected before the actual merge.

Next two blocks of code find both vendor records for further updating.

Calling member method `merge()` on the record to be deleted transfers all of its data and related records to the destination, which is specified as a first argument.

The last thing to do is to save the destination record and delete the first one.

Such a technique can be used to merge two or even more records. Besides vendors, it could also be customers, ledger accounts, and other such similar records. Every case has to be investigated separately as each record type contains different relations with other tables.

# Adding document handling notes

It is a good practice to add some kind of note to the record when doing data renaming, merging, or any other data manipulation task, whether it's manual or automatic. Dynamics AX allows adding a note or a file to any records by using the so called **Document handling** feature.

By default, it is enabled for all tables, but can be restricted to fewer tables by changing its configuration parameters.

**Document handling** can be accessed from the form toolbar by selecting the **Document handling** icon or choosing **Document handling** from the **Command** menu. A form appears, which allows adding notes or files to any currently selected record.

Dynamics AX also allows us to add document handling notes from the code, which helps developers or consultants to add additional information when doing various data migration or conversion tasks.

In this recipe, we will add a note to vendor account **5001**.

## How to do it...

1. Open AOT and create a new job called **VendAccountDocu**, and enter the following code:

```
static void VendAccountDocu(Args _args)
{
    DocuRef docuRef;
    #define.vend('5001')
    #define.docuType('Note')
    ;

    docuRef.RefCompanyId = curext();
    docuRef.RefTableId   = tablenum(VendTable);
    docuRef.RefRecId     = VendTable::find(#vend).RecId;
    docuRef.TypeId       = #docuType;
    docuRef.Name         = 'Imported';
    docuRef.Notes        = 'This vendor was imported.';
    docuRef.insert();
}
```

2. Run the job to create the note.

3. Open **Accounts payable | Vendor Details**, and locate the vendor account:

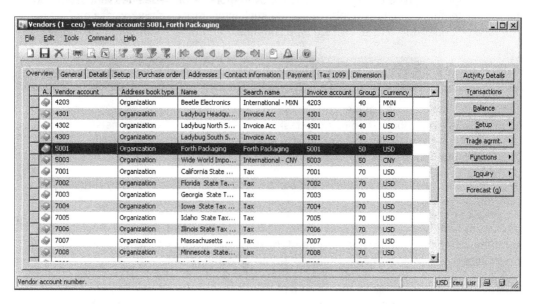

4. Click the **Document handling** button on the form toolbar or select **Document handling** from the **Command** menu to view the note added by our code:

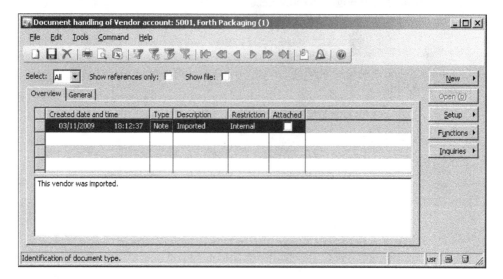

## How it works...

All document handling notes are stored in the **DocuRef** table, where three fields, **RefCompanyId**, **RefTableId**, and **RefRecId** are used to identify the parent record. In our recipe, we set those fields to the current company account, vendor table ID, and vendor account record ID respectively.

Next, we set note type, name, and description and insert the document handling record. In this way, we added a note to the record. The code in this recipe could be also added to a separate method for further reuse.

# Using a normal table as temporary table

Standard Dynamics AX contains numerous temporary tables, which are used by the application and could be used in custom modifications too. Although new temporary tables could also be easily created using AOT, sometimes it is not effective. One of the cases could be when the temporary table is very similar or exactly the same as an existing "real" one. The goal of this recipe is to demonstrate an approach to how standard non-temporary tables could be used as temporary.

As an example, we will use the vendor table to insert and display a couple of temporary records without affecting actual data.

## How to do it...

1. In AOT, create a new class called **VendTableTmp** with the following code:

```
class VendTableTmp
{
}
server static void main(Args _args)
{
    VendTable    vendTable;
    ;

    vendTable.setTmp();
    vendTable.AccountNum = '1000';
    vendTable.Name       = 'Vendor 1';
    vendTable.PartyId    = '1';
    vendTable.doInsert();
    vendTable.clear();
    vendTable.AccountNum = '1002';
    vendTable.Name       = 'Vendor 2';
    vendTable.PartyId    = '2';
    vendTable.doInsert();
    while select vendTable
```

```
        {
            info(strfmt(
                "%1 - %2",
                vendTable.AccountNum,
                vendTable.Name));
        }
    }
```

2.   Run the class to see results:

## How it works...

The principle of this recipe is in the `setTmp()` method. It is available on all tables, and it declares the current table instance to behave as a temporary table in the current scope. So in this recipe, we first call `setTmp()` on the `vendTable` table to make it temporary in the scope of this method. That means any data manipulations will be lost once the execution of this method is over and actual table content will not be affected.

Next, we insert couple of test records. Here, we use `doInsert()` to bypass any validation rules that are not required in this recipe.

The last thing to do is to check for newly created records by listing the `vendTable` table. We can see that although the table contains many actual records, only the ones which we have inserted here are listed.

## See also

Working with Data in Forms, Creating default data wizards

# Copying a record

I've experienced that one of the tasks often used when manipulating data is record copying. For various reasons, an existing record needs to be modified and saved as a new one. The most obvious example could be when a user requires a function that allows him or her to quickly duplicate records on any of the existing forms.

There are several ways of copying one record into another in X++. In this recipe, we will explain the usage of table `data()` method, global `buf2buf()` function, and their differences. As an example, we will copy one of the existing customer records into a new one. Normally, copying a customer involves more data around the customer like customer contacts, bank accounts, printing settings, and similar, but for demonstration purposes, we will assume that our goal is only to copy the customer record itself without worrying about related data.

## How to do it...

1.  Open **Accounts receivable | Customer Details**, and find the customer to be copied. In this example, we will use **1104**:

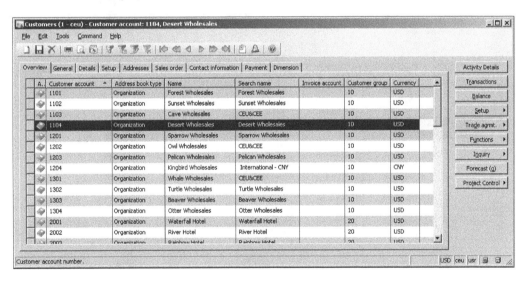

2.  Open AOT, create a new job called **CustTableCopy** with the following code and run it:

```
static void CustTableCopy(Args _args)
{
    CustTable custTable1;
    CustTable custTable2;
    ;
```

```
custTable1 = CustTable::find('1104');

ttsbegin;

custTable2.data(custTable1);

custTable2.AccountNum = '1105';

custTable2.PartyId = '';
custTable2.PartyId = DirParty::createPartyFromCommon(
    custTable2).PartyId;

if (!custTable2.validateWrite())
{
    throw Exception::Error;
}

custTable2.insert();

ttscommit;
}
```

3.  Open **Accounts receivable | Customer Details** again, and notice that there two identical customer records now:

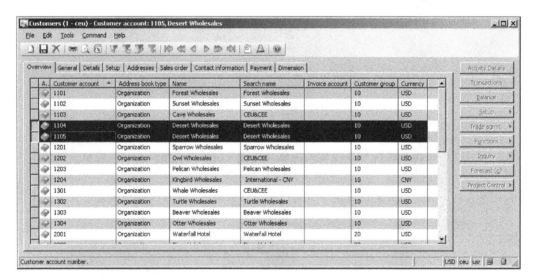

## How it works...

In this recipe, we have two variables—`custTable1` for original record and `custTable2` for new one. First, we find the original record by calling `find()` on the **CustTable** table.

Next, we copy it to the new one. Here, we use the `data()` table member method, which copies all data fields from one variable to another.

After that, we set a new customer account number and new address book ID (we have to clear it before). These two fields are part of unique table indexes, and the system would issue an error if one of them is already used.

Finally, we call insert() on the table, if validateWrite() is successful. In this way, we have created a new customer record, which is exactly the same as the existing one apart from the two fields.

## There's more...

As we saw before, the data() method copies all table fields including system fields like record ID, company account, created user, and so on. Most of the time, it is OK because when the new record is saved, the system fields are overwritten with the new values. But this is not the case when copying records between different companies.

If we were to modify the previously created job to include the changecompany() statement, the job would not work. Company ID would still be copied from original record to the new one and would not be changed during the insert.

To solve similar problems, Dynamics AX provides another function called buf2buf(). It is very similar to the table's data() method with one major difference. buf2buf() copies all data fields excluding the system ones. The code in the function is as follows:

```
static void buf2Buf(
    Common   _from,
    Common   _to)
{
    DictTable   dictTable = new DictTable(_from.TableId);
    fieldId     fieldId   = dictTable.fieldNext(0);

    while (fieldId && ! isSysId(fieldId))
    {
        _to.(fieldId)   = _from.(fieldId);
        fieldId         = dictTable.fieldNext(fieldId);
    }
}
```

We can clearly see that during the copying process, all the table fields are traversed, but the system fields are excluded. We can also see that this function is slower than the internal data(), as it checks and copies field-by-field.

Now that we have learned about this function, let's use it. Let's update a previous example to copy customer records from one Dynamics AX company to another. Do not forget that in practice, such copying would not make any sense as much customer related data will not be copied, but here it will be used as a good example. Update the previous job to (replace TST with your company):

```
static void CustTableCopy(Args _args)
{
    CustTable custTable1;
    CustTable custTable2;
    ;

    custTable1 = CustTable::find('1104');
    changecompany('TST')
    {
        ttsbegin;
        buf2buf(custTable1, custTable2);
        custTable2.AccountNum = '1105';
        custTable2.PartyId    = '';
        custTable2.PartyId = DirParty::createPartyFromCommon(
            custTable2).PartyId;
        if (!custTable2.validateWrite())
        {
            throw Exception::Error;
        }
        custTable2.insert();
        ttscommit;

    }
}
```

There are only two differences here. First we change the current company before we start creating a new record. Second, we replace `data()` with `buf2buf()`. The latter function accepts two records as arguments—source and destination. When we run this job, a new record will be created in another company.

# Building a query object

Query objects are used to visually build SQL statements. They are used by Dynamics AX reports, views, forms, and other objects. Normally queries are stored in AOT, but they can also be created from code dynamically. This is normally done when visual tools cannot handle complex and dynamic queries. In this recipe, we will create one dynamically from code.

As an example, we will build a query that selects all active customers who belong to group **10** and have at least one sales order.

## How to do it...

1. Open AOT, create a new job called **CustTableSales**, and enter the following code:

```
static void CustTableSales(Args _args)
{
    Query                   query;
    QueryBuildDataSource    qbds1;
    QueryBuildDataSource    qbds2;
    QueryBuildRange         qbr1;
    QueryBuildRange         qbr2;
    QueryRun                queryRun;
    CustTable               custTable;
    ;

    query = new Query();

    qbds1 = query.addDataSource(tablenum(CustTable));
    qbds1.addSortField(
        fieldnum(CustTable, Name),
        SortOrder::Ascending);

    qbr1 = qbds1.addRange(fieldnum(CustTable,Blocked));
    qbr1.value(queryvalue(CustVendorBlocked::No));

    qbr2 = qbds1.addRange(fieldnum(CustTable,CustGroup));
    qbr2.value(queryvalue('10'));

    qbds2 = qbds1.addDataSource(tablenum(SalesTable));
    qbds2.relations(false);
    qbds2.joinMode(JoinMode::ExistsJoin);
    qbds2.addLink(
        fieldnum(CustTable,AccountNum),
        fieldnum(SalesTable,CustAccount));

    queryRun = new QueryRun(query);

    while (queryRun.next())
    {
        custTable = queryRun.get(tablenum(CustTable));
        info(strfmt(
            "%1 - %2",
            custTable.Name,
            custTable.AccountNum));
    }
}
```

2. Run the job, and the following screen should appear:

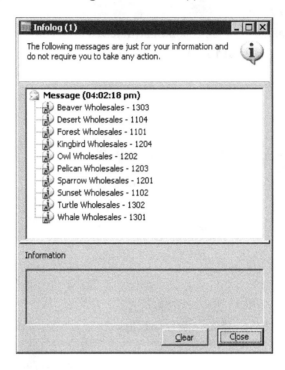

## How it works...

First, we create a new `query` object. Next, we add a new **CustTable** data source to the `query` by calling its `addDataSource()` member method. The method returns a reference to the **QueryBuildDataSource** object—`qbds1`. Here, we call `addSortField()` to enable sorting by customer name.

The following two blocks of code creates two filter ranges. The first is to show only active customers and the second one is to list only customers belonging to a single group **10**. Those two filters are automatically added together using the SQL AND operator. **QueryBuildRange** objects are created by calling the `addRange()` member method of the **QueryBuildDataSource** object with the field ID number as argument. Range value is set by calling `value()` on the **QueryBuildRange** object itself. It is a good practice to use `queryvalue()` or a similar function to process values before applying them as a range. More functions like `querynotvalue()`, `queryrange()`, and so on can be found in the **Global** application class. Note that these functions actually process data using the **SysQuery** application class, which in turn has even more interesting helper methods that might be handy for every developer.

Adding another data source to an existing one connects both data sources using the SQL JOIN operator. It this example, we are displaying customers that have at least one sales order. We start by adding the **SalesTable** table as another data source. We are going to use custom relations between those tables, so we need to disable standard relations by calling the relations() method with false as an argument. Calling joinMode() with JoinMode::ExistsJoin as a parameter ensures that a record from a parent data source will be displayed only if the relation exists in its attached data source. And finally, we create a relation by calling addLink() and passing the field ID number of both tables.

Last thing to do is to create and run the queryRun object and show the selected data on the screen.

## There's more...

It is worth mentioning a couple of specific cases when working with query objects from code. One of them is how to use the **OR** operator and the other one is how to address array fields.

### Using the OR operator

As you have already noted, regardless of how many ranges are added, all of them will be added together using the SQL AND operator. In most cases, it is fine, but sometimes complex user requirements demand ranges to be added using SQL OR. There might be a number of work-arounds, like using temporary tables or similar, but I use the Dynamics AX feature that allows passing raw SQL as a range.

In this case, the range has to be formatted like the fully qualified SQL WHERE clause including field names, operators, and values. Each separate clause has to be in brackets. It is also very important that filter values, especially if they are specified by the user, have to be properly formatted before using them in a query.

Let's replace the code from the previous example:

```
qbr2.value(queryValue('10'));
```

with the new code:

```
qbr2.value(strfmt(
    '((%1 = "%2") || (%3 = "%4"))',
    fieldstr(CustTable,CustGroup),
    queryvalue('10'),
    fieldstr(CustTable,Currency),
    queryvalue('EUR')));
```

Now, the result would also include all the customers having the default currency **EUR**.

## Using arrays fields

Some table fields in Dynamics AX are based on extended data types, which contains more than one array element. An example in a standard application could be financial dimensions based on the **Dimension** extended data type or project sorting based on **ProjSortingId**. Although such fields are very much the same as normal fields, in queries, they should be addressed slightly different. To demonstrate the usage, let's modify the example by filtering the query to list only customers containing a specific **Purpose** value. In the standard application, **Purpose** is the third financial dimension, where the first is **Department** and the second is **Cost centre**.

First, let's declare a new **QueryBuildRange** object in the variable declaration section:

```
QueryBuildRange qbr3;
```

Next, we add the following code right after the `qbr2.value(...)` code:

```
qbr3 = qbds1.addRange(
    fieldid2ext(fieldnum(CustTable,Dimension),3));
qbr3.value(queryvalue('Site1'));
```

Notice that we use the global `fieldid2ext()` function, which converts the field ID and the array number into a valid number to be used by `addRange()`. This function can also be used anywhere, where addressing the dimension fields is required. The value **3** as its second argument here means that we are using a third dimension, that is, **Purpose**. In my application, I have purposes defined as **Site1**, **Site2**, and **Site3**, so I simply use the first one as filter criteria.

Now, when we run this job, the customer list based on previous criteria will be reduced even more to match customers having only a specific **Purpose** set.

## See also

Working with Data in Forms, Creating custom filters

Building Lookups, Using a form for lookup building

# Using a macro in a SQL statement

In a standard Dynamics AX application, there are macros like **InventDimJoin** and **InventDimSelect**, which are reused numerous times across the application. Those macros are actually full or partial X++ SQL queries, which can be called with various arguments. Such approach saves developing time and makes upgrades easier.

In this recipe, we will create a small macro, which holds a single `where` clause to display only active vendor records. Then, we will create a job which uses created macro for displaying a vendor list.

## How to do it...

1. Open AOT, and create a new macro called **VendTableNotBlocked** with the following code:

```
(%1.Blocked == CustVendorBlocked::No)
```

2. In AOT, also create a new job called **VendTableMacro** with the following code:

```
static void VendTableMacro(Args _args)
{
    VendTable    vendTable;
    ;

    while select vendTable
        where #VendTableNotBlocked(vendTable)
    {
        info(strfmt(
            "%1 - %2",
            vendTable.AccountNum,
            vendTable.Name));
    }
}
```

3. Run the job, and inspect the results, as displayed on the screen:

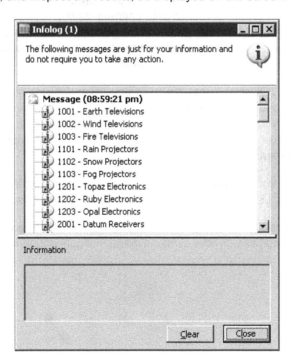

## How it works...

First, we define a macro that holds our `where` clause. Normally, the purpose of defining SQL in a macro is to reuse it a number of times in various places. We use `%1` as an argument. More arguments could be used.

Next, we create a job with the `select` statement. Here, we use the previously created macro in a `where` clause. We pass `vendTable` as an argument.

The query works like any other query, but the advantage is that the code in the macro could be reused elsewhere.

Note that although using a macro in a SQL statement can reduce the amount of code, too much code in it might reduce the SQL statement's readability for other developers. So keep it balanced.

# Executing a direct SQL statement

Dynamics AX allows developers to build X++ SQL statements flexible enough to fit any custom business process. But in several cases, the usage of X++ SQL is either not effective or not possible at all.

One of the cases is when we run data upgrade tasks during an application version upgrade. The standard application contains a set of data upgrade tasks to be completed during the version upgrade. If the application is highly customized, then most likely, the standard tasks has to be modified to reflect data dictionary customizations or even a new set of tasks have to be created to make sure data is handled correctly during the upgrade.

Normally, at this stage, SQL statements are so complex that they can only be created using database-specific SQL and executed directly in the database. Additionally, running direct SQL statements dramatically increases data upgrade performance because most of the code is executed on the database server where all data resides. This is very important while working with large volumes of data.

Another case when we would need to use direct SQL statements is when we want to connect to an external database using the ODBC driver. In this case, X++ SQL is not supported at all.

This recipe will demonstrate how to execute direct SQL statements. We will connect to the current Dynamics AX database directly using an additional connection and will retrieve the list of vendor accounts.

## How to do it...

1. Open AOT, and create a new class called **vendTableSql** with the following code:

```
class VendTableSql
{
}
server static void main(Args _args)
{
    UserConnection              userConnection;
    Statement                   statement;
    str                         sqlStatement;
    SqlSystem                   sqlSystem;
    SqlStatementExecutePermission  sqlPermission;
    ResultSet                   resultSet;
    DictTable                   tblVendTable;
    DictField                   fldAccountNum;
    DictField                   fldName;
    DictField                   fldDataAreaId;
    DictField                   fldBlocked;
    ;

    tblVendTable = new DictTable(tablenum(VendTable));
    fldAccountNum = new DictField(
        tablenum(VendTable),
        fieldnum(VendTable,AccountNum));
    fldName = new DictField(
        tablenum(VendTable),
        fieldnum(VendTable,Name));
    fldDataAreaId = new DictField(
        tablenum(VendTable),
        fieldnum(VendTable,DataAreaId));
    fldBlocked = new DictField(
        tablenum(VendTable),
        fieldnum(VendTable,Blocked));
    sqlSystem = new SqlSystem();
    sqlStatement = 'SELECT %2, %3 FROM %1 ' +
        'WHERE %4 = %6 AND %5 = %7';
    sqlStatement = strfmt(
        sqlStatement,
        tblVendTable.name(DbBackend::Sql),
        fldAccountNum.name(DbBackend::Sql),
        fldName.name(DbBackend::Sql),
        fldDataAreaId.name(DbBackend::Sql),
        fldBlocked.name(DbBackend::Sql),
```

```
        sqlSystem.sqlLiteral(curext(), true),
        sqlSystem.sqlLiteral(CustVendorBlocked::No, true));

    userConnection = new UserConnection();
    statement      = userConnection.createStatement();

    sqlPermission = new SqlStatementExecutePermission(
        sqlStatement);

    sqlPermission.assert();

    resultSet      = statement.executeQuery(sqlStatement);

    CodeAccessPermission::revertAssert();

    while (resultSet.next())
    {
        info(strfmt(
            "%1 - %2",
            resultSet.getString(1),
            resultSet.getString(2)));
    }
}
```

2. Run the class, and notice the list of vendors retrieved directly from the database:

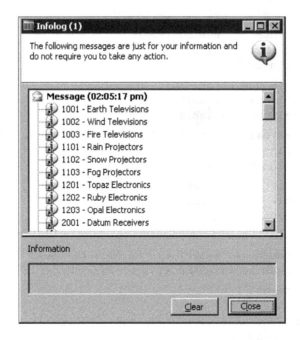

## How it works...

We start the code by creating **DictTable** and **DictField** objects for handling the vendor table and its fields later in the query.

A new **SqlSystem** object also has to be created. It will be used to convert Dynamics AX types to SQL types.

Next, we set up a SQL statement with %1, %2, and other placeholders for table or field names or values to be inserted later.

The main query creation happens next when the query placeholders are replaced with the right values. Here we use previously created **DictTable** and **DictField** type objects by calling their name() methods with the **DbBackend::Sql** enumeration as an argument. This ensures that we pass the name exactly how it is used in the database. For example, the **Dimension** field in **VendTable** actually consists of a set of three fields, which are named in the database DIMENSION, DIMENSION2_, and DIMENSION3_ respectively and using **DbBackend::Sql** would return us exactly that.

We also use the sqlLiteral() of the previously created sqlSystem object to properly format SQL values to make sure that they do not have any unsafe characters.

Once the SQL statement is ready, we initialize a direct connection to the database and run the statement. The result is a resultSet object, and we get the results by using the while statement and calling its next() until the end.

Note that we create an sqlPermission object of type **SqlStatementExecutePermission** here and call its assert() before executing the statement. This is required in order to comply with Dynamics AX **SQL** execution security requirements.

Another thing to mention is that when building direct SQL queries, special attention has to be paid to license, configuration, and security keys. Some tables or fields might be disabled in the application and may not be present in the database.

The code in this recipe can be also used to connect to the external ODBC databases. We only need to replace the UserConnection class with OdbcConnection and use text names instead of **DictTable** and **DictField**.

## There's more...

The Standard Dynamics AX application provides an alternate way of building direct SQL statements by using a set of **SQLBuilder** classes. By using those classes, we can create SQL statements as objects as oppose to text. We will demonstrate next how to use a set of **SQLBuilder** classes. We will create the same SQL statement as before.

First in AOT, we create another class called **VendTableSqlBuilder** with the following code::

```
class VendTableSqlBuilder
{
}
server static void main(Args _args)
{
    UserConnection                  userConnection;
    Statement                       statement;
    str                             sqlStatement;
    SqlStatementExecutePermission   sqlPermission;
    ResultSet                       resultSet;
    SQLBuilderSelectExpression      selectExpr;
    SQLBuilderTableEntry            vendTable;
    SQLBuilderFieldEntry            accountNum;
    SQLBuilderFieldEntry            name;
    SQLBuilderFieldEntry            dataAreaId;
    SQLBuilderFieldEntry            blocked;
    ;

    selectExpr = SQLBuilderSelectExpression::construct();

    vendTable = selectExpr.addTableId(
        tablenum(VendTable));

    accountNum = vendTable.addFieldId(
        fieldnum(VendTable,AccountNum));

    name = vendTable.addFieldId(
        fieldnum(VendTable,Name));

    dataAreaId = vendTable.addFieldId(
        fieldnum(VendTable,DataAreaId));

    blocked = vendTable.addFieldId(
        fieldnum(VendTable,Blocked));

    vendTable.addRange(dataAreaId, curext());
    vendTable.addRange(blocked, CustVendorBlocked::No);

    selectExpr.addSelectFieldEntry(
        SQLBuilderSelectFieldEntry::newExpression(
            accountNum,
            'AccountNum'));

    selectExpr.addSelectFieldEntry(
        SQLBuilderSelectFieldEntry::newExpression(
            name,
            'Name'));

    sqlStatement   = selectExpr.getExpression(null);
```

```
userConnection = new UserConnection();
statement       = userConnection.createStatement();

sqlPermission = new SqlStatementExecutePermission(
    sqlStatement);

sqlPermission.assert();

resultSet = statement.executeQuery(sqlStatement);

CodeAccessPermission::revertAssert();

while (resultSet.next())
{
    info(strfmt(
        "%1 - %2",
        resultSet.getString(1),
        resultSet.getString(2)));
}
}
```

In this method, we first create a new `selectExpr` object, which is based on the **SQLBuilderSelectExpression** class. It represents the object of the SQL statement.

Next, we add the **VendTable** table to it by calling its member method `addTableId()`. The method returns a reference to the `vendTable` object of type **SQLBuilderTableEntry**, which corresponds to a table node in a SQL query.

Then, we create four field objects of type **SQLBuilderFieldEntry** to be used later and two ranges to show only this company account and only active vendor accounts.

We use `addSelectFieldEntry()` to add two fields to be selected. Here we use the previously created field objects.

The SQL statement is generated once `getExpression()` is called and the rest of the code is the same as in the previous example.

Running the class would give us results exactly like the ones we got before.

# Enhancing the data consistency check

It is highly recommended from time-to-time to run the standard Dynamics AX data consistency check found in **Basic | Periodic | Consistency check** to check system data integrity. This function finds orphan data, validates parameters, and does many other things. But in one of my recent projects, I have noticed that it does not do everything. For example, it does not check the data in the **AssetLedgerAccounts** table, which holds the set up fixed asset posting profiles.

In this recipe, we will see how we can enhance the standard Dynamics AX consistency check to include more tables in its data integrity validation.

## Getting ready

Before we start, we need to create an invalid setup to make sure we can simulate data inconsistency. Open **General ledger | Chart of Account Details** and create a new ledger account, for instance, **000009**:

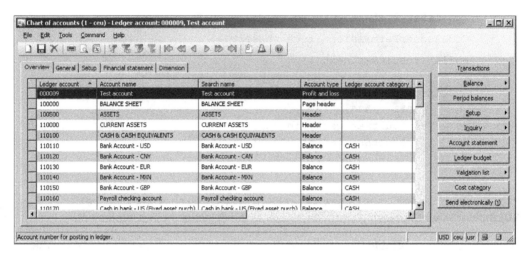

Open **General ledger | Setup | Fixed assets | Posting profiles** and specify the new account in the **Ledger account** field, for example, for any records:

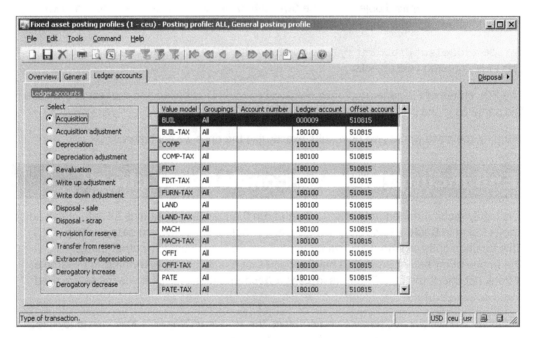

Go back to the **Chart of accounts** form, and delete the previously created account.

Now, we have a non-existing ledger account in the fixed asset posting settings.

## How to do it...

1. Open the **LedgerConsistencyCheck** class in AOT, and add the following code to the end of its `run()`:

   ```
   this.kernelCheckTable(tablenum(AssetLedgerAccounts));
   ```

2. Open **Basic | Periodic | Consistency check**, select **General ledger** node, and click **Execute** on the right-hand side:

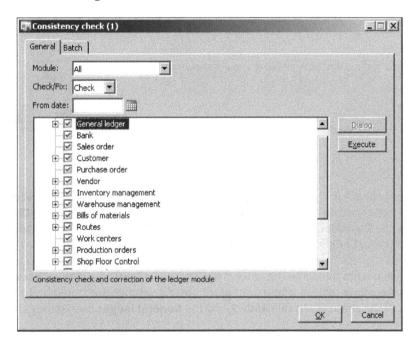

3.   Now, the message displayed in **Infolog** tells us that the account is missing in the fixed asset posing settings:

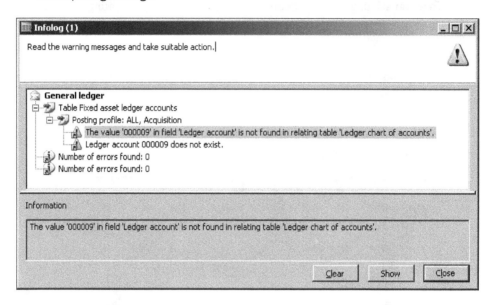

## How it works...

The consistency check in Dynamics AX validates only the predefined list of tables for each module. The system contains a number of classes derived from **SysConsistencyCheck**. For example, the **CustConsistencyCheck** class is responsible for validating the **Accounts receivable** module, **LedgerConsistencyCheck**—for **General ledger** and so on. Each class performs a check for the tables defined in its run().In this recipe, we include the **AssetLedgerAccounts** table into the latter class, that is, **LedgerConsistencyCheck**. **AssetLedgerAccounts** table is where fixed asset posting settings are stored and in this way, we ensure that the settings are validated during the **General ledger** consistency check.

## There's more...

For custom modules, a new separate consistency check class could be created. The class should extend **SysConsistencyCheck** and follow similar development principles to existing ones. The newly created class will also automatically appear in the **Consistency check** form tree.

# Exporting to an XML file

Briefly, **Extensible Markup Language** (**XML**) defines a set of rules for encoding documents electronically. It allows creating of all kind of structured documents. In Dynamics AX, **XML** files are widely used across the application. For example, user profiles can be exported as **XML** files. Business data like financial statements can also be exported as **XBRL** (**eXtensible Business Reporting Language**) files, which are based on **XML**.

Probably, the main thing that is associated with **XML** in Dynamics AX is the **Application Integration Framework**. It is an infrastructure that allows exposing business logic or exchanging data with other external systems. The communication is done by using XML formatted documents. By using existing **XML** framework application classes prefixed with **Axd,** you can export or import data from or to the system in an XML format. It is also possible to create new **Axd** classes using the **AIF Document Service Wizard** from the **Tools | Development tools | Wizards** menu to support exporting and importing newly created tables.

Dynamics AX also contains a set of application classes prefixed with **Xml** like **XmlDocument**, and **XmlNode**. Basically, those classes are wrappers around the **System.XML** namespace in **.NET Framework**.

In this recipe to show the principle of **XML**, we will create a new simple **XML** document by using the latter classes. We will create the file with the data from the chart of accounts table and will save it as an **XML** file.

## How to do it...

1.  Open AOT and create a new class called **CreateXmlFile** with the following code. Replace `<documents>` with your own path (use double backslashes for folder separation, that is, `\\`):

```
class CreateXmlFile
{
}
public static void main(Args _args)
{
    XmlDocument doc;
    XmlElement  nodeXml;
    XmlElement  nodeTable;
    XmlElement  nodeAccount;
    XmlElement  nodeName;
    LedgerTable ledgerTable;
    #define.filename('<documents>\\accounts.xml')
    ;

    doc     = XmlDocument::newBlank();
    nodeXml = doc.createElement('xml');
```

```
        doc.appendChild(nodeXml);
    while select ledgerTable
    {
        nodeTable = doc.createElement(tablestr(LedgerTable));
        nodeTable.setAttribute(
            fieldstr(LedgerTable, RecId),
            int642str(ledgerTable.RecId));
        nodeXml.appendChild(nodeTable);
        nodeAccount = doc.createElement(
            fieldstr(LedgerTable, AccountNum));
        nodeAccount.appendChild(
            doc.createTextNode(ledgerTable.AccountNum));
        nodeTable.appendChild(nodeAccount);
        nodeName = doc.createElement(
            fieldstr(LedgerTable, AccountName));
        nodeName.appendChild(
            doc.createTextNode(ledgerTable.AccountName));
        nodeTable.appendChild(nodeName);
    }
    doc.save(#filename);
}
```

2.  Run the class. The XML file **accounts.xml** should be created in the specified folder. Open it using **Internet Explorer**, and review the created XML structure:

## How it works...

We start by creating a new **XmlDocument**, which represents an **XML** structure using its `newBlank()` method. Then we create its root node named `xml` using `createElement()`, and add the node to the document by calling the document's `appendChild()` method.

Next, we go though the **LedgerTable** table and do the following for each record:

- ▶ Create a new **XmlElement** node, which is named exactly as the table name, and add this node to the root node.
- ▶ Create a node representing the account number field and its child node representing its value. The account number node is created using `createElement()`, and its value is created using `createTextNode()`. The `createTextNode()` method basically adds a value as text with no XML tags.
- ▶ Add the account number node to the table node.
- ▶ Create a node representing the account name field and its child node representing its value.
- ▶ Add the account name node to the table node.

Finally, we save the created **XML** document as a file.

In this way, we could create documents having virtually any structure.

# Importing from an XML file

The exporting to an **XML** file recipe has already explained the importance of **XML** in Dynamics AX, and how **XML** documents could be used for exporting data from the system.

In this recipe, we will continue about **XML**. We will create a piece of code that reads **XML** files. As a source file, we will use the previously created **accounts.xml** file.

## How to do it...

1. Open AOT, and create a new class called **ReadXmlFile** with the following code. Replace <documents> with your own path (use double backslashes for folder separation, i.e. \\):

```
class ReadXmlFile
{
}

public static void main(Args _args)
{
    XmlDocument doc;
    XmlNodeList data;
    XmlElement  nodeTable;
    XmlElement  nodeAccount;
    XmlElement  nodeName;
    #define.filename('<documents>\\accounts.xml')
    ;

    doc  = XmlDocument::newFile(#filename);
    data = doc.selectNodes('//'+tablestr(LedgerTable));
    nodeTable = data.nextNode();

    while (nodeTable)
    {
        nodeAccount = nodeTable.selectSingleNode(
            fieldstr(LedgerTable, AccountNum));
        nodeName = nodeTable.selectSingleNode(
            fieldstr(LedgerTable, AccountName));

        info(strfmt(
            "%1 - %2",
            nodeAccount.text(),
            nodeName.text()));
        nodeTable = data.nextNode();
    }
}
```

2. Run the class. **Infolog** should display the contents of the `accounts.xml` file on the screen:

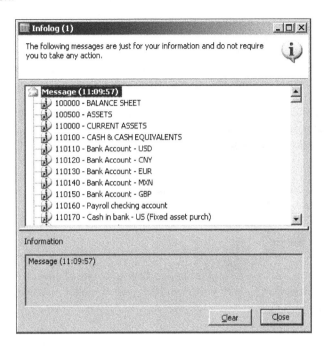

## How it works...

In this recipe, we first create a new **XmlDocument**. We create it from the file and hence we have to use `newFile()`. Then we get all the document nodes of the table as **XmlNodeList**. We also get its first element by calling `nextNode()`.

Next, we loop through all the list elements and do the following:

- ▸ Get an account number node as an **XmlElement**.
- ▸ Get an account name node as an **XmlElement**.
- ▸ Display the text of both nodes in **Infolog**. Normally, this should be replaced with more sensible code to process the data.
- ▸ Get the next list element.

In this way, we retrieve the data from the **XML** file. A similar approach could be used to read any other **XML** file.

# Creating a comma-separated value file

Comma-separated value (**CSV**) files are widely used across various systems. Although nowadays modern systems use **XML** formats for data exchange, **CSV** files are still popular because of the simplicity of their format. Normally, the data in the file is organized so one line corresponds to one record and each line contains a number of values normally separated by commas. Record and value separators could be any other symbol depending on the system requirements.

I have been successfully using **CSV** files for custom data migration tasks from/to Dynamics AX when the standard **Data export/import** utility is not enough. Speaking about Dynamics AX **Data export/import** utility, I have to mention that besides Binary and Excel formats, it can also handle **CSV** files.

In this recipe, we will learn how to create a custom comma-separated file from code. We will export a list of ledger accounts—account number and name.

## How to do it...

1. Open AOT, and create a new class called **CreateCommaFile** with the following code. Replace `<documents>` with your own path (use double backslashes for folder separation, i.e. \\):

```
class CreateCommaFile
{
}
public static client void main(Args _args)
{
    CommaIo     file;
    container   line;
    LedgerTable ledgerTable;
    #define.filename('<documents>\\accounts.csv')
    #File
    ;

    file = new CommaIo(#filename, #io_write);
    if (!file || file.status() != IO_Status::Ok)
    {
        throw error("File cannot be opened.");
    }
    while select ledgerTable
    {
        line = [
            ledgerTable.AccountNum,
            ledgerTable.AccountName];
        file.writeExp(line);
    }
}
```

2. Run the class. A new file called `accounts.csv` should be created in the specified folder. Open that file with **Notepad** to view the results:

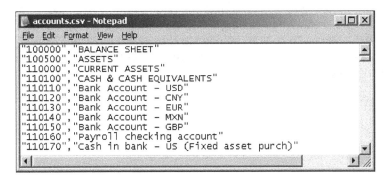

## How it works...

In the variable declaration section of the `main()` method of the **CreateCommaFile** class along with other variables we define a name for the output file. Normally, this should be replaced with a proper input variable. Here, we also define a standard `#File` macro which contains a number of file-handling modes like `#io_read`, `#io_write`, `#io_append`, etc., file types, delimiters, and other things.

Next, we create a new CSV file by calling `new()` on a standard **CommaIo** class. It accepts two parameters—filename and mode. For mode, we use `#io_write` from the `#File` macro to make sure a new file is created and opened for further writing. If a file with the given name already exists, then it will be overwritten. To make sure that a file is created successfully, we check if the object `file` exists and its status is valid, otherwise we show an error message.

In multilingual environments, it is better to use **CommaTextIo**. It behaves the same way as **CommaIo** does plus it supports Unicode, which allows us to process data with various language-specific symbols.

And finally, we loop though the **LedgerTable** table, store its account number and name fields into a container, and write them to the file using `writeExp()`.

In this way, we create a new comma-separated value file with the list of ledger accounts.

## There's more...

You probably already noticed that the `main()` method has a `client` modifier, which forces its code to run on the client. When dealing with large amounts of data, it is more effective to run the code on the server. To do that, we need to change the modifier to `server`. The class below generates exactly the same file as before, except that this file is created on the folder on the server's file system:

```
class CreateCommaFileServer
{
}
public static server void main(Args _args)
{
    CommaIo          file;
    container        line;
    LedgerTable      ledgerTable;
    FileIoPermission perm;
    #define.filename('<documents>\\accounts.csv')
    #File
    ;

    perm = new FileIoPermission(#filename, #io_write);
    perm.assert();

    file = new CommaIo(#Filename, #io_write);
    if (!file || file.status() != IO_Status::Ok)
    {
        throw error("File cannot be opened.");
    }
    while select ledgerTable
    {
        line = [
            ledgerTable.AccountNum,
            ledgerTable.AccountName];
        file.writeExp(line);
    }
    CodeAccessPermission::revertAssert();
}
```

Make sure you replace <documents> with your own folder on the server. Use double backslashes for folder separation, i.e. \\.

File manipulation on the server is protected by Dynamics AX code access security and we must use the **FileIoPermission** class to make sure we match the requirements. That's why we have to call the following code before opening the file to assert permissions:

```
perm = new FileIoPermission(#Filename, #io_write);
perm.assert();
```

and the following code after we completed all file operations to make sure we clear assertions:

```
CodeAccessPermission::revertAssert();
```

# Reading a comma-separated value file

Besides data import/export, CSV files could be used for integration between systems. It is probably the most simple integration approach. I've seen and worked on a number of projects where an external application, for example a specialized billing system, generates CSV files every day. Dynamics AX runs a periodic batch job, which reads the generated files every night and imports the data, for instance, sales orders. Although this is not a real-time integration, in most cases it does the job and does not require any additional components like Dynamics AX Application Integration Framework or something similar.

Another well known example is when external companies are hired to manage the payroll. On a periodic basis, they send CSV files to the finance department, which are then loaded into the **General journal** in Dynamics AX and processed as usual.

In this recipe, we will learn how to read CSV files from code. As an example, we will process the file created in a pervious recipe.

## How to do it...

1.  In AOT, create a new class named **ReadCommaFile** with the following code. Replace <documents> with your own path (use double backslashes for folder separation, i.e. \\):

```
class ReadCommaFile
{
}
public static client void main(Args _args)
{
    CommaIo    file;
    container line;
```

```
#define.filename('<documents>\\accounts.csv')
#File
;

file = new CommaIo(#filename, #io_read);
if (!file || file.status() != IO_Status::Ok)
{
    throw error("File cannot be opened.");
}

while (file.status() == IO_Status::Ok)
{
    line = file.read();
    if (line != connull())
    {
        info(con2str(line, ' - '));
    }
}
}
```

2.   Run the class to view the file's content:

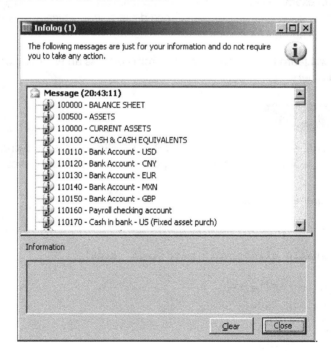

## How it works...

As in the previous recipe, we first create a new `file` object using **CommaIo**. This time we use `#io_read` as the mode to make sure that the existing file is opened for reading only. We also perform the same validations to make sure that the file object is correctly created, otherwise we show an error message.

Next and finally, we read the file line by line until we reach the end of the file. Here we use the `while` loop until the file status changes from `IO_Status::OK` to `IO_Status::FileTooShort`, which means no more lines exist in the file. Inside the loop, we call `read()` on the `file` object, which returns the current line as a container and moves the internal file cursor to the next line. File data is then simply outputted to the screen using the standard global `info()` function in conjunction with `con2str()`, which converts a container to a string for displaying.

The last element of code where data is outputted normally should be replaced by proper code that processes the incoming data.

## There's more...

File reading, like file writing, could also be executed on a server to improve performance. The modifier `client` has to be changed to `server`, and code with the **FileIoPermission** class has to be added to fulfill the code access security requirements. The modified class should look like the following:

```
class ReadCommaFileServer
{
}
public static server void main(Args _args)
{
    CommaIo         file;
    container       line;
    FileIoPermission perm;
    #define.filename('<documents>\\accounts.csv')
    #File
    ;

    perm = new FileIoPermission(#filename, #io_read);
    perm.assert();

    file = new CommaIo(#Filename, #io_read);
    if (!file || file.status() != IO_Status::Ok)
    {
```

```
        throw error("File cannot be opened.");
    }

    while (file.status() == IO_Status::Ok)
    {
        line = file.read();
        if (line != connull())
        {
            info(con2str(line, ' - '));
        }
    }

    CodeAccessPermission::revertAssert();
}
```

# Deleting all company transactional data

Normally, during the testing stage of any Dynamics AX project, system configuration is adjusted depending on the testing results. This process may be performed as many times as required until the system is ready. During this process, it might appear that at some point the system have too many transactions, which may impact further tests. If this happens, then the data is wiped out by exporting configuration data, deleting whole company, and importing configuration data back. Data clean-up is also required when "fresh" retesting is required.

Although the described process does the job, it might be slightly time consuming. During my developments, I found the undocumented class called **SysDatabaseTransDelete** in the standard Dynamics AX application. Once started, it deletes all transactional data in the current company. It allows us to quickly get rid of all transactions and leaves configuration data intact.

But although this class is useful during the testing stages, it definitely should not be used in production environments.

In this recipe, we will explore how to delete all transactional data using the mentioned application class.

## How to do it...

1. First, we need to make a copy of an existing company account to make sure we are not deleting the data in the current company. Open **Administration | Company accounts**, and select the current company:

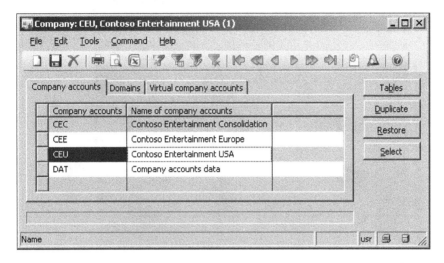

2. Click on the **Duplicate** button, and then type in the details for a new company:

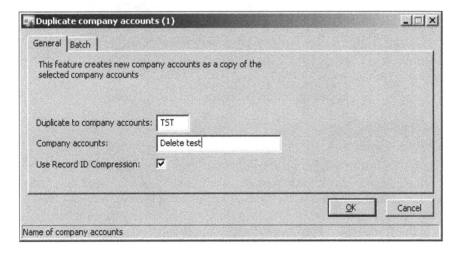

3. After a couple of moments, a new company should be created. Select it in the form and click on the **Select** button to make sure you start working in it:

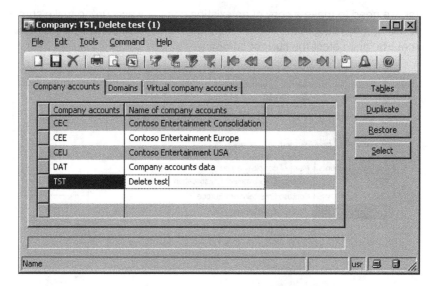

4. Next open AOT, find the **SysDatabaseTransDelete** class in AOT, and run it.

5. Click **Yes** to acknowledge that you want to delete all transactions:

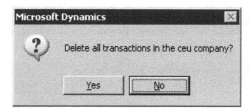

## How it works...

In this recipe, we use the **SysDatabaseTransDelete** class, which is included in the standard Dynamics AX application. No additional coding is required. We simply need to run it in the company that we want to clean up. This class is not included in any menu, so it has to be started from AOT. The class deletes all data in the current company account from all tables belonging to the **Transaction**, **WorksheetHeader**, and **WorksheetLine** table groups.

# 2
# Working with Forms

In this chapter, we will cover:

- ▸ Creating dialogs
- ▸ Handling dialog events
- ▸ Creating dynamic menu buttons
- ▸ Building dynamic form
- ▸ Adding form splitters
- ▸ Creating modal form
- ▸ Changing common form appearance
- ▸ Storing last form values
- ▸ Using tree controls
- ▸ Building checklists
- ▸ Adding a "Go to the Main Table Form" link
- ▸ Modifying the User setup form
- ▸ Modifying application version

## Introduction

Forms in Dynamics AX represent the user interface and are mainly used for entering or modifying data. They are also used for running reports, executing user commands, validating data, and so on.

Normally, forms are created using AOT by creating a form object and adding form controls like tabs, tab pages, grids, groups, data fields, images, and other. Form behavior is controlled by its properties or the code in its member methods. The behavior and layout of form controls are also controlled by their properties and the code in their member methods. Although it is very rare, forms can also be created dynamically from code.

In this chapter, we will cover various aspects of using Dynamics AX forms. We start with building Dynamics AX dialogs, which actually are dynamic forms, and explain how to handle their events. The chapter will also show how to add dynamic controls to existing forms, how to build dynamic forms from scratch, how to make forms modal, and how to change the appearance of all application forms with a few lines of code.

This chapter also discusses the usage of splitters, tree controls, creating checklists, saving last user selections, modifying application version, and other things.

# Creating Dialogs

Dialogs are a way to present users with a simple input form. They are commonly used for small user tasks like filling in report values, running batch jobs, presenting only the most important fields to the user when creating a new record, etc. Dialogs are normally created from X++ code without storing actual layout in AOT.

The application class `Dialog` is used to build dialogs. Other application classes like `DialogField`, `DialogGroup`, `DialogTabPage`, and so on, are used to create dialog controls. One of the common ways is to use dialogs within `RunBase` framework classes that need user input.

In this example, we will see how to build a dialog from code using the `RunBase` framework class. The dialog will contain customer table fields shown in different groups and tabs for creating a new record. There will be two tab pages, **General** and **Details**. The first page will have **Customer account** and **Name** input controls. The second page will be divided into two groups, **Setup** and **Payment**, with relevant fields. The actual record will not be created, as it is out of scope of this example. However, for demonstration purposes, the information specified by the user will be displayed in the **Infolog**.

## How to do it...

1. Open AOT, and create a new class `CustCreate` with the following code:

```
class CustCreate extends RunBase
{
    DialogField     fieldAccount;
    DialogField     fieldName;
    DialogField     fieldGroup;
    DialogField     fieldCurrency;
    DialogField     fieldPaymTermId;
    DialogField     fieldPaymMode;
    CustAccount     custAccount;
    CustName        custName;
    CustGroupId     custGroupId;
    CurrencyCode    currencyCode;
    CustPaymTermId  paymTermId;
```

```
        CustPaymMode    paymMode;
}
public container pack()
{
    return connull();
}
public boolean unpack(container packedClass)
{
    return true;
}
protected Object dialog()
{
    Dialog          dialog;
    DialogTabPage   tabGeneral;
    DialogTabPage   tabDetails;
    DialogGroup     groupCustomer;
    DialogGroup     groupPayment;
    ;

    dialog = super();
    dialog.caption("Customer information");
    tabGeneral      = dialog.addTabPage("General");
    fieldAccount    = dialog.addField(
        typeid(CustVendAC),
        "Customer account");
    fieldName       = dialog.addField(typeid(CustName));
    tabDetails      = dialog.addTabPage("Details");
    groupCustomer   = dialog.addGroup("Setup");
    fieldGroup      = dialog.addField(typeid(CustGroupId));
    fieldCurrency   = dialog.addField(typeid(CurrencyCode));
    groupPayment    = dialog.addGroup("Payment");
    fieldPaymTermId = dialog.addField(typeid(CustPaymTermId));
    fieldPaymMode   = dialog.addField(typeid(CustPaymMode));
    return dialog;
}
public boolean getFromDialog()
{;
    custAccount  = fieldAccount.value();
    custName     = fieldName.value();
    custGroupId  = fieldGroup.value();
    currencyCode = fieldCurrency.value();
    paymTermId   = fieldPaymTermId.value();
    paymMode     = fieldPaymMode.value();
    return true;
```

```
    }

public void run()
{;
    info("You have entered customer information:");
    info(strfmt("Account: %1", custAccount));
    info(strfmt("Name: %1", custName));
    info(strfmt("Group: %1", custGroupId));
    info(strfmt("Currency: %1", currencyCode));
    info(strfmt("Terms of payment: %1", paymTermId));
    info(strfmt("Method of payment: %1", paymMode));
}

static void main(Args _args)
{
    CustCreate custCreate = new CustCreate();
    ;

    if (custCreate.prompt())
    {
        custCreate.run();
    }
}
```

2.  To test the dialog, run the class. The following form should appear with the **General** tab page open initially:

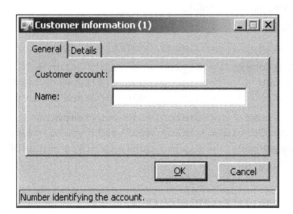

3. When you click on the **Details** tab page, you will see the following screen:

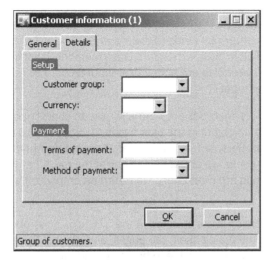

4. Enter some information into the fields, and click **OK**. The results are displayed in the **Infolog**:

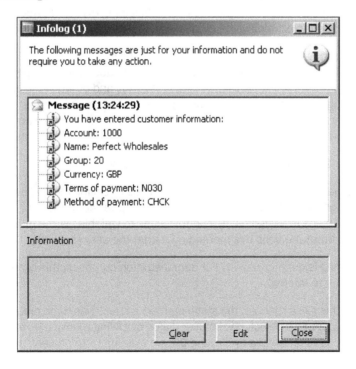

## How it works...

Firstly, we create a new class `CustCreate`. By extending it from `RunBase`, we utilize the standard approach of running such kinds of dialogs. `RunBase` will also automatically add the required buttons to the dialog. Then we declare class member variables, which will be used later. `DialogField` type variables are actual user input fields. The rest are used to store the values returned from user input.

The `pack()` and `unpack()` methods are normally used to convert an object to a container, which is a format to store an object in the user cache (`SysLastValue`) or to transfer it between Server and Client tiers. `RunBase` requires those two methods to be present in all its subclasses. In this example, we are not using any of the `pack()`/`unpack()` features, but because those methods are mandatory, we return an empty container from `pack()` and `true` from `unpack()`.

The layout of the actual dialog is constructed in the `dialog()` member method. Here, we define local variables for the dialog itself, tab pages, and groups. Those variables, as opposed to the dialog fields, do not store any value to be processed further.

The `super()` of the **RunBase** framework creates the initial `dialog` object for us. The object is created using the **Dialog** application class. The class actually uses the Dynamics AX form as a base, automatically adds the relevant controls, including **OK** and **Cancel** buttons, and presents it to the user as a dialog.

Additional dialog controls are added to the dialog by using the `addField()`, `addGroup()`, and `addTabPage()` methods. There are more methods to add different types of controls like `addText()`, `addImage()`, `addMenuItemButton()`, and others. All controls have to be added to the dialog object directly. Adding an input control to groups or tabs is done by calling `addField()` right after `addGroup()` or `addTabPage()`. In the example above, we add tab pages, groups, and fields in logical sequence, so every control appears in the right position.

The method returns a prepared dialog object for further processing.

Values from the dialog controls are assigned to variables by calling the `value()` member method of `DialogField`. If a dialog is used within the `RunBase` framework, as in this example, the best place to assign dialog control values to variables is the `getFormDialog()` member method. `RunBase` calls this method right after the user clicks **OK**.

The main processing is done in `run()`. For demonstration purposes, this example contains only variable output to **Infolog**.

In order to make this class runable, the static method `main()` has to be created. Here, we create a new `CustCreate` object, invoke user dialog by calling `prompt()`, and once the user finishes entering customer details by clicking **OK**, we call `run()` to process the data.

# Handling dialog events

Sometimes, the user interface requires us to change the status of a field, depending on the status of another field. For example, if the user marks the **Show filter** checkbox, another field, **Filter**, appears or becomes enabled. In standard Dynamics AX forms, this can be done using input control event `modified()`. But sometimes such features are required on dialogs where handling events is not that straightforward.

Very often, I find myself in a situation where existing dialogs need to be adjusted to support events. The easiest way of doing that is of course to build a form in AOT, which will replace the original dialog. But in cases when the existing dialog is complex enough, probably a more cost effective solution would be to implement dialog event handling. It is not as flexible as AOT forms, but in most cases it does the job.

In this recipe, we will create a dialog very similar to the previous one, but instead of entering the customer number, we will be able to select it from the list. Once the customer is selected, the rest of the fields will be filled automatically by the system from the customer record.

## How to do it...

1. In AOT, create a new class named **CustSelect** with the following code:

```
class CustSelect extends RunBase
{
    DialogField fieldAccount;
    DialogField fieldName;
    DialogField fieldGroup;
    DialogField fieldCurrency;
    DialogField fieldPaymTermId;
    DialogField fieldPaymMode;
}
public container pack()
{
    return connull();
}

public boolean unpack(container packedClass)
{
    return true;
}

protected Object dialog()
{
    Dialog          dialog;
    DialogTabPage   tabGeneral;
    DialogTabPage   tabDetails;
    DialogGroup     groupCustomer;
    DialogGroup     groupPayment;
```

```
    ;

        dialog = super();
        dialog.caption("Customer information");
        dialog.allowUpdateOnSelectCtrl(true);
        tabGeneral      = dialog.addTabPage("General");
        fieldAccount    = dialog.addField(
            typeid(CustAccount),
            "Customer account");
        fieldName       = dialog.addField(typeid(CustName));
        fieldName.enabled(false);
        tabDetails      = dialog.addTabPage("Details");
        groupCustomer   = dialog.addGroup("Setup");
        fieldGroup      = dialog.addField(typeid(CustGroupId));
        fieldCurrency   = dialog.addField(typeid(CurrencyCode));
        fieldGroup.enabled(false);
        fieldCurrency.enabled(false);
        groupPayment    = dialog.addGroup("Payment");
        fieldPaymTermId = dialog.addField(typeid(CustPaymTermId));
        fieldPaymMode   = dialog.addField(typeid(CustPaymMode));
        fieldPaymTermId.enabled(false);
        fieldPaymMode.enabled(false);
        return dialog;
    }
    public void dialogSelectCtrl()
    {
        CustTable custTable;
        ;

        custTable     = CustTable::find(fieldAccount.value());
        fieldName.value(custTable.Name);
        fieldGroup.value(custTable.CustGroup);
        fieldCurrency.value(custTable.Currency);
        fieldPaymTermId.value(custTable.PaymTermId);
        fieldPaymMode.value(custTable.PaymMode);
    }
    static void main(Args _args)
    {
        CustSelect custSelect = new CustSelect();
        ;

        if (CustSelect.prompt())
        {
            CustSelect.run();
        }
    }
```

2. Run the class, select any customer from the list, and move the cursor to the next control. Notice how the rest of the fields were populated automatically with the customer information:

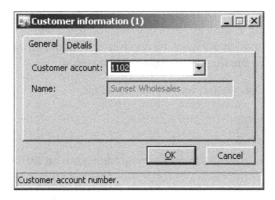

3. When you click on **Details** tab page, you will see the details as in following screenshot:

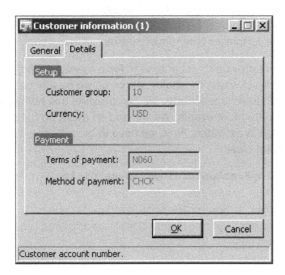

## How it works...

The new class `CustSelect` is a copy of `CustCreate` from the previous recipe with few changes. In its declaration, we leave all `DialogField` declarations. We remove all other variables apart from Customer account. The Customer account input control is the only editable field on the dialog, so we have to keep it for storing its value.

The methods `pack()`/`unpack()` remain the same as we are not using any of their features.

In the `dialog()` member method, we call `allowUpdateOnSelect()` with the argument `true` to enable input control event handling. We also disable all fields apart from Customer account by calling `enable()` with parameter `false` for every field.

The member method `dialogSelectCtrl()` of the `RunBase` class is called every time the user modifies any input control in the dialog. It is the place where we have to add all the required code to ensure that, in our case, all controls are populated with the correct data from the customer record, once the Customer account is chosen.

Static `main()` method ensures that we can run this class.

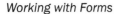

## There's more...

Usage of `dialogSelectCtrl()` sometimes might appear a bit limited as this method is only invoked when the dialog control loses its focus. No other events can be controlled, and it can become messy if more controls needs to be processed. Actually, this method is called from the `selectControl()` of the form, which is used as a base for the dialog.

As mentioned earlier, dialogs created using the **Dialog** class are actually forms, which are dynamically created during runtime. So in order to extend event handling functionality on dialogs, we should utilize form event handling features.

The **Dialog** class does not provide direct access to form event handling functions, but we can easily access the form object within the dialog. Although we cannot create the usual event handling methods on runtime form controls, we can override this behavior. Let's modify the previous example to include more events. We will add an event on the second tab page, which is triggered once the page is activated. First, we have to override the `dialogPostRun()` method on the **CustSelect** class:

```
public void dialogPostRun(DialogRunbase dialog)
{;
    dialog.formRun().controlMethodOverload(true);
    dialog.formRun().controlMethodOverloadObject(this);
    super(dialog);
}
```

Here, we enable event overriding on the form after it is fully created and is ready for displaying on the screen. We also pass the **CustSelect** object as argument for the `controlMethodOverloadObject()` to make sure that form "knows" where overridden events are located.

Next, we have to create the method that overrides the tab page event:

```
void TabPg_2_pageActivated()
{;
    info('Tab page activated');
}
```

The method name consists of the control name and event name joined with an underscore. But before creating such methods, we first have to get the name of the runtime control. This is because the dialog form is created dynamically, and Dynamics AX defines control names automatically without allowing the user to choose them. In this example, I have temporary added the following code to the bottom of `dialog()`, which displayed the name of the **Details** tab page control when the class was executed:

```
info(tabDetails.name());
```

Now, run the class again, and select the **Details** tab page. The message should be displayed in the **Infolog**.

# Creating dynamic menu buttons

Normally, Dynamics AX forms are created in AOT by adding various controls to the form's design and do not change during runtime. But besides that, Dynamics AX allows developers to add controls dynamically during form runtime.

Probably, you have already noticed that the **Document handling** form in the standard Dynamics AX application has a nice option to create a new record by clicking the **New** button and selecting the desired document type from the list. This feature does not add any new functionality to the application, but it provides an alternative way of quickly creating a new record and it makes the form more user-friendly. The content of this button is actually generated dynamically during the initialization of the form and may vary depending on the document handling setup.

There might be other cases when such features can be used. For example, dynamic menu buttons could be used to display a list of statuses, which depends on the type of the selected record.

In this recipe, we will explore the code behind this feature. As an example, we will modify the **Ledger budget** button on the **Chart of accounts** form to display a list of available budget models relevant only for the selected ledger account. That means the list is going to be generated dynamically and may be different for different accounts.

## How to do it...

1. Open the **LedgerTable** form in AOT.
2. Add the following variable to its class declaration:
   ```
   Map modelMap;
   ```
3. Delete the **ButtonBudget** menu item button located in the form's **ButtonGroup**.

4. Create a new button of type **MenuButton** instead in the same place as **ButtonBudget** with the following properties:

| Property | Value |
|---|---|
| Name | ButtonBudget |
| AutoDeclaration | Yes |
| Text | Ledger budget |

5. Override its `clicked()` method:

```
void clicked()
{
    MapIterator              mapIterator;
    BudgetModel              model;
    LedgerBudget             budget;
    FormFunctionButtonControl menuItemButton;
    ;

    if (modelMap)
    {
        mapIterator = new MapIterator(modelMap);
        mapIterator.begin();
        while (mapIterator.more())
        {
            element.design().removeControl(mapIterator.key());
            mapIterator.next();
        }
    }
    modelMap = new Map(Types::Integer, Types::String);
    while select model
        where model.Type      == HeadingSub::Heading
           && model.Blocked == NoYes::No
        exists join budget
        where budget.ModelNum   == model.ModelId
           && budget.AccountNum == LedgerTable.AccountNum
    {
        menuItemButton = ButtonBudget.addControl(
            FormControlType::MenuFunctionButton,
            'LedgerBudgetModel');
        menuItemButton.text(model.Txt);
        modelMap.insert(menuItemButton.id(), model.ModelId);
    }
    super();
}
```

6. Add a new **MenuItemButton** to this **MenuButton** with properties:

| Property | Value |
|----------|-------|
| Name | LedgerBudget |
| MenuItemType | Display |
| MenuItemName | LedgerBudget |
| Text | All models |

7. Insert a **Separator** afterwards.

8. The form should look like this in AOT:

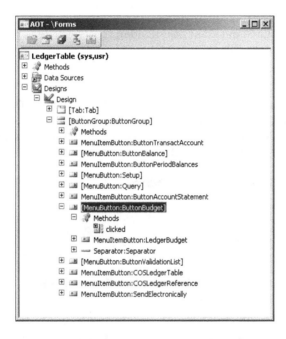

9. Next, add the following code to the top of the form's run() right after the variable declaration section:

```
element.controlMethodOverload(true);
```

10. And finally, create a new form method:

```
public void ledgerBudgetModel_clicked()
{
    FormFunctionButtonControl  menuItemButton;
    BudgetModelId              modelId;
    Args                       args;
    FormRun                    formRun;
    FormDataSource             fds;
    QueryBuildDataSource       qbds;
```

```
QueryBuildRange              qbr;
;

menuItemButton = element.controlCallingMethod();
modelId        = modelMap.lookup(menuItemButton.id());
args = new Args(formstr(LedgerBudget));
args.record(LedgerTable);
formRun = classfactory.formRunClass(args);
formRun.init();
fds = formRun.dataSource();
qbds = fds.query().dataSourceTable(
    tablenum(LedgerBudget));
qbr  = qbds.addRange(fieldnum(LedgerBudget,ModelNum));
qbr.value(queryvalue(modelId));
qbr.status(RangeStatus::Hidden);
formRun.run();
formRun.wait();
}
```

11. To test the results, open **General ledger | Chart of Account Details**, and expand the **Ledger budget** menu button for several accounts containing budgets for different models. Notice how the content of the **Ledger budget** menu changes depending on what budgets are configured for the selected account:

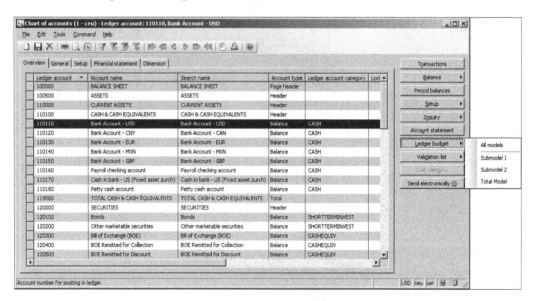

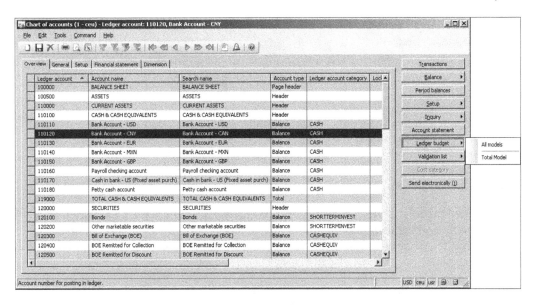

12. If you click on one of the available options, for example, **Total Model** for account **110110**, then you get a list of ledger budget records for this particular account and this particular model:

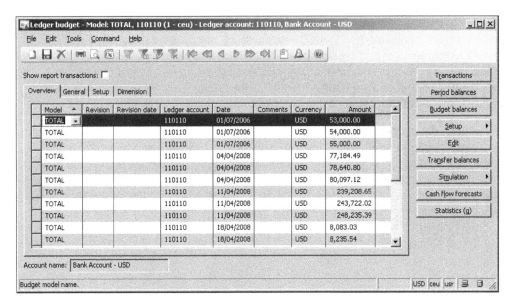

## How it works...

We start the example by adding a new **Map** variable to the form's class declaration section. We will use it temporarily for storing a list of available budget models along with dynamically created control numbers.

The next step is to replace the existing **Ledger budget** menu item button with a menu button. This will allow a user to expand it and select one of the options inside it. Notice that the new button is named exactly the same as the previous one. This is because there is a standard code on the form that handles the button's availability depending on the type of selected account. By leaving the same name, we ensure that the code will compile and work properly.

Now, we need to override the button's `clicked()`. The code in here will be executed once the user has clicked on the **Ledger budget** button, and it will create dynamic menu item buttons. The code has to be before `super()` to make sure the `super()` "knows" about all the controls in this menu button.

The code starts with first removing all existing items, in case they were created previously. We have to perform this operation, otherwise the list will keep increasing with every user click. We loop though the `modelMap` variable and remove every control from the form's design that matches the value in the **Map**. This part of the code is not executed when a user opens the **Ledger budget** menu button for the first time, because `modelMap` is not initialized yet. After this, we reset the **Map** by recreating it.

The second part of this method loops through existing budget models for the currently selected ledger account and creates a new menu item button for every model. Here, we also prepare the `modelMap` variable for further use by storing the number of the newly created control and the budget model ID. Notice that we have set the same name `LedgerBudgetModel` for every control created. As we will see later, this is done on purpose.

To finish with the **Ledger budget** menu button, we also add a menu item button pointing to the original **Ledger budget** form along with a separator. There are two reasons for this. First, we still want to keep the original functionality allowing the user to open the **Ledger budget** form if there are no budget records. And secondly, by having something inside the **Ledger budget** menu button, we force it to be displayed during the initialization of the form. If this menu button was empty, it would simply not be displayed on the form and the code in its `clicked()` method would never be executed. Lastly, the separator simply distinguishes the static and dynamic parts of the content.

Finally, we have to ensure that the correct form is opened once the user selects one of the dynamic options. We could have assigned the **LedgerBudget** menu item to every control created, but this would not filter the opened **Ledger budget** form with the chosen budget model. In order to achieve that, we have to override the button's event with our code. By calling `controlMethodOverload(true)`, we enable form control event overriding. Now, we have to create a new form method with a name consisting of the control name and event name separated by an underscore, i.e. for our dynamic control named **LedgerBudgetModel**, we have to create `ledgerBudgetModel_clicked()`. In this method, we retrieve the value of the currently selected budget model, create and initialize the **LedgerBudget** form, apply the budget model filter to its data source, and run it. In this way, we simulate the execution of the **LedgerBudget** menu item and also set the required filter.

The last thing to mention here is about the security. When building dynamic controls, it is very important that the created functionality can still be properly controlled by the Dynamics AX security system. For example, in this recipe, if a user does not have access to the **LedgerBudget** menu item, then the **Ledger budget** menu button will be automatically inaccessible, and there will be no further access to dynamic buttons inside it. This is because during form initialization, only "real" controls are considered so as only the menu button control's **LedgerBudget** menu item is disabled by the security, the whole menu button will be hidden too.

# Building dynamic form

A standard approach for creating forms in Dynamics AX is to create and store form objects in AOT. This ensures system performance and a high level of complexity. But in a number of cases, it is required to have forms created dynamically. Looking at the standard Dynamics AX application, we can see that application objects like the **Table browser** form, various lookups, or dialogs are built dynamically.

In this recipe, we will create a dynamic form. To show how flexible it can be, we will replicate the layout of the existing transaction type form in the **Bank** module. It can be opened from **Bank | Setup | Bank transaction type**.

## How to do it...

1. In AOT, create a new class called **BankTransTypeDynamic** with the following code:

```
static void main(Args _args)
{
    DictTable               dictTable;
    Form                    form;
    FormBuildDesign         design;
    FormBuildDataSource     ds;
    FormBuildTabControl     tab;
    FormBuildTabPageControl tp1;
    FormBuildTabPageControl tp2;
```

```
FormBuildGridControl      grid;
FormBuildGroupControl     grp1;
FormBuildGroupControl     grp2;
FormBuildGroupControl     grp3;
Args                      args;
FormRun                   formRun;
;

dictTable = new DictTable(tablenum(BankTransType));

form = new Form();
form.name("BankTransTypeDynamic");

ds = form.addDataSource(dictTable.name());
ds.table(dictTable.id());

design = form.addDesign('design');
design.caption("Bank transaction type");

tab = design.addControl(FormControlType::Tab, "Tab");
tab.widthMode(FormWidth::ColumnWidth);
tab.heightMode(FormHeight::ColumnHeight);

tp1 = tab.addControl(FormControlType::TabPage, "Tp1");
tp1.caption("Overview");

tp2 = tab.addControl(FormControlType::TabPage, "Tp2");
tp2.caption("General");

grid = tp1.addControl(FormControlType::Grid, "Grid");
grid.dataSource(ds.name());
grid.widthMode(FormWidth::ColumnWidth);
grid.heightMode(FormHeight::ColumnHeight);

grid.addDataField(
    ds.id(),
    fieldnum(BankTransType, BankTransType));

grid.addDataField(
    ds.id(),
    fieldnum(BankTransType, Name));

grid.addDataField(
    ds.id(),
    fieldnum(BankTransType, LedgerAccountNum));

grp1 = tp2.addControl(FormControlType::Group, "Grp1");
grp1.dataSource(ds.id());
grp1.autoDataGroup(true);
grp1.dataGroup(
    tablefieldgroupstr(BankTransType, Identification));
```

```
grp2 = tp2.addControl(FormControlType::Group, "Grp2");
grp2.dataSource(ds.id());
grp2.autoDataGroup(true);
grp2.dataGroup(tablefieldgroupstr(BankTransType, Name));

grp3 = tp2.addControl(FormControlType::Group, "Grp3");
grp3.dataSource(ds.id());
grp3.autoDataGroup(true);
grp3.dataGroup(tablefieldgroupstr(BankTransType, Ledger));

args = new Args();
args.object(form);

formRun = classfactory.formRunClass(args);
formRun.init();
formRun.run();

formRun.detach();
}
```

2.  To test the form, run the class. Notice that the form is very much similar to the one in
    **Bank | Setup | Bank transaction type**:

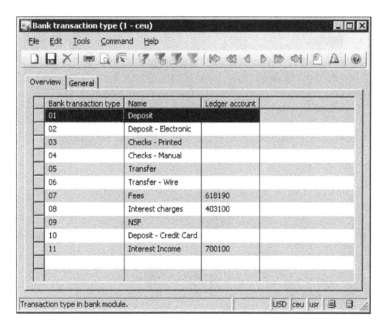

3. Click on the **General** tab page to display additional information:

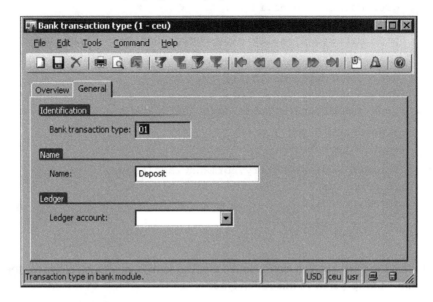

## How it works...

We start the code with declaring variables. Note that most of them begin with **FormBuild**, which is a set of application classes used for building dynamic controls. Each of those types corresponds to the control types manually used when building forms in AOT.

Right after the variable declaration, we create a `dictTable` object based on the **BankTransType** table. We will reuse this object later a number of times.

Next, we create a form object and assign a name by calling:

```
form = new Form();
form.name("BankTransTypeDynamic");
```

The form should have a data source, so we add one by calling `addDataSource()` on the `form` object:

```
ds = form.addDataSource(dictTable.name());
ds.table(dictTable.id());
```

Every form has a design; so does ours:

```
design = form.addDesign('design');
design.caption("Bank transaction type");
```

Once the design is ready, we can start adding controls. First, we add a tab control by automatically expanding width and height:

```
tab = design.addControl(FormControlType::Tab, "Tab");
tab.widthMode(FormWidth::ColumnWidth);
tab.heightMode(FormHeight::ColumnHeight);
```

Then we add two tab pages, **Overview** and **General**:

```
tp1 = tab.addControl(FormControlType::TabPage, "Tp1");
tp1.caption("Overview");

tp2 = tab.addControl(FormControlType::TabPage, "Tp2");
tp2.caption("General");
```

The first tab page contains a grid pointing to the data source and automatically expanding height and width:

```
grid = tp1.addControl(FormControlType::Grid, "Grid");
grid.dataSource(ds.name());
grid.widthMode(FormWidth::ColumnWidth);
grid.heightMode(FormHeight::ColumnHeight);
```

We add three controls pointing to relevant table fields by calling addDataField() on grid:

```
grid.addDataField(
    ds.id(),
    fieldnum(BankTransType, BankTransType));

grid.addDataField(
    ds.id(),
    fieldnum(BankTransType, Name));

grid.addDataField(
    ds.id(),
    fieldnum(BankTransType, LedgerAccountNum));
```

The second tab page contains three groups, which we add by `addControl()` with the first argument `FormControlType::Group`. Here, we save some time and code by making those groups automatic by calling `autoDataGroup()` with `true`:

Group 1:

```
grp1 = tp2.addControl(FormControlType::Group, "Grp1");
grp1.dataSource(ds.id());
grp1.autoDataGroup(true);
grp1.dataGroup(
    tablefieldgroupstr(BankTransType, Identification));
```

Group 2:

```
grp2 = tp2.addControl(FormControlType::Group, "Grp2");
grp2.dataSource(ds.id());
grp2.autoDataGroup(true);
grp2.dataGroup(tablefieldgroupstr(BankTransType, Name));
```

Group 3:

```
grp3 = tp2.addControl(FormControlType::Group, "Grp3");
grp3.dataSource(ds.id());
grp3.autoDataGroup(true);
grp3.dataGroup(tablefieldgroupstr(BankTransType, Ledger));
```

The last lines of code initialize and run the form.

# Adding form splitters

Commonly used forms like **Sales orders** or **Projects** in Dynamics AX have multiple grids. Normally, one grid is in the upper section and another one is in the bottom section of the form. Sometimes grids are placed next to each other.

The size of the data in each grid may vary, and that's why most of the forms with multiple grids have splitters in the middle so users can resize both grids at once by dragging the splitter with the help of a mouse. It is a good practice to add splitters to newly created forms.

Although Microsoft developers did a good job by adding splitters to most of the multi-grid forms, there is still at least one that has not got it. It is the **Account reconciliation** form in the **Bank** module, which is one of the most commonly used forms. It can be opened from **Bank | Bank Account Details**, **Functions | Account reconciliation** button, and then the **Transactions** button. In the following screenshot, you can see that the size of the bottom grid cannot be changed:

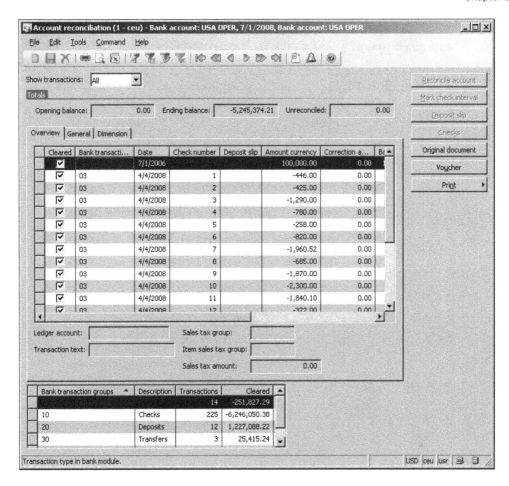

In this recipe, we will demonstrate the usage of splitters by resolving this situation. We will add a form splitter in the middle of the two grids in the mentioned form. It will allow users to define the sizes of both grids to make sure that the data is displayed optimally.

## How to do it...

1.  Open the **BankReconciliation** form in AOT, and create a new **Group** at the very top of the form's design with the following properties:

| Property | Value |
| --- | --- |
| Name | Top |
| AutoDeclaration | Yes |
| FrameType | None |
| Width | Column width |

2. Move the **AllReconciled**, **Balances**, and **Tab** controls into the newly created group.

3. Create a new **Group** right below the **Top** group with properties:

| Property | Value |
|---|---|
| Name | Splitter |
| AutoDeclaration | Yes |
| Width | Column width |
| Height | 5 |
| FrameType | Raised 3D |
| BackgroundColor | Window background |
| HideIfEmpty | No |
| AlignChild | No |

4. Add the following line of code to the bottom of the form's class declaration:

```
SysFormSplitter_Y fs;
```

5. Add the following line of code to the bottom of the form's `init()`:

```
fs = new SysFormSplitter_Y(Splitter, Top, element);
```

6. Override three methods in the **Splitter** group with the following code:

```
public int mouseDown(
    int     _x,
    int     _y,
    int     _button,
    boolean _ctrl,
    boolean _shift)
{
    return fs.mouseDown(_x, _y, _button, _ctrl, _shift);
}

public int mouseMove(
    int     _x,
    int     _y,
    int     _button,
    boolean _ctrl,
    boolean _shift)
{
    return fs.mouseMove(_x, _y, _button, _ctrl, _shift);
}

public int mouseUp(
    int     _x,
```

```
    int     _y,
    int     _button,
    boolean _ctrl,
    boolean _shift)
{
    return fs.mouseUp(_x, _y, _button, _ctrl, _shift);
}
```

7.  Change the following properties of the existing **BankTransTypeGroup** group:

| Property | Value |
| --- | --- |
| Top | Auto |
| Width | Column width |
| Height | Column height |

8.  Change the following property of the exiting **TypeSums** grid located in **BankTransTypeGroup** group:

| Property | Value |
| --- | --- |
| Height | Column height |

9.  In AOT the Modified **BankReconciliation** form should look like the following screenshot:

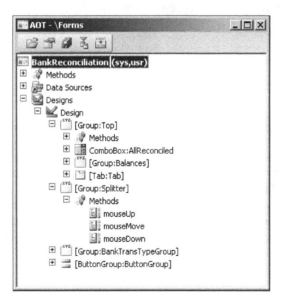

10. Now, to test the results, open **Bank | Bank Account Details**, select any bank account, click **Functions | Account reconciliation**, choose an existing or create a new account statement, and click the **Transactions** button. Notice that now the form has a nice splitter in the middle, which makes the form look better and allows defining the size of each grid:

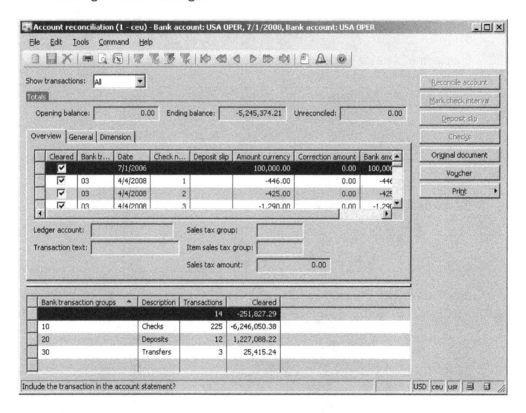

## How it works...

Normally a splitter is placed between two form groups. In this recipe, to follow that rule, we need to adjust the **BankReconciliation** form's design. The filter **AllReconciled**, the group **Balances** and the tab **Tab** are moved to a new group called **Top**. We do not want this new group to be visible to user, so we set **FrameType** to **None**. Setting **AutoDeclaration** to **Yes** allows us to access this object from X++ code. And finally, we make this group automatically expand in the horizontal direction by setting its **Width** to **Column width**. At this stage, visual form layout did not change, but now we have the upper group ready.

The **BankTransTypeGroup** group could be used as a bottom group with slight changes. We change its **Top** behavior to **Auto** and make it fully expandable in the horizontal and vertical directions. The **Height** of the grid inside this group also has to be changed to **Column height** in order to fill all the vertical space.

In the middle of those two groups, we add a splitter. The splitter is nothing else but another group, which looks like a splitter. In order to achieve that, we set **Height** to **5**, **FrameType** to **Raised 3D**, and **BackgroundColor** to **Windows background**. This group does not hold any other controls inside. Therefore, in order to make it visible, we have to set the property **HideIfEmpty** to **No**. The value **No** of the property **AlignChild** makes the splitter begin on the very left side of the form and the **Column width** value of the property **Width** forces the splitter to automatically fill the form's width.

Mouse events are handled by the **SysFormSplitter_Y** application class. After it has been declared in the form's class declaration, we create the actual object in the form's init(). We pass the name of the splitter control, the name of the top group and the form itself as arguments when creating it.

A fully working splitter requires three mouse event handlers. It is implemented by overriding the mouseMove(), mouseDown(), and mouseUp() methods in the splitter group control. All arguments are passed to the respective member methods of the **SysFormSplitter_Y** class which does all the job.

In this way, horizontal splitters can be easily added to any form. The Dynamics AX application also contains nice examples about splitters, which can be found in AOT in the **Tutorial_Form_Split** form. Vertical splitters can also be added to forms using a very similar approach. For this, we need to use another application class called **SysFormSplitter_X**.

# Creating modal forms

During my trainings and working with Dynamics AX users, I noticed that people who are not familiar with computers and software tend to get lost among open application windows. The same could be applied to Dynamics AX. I experienced many times when a user opened one form, clicked some button to open another one, and then went back to the first one without closing the second one. Sometimes this happens intentionally, sometimes—not, but the result is that the second form is hidden behind the first one and the user starts wondering why it is not possible to close or edit the first form.

Such issues could be easily solved by making the child form a modal window. In other words, the second form always stays on top of the first one until closed. In this recipe, we will do exactly that. As an example, we will make the **Create sales order** form a modal window.

## How to do it...

1. Open the **SalesCreateOrder** form in AOT, and set its **Design** property:

   | Property | Value |
   | --- | --- |
   | WindowType | Popup |

2. To test, open **Accounts receivable | Sales Order Details**, and start creating a new order. Notice that now the sales order creation form always stays on top of the **Sales order** form:

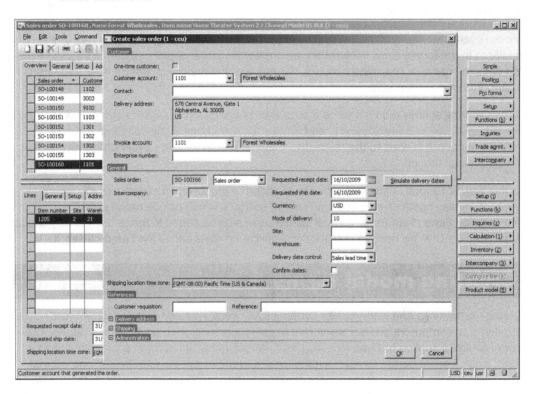

## How it works...

Dynamics AX form design has a **WindowType** property, which is set to **Standard** by default. In order to make a form behave as a modal window, we have to change it to **Popup**. Such forms will always stay on top of the parent form.

## There's more...

We already know that some of the Dynamics AX forms are created dynamically using the **Dialog** class. If we look deeper into the code, we could find that the **Dialog** class actually creates a runtime Dynamics AX form. That means we can apply the same principle, i.e. change the relevant form's design property. The following code could be added to the **Dialog** object and would do the job:

```
dialog.dialogForm().buildDesign().windowType(
    FormWindowType::Popup);
```

We get a reference to the form's design, by first using `dialogForm()` of the **Dialog** object to get a reference to the **DialogForm** object, and then we call `buildDesign()` on the latter object. Then, we set the design's property by calling its `windowType()` with an argument `FormWindowType::Popup`.

# Changing common form appearance

In every single multi-company Dynamics AX project, in order to prevent user mistakes, I was asked to add functionality that allows setting the background color of every form per company. By doing that, users clearly see in which company account they are at the moment and can easily work within multiple companies at the same time.

In this recipe, we will modify **SysSetupFormRun** class to change the background color for every form in Dynamics AX.

## How to do it...

1. Open **SysSetupFormRun** in AOT, and override its `run()` with the following code:

```
public void run()
{;
    super();
    this.design().colorScheme(FormColorScheme::RGB);
    this.design().backgroundColor(WinAPI::RGB2int(255,0,0));
}
```

2. To test the results, open any Dynamics AX form, for example, **General ledger | Chart of Accounts Details** and notice how the background color is changed to red:

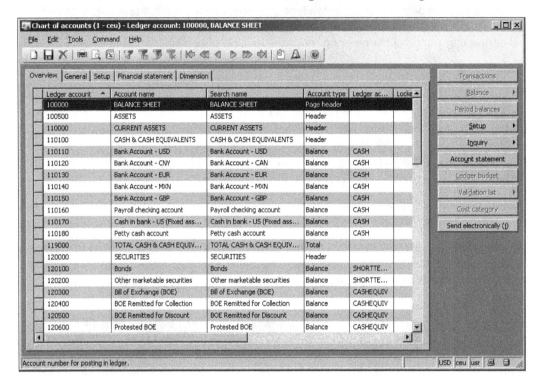

## How it works...

`SysSetupFormRun` is the application class that is called by the system every time a user runs a form. The best place to add our custom code is to override the `run()` method and place it under the `super()`.

We use `this.design()` to get a reference to the form's design. By calling `colorScheme()` and `backgroundColor()`, we set the color scheme to red/green/blue and the color code to red.

We use `WinAPI::RGB2int()` to transform the human-readable red/green/blue code into the numeric color code.

## There's more...

This recipe showed a very basic principle of how to change the common appearance of all forms with few lines of code. You noticed that the color in this recipe does not fill all areas of the form, which does not make the form look nice. An alternative to this could be to dynamically add a colored rectangle or something similar to the top of the form. The possibilities are endless here. New controls like input fields, buttons, menu items, and others could also be added to all forms dynamically using this class. But do not overdo as it may impact system performance.

For example, this recipe could be combined with one of the later recipes, Picking a color from Chapter 4, Building Lookups. In this recipe, one color could be set per each Dynamics AX company in the **Company information** form, and this value could be used in the `run()` of the **SysSetupFormRun** class. This would ensure that all forms are colored differently for each Dynamics AX company to make sure users do not get lost among forms when working in multi-company environments.

## See also

Building Lookups, Picking a color

# Storing last form values

Dynamics AX has a very useful feature, which allows saving the latest user choices per user per form. This feature is implemented across a number of standard reports, periodic jobs, and other objects, which require user input.

When developing a new functionality for Dynamics AX, I always try to keep that practice. One of the frequently used areas is custom filters for grid-based forms. Although, Dynamics AX allows users to use standard filtering for any grid, in practice sometimes it is not very useful, especially when the user requires something specific.

In this recipe, we will see how to store the latest user filter selections. To make it as simple as possible, we will use existing filters on the **General journal** form, which can be opened from **General ledger | Journals | General journal**. This form contains two filters—**Show** and **Show user-created only**. **Show** allows displaying journals by their posting status and **Show user-created only** toggles between all journals and the currently logged user's journals.

## How to do it...

1. Find the **LedgerJournalTable** form in AOT, and add the following code to the bottom of its class declaration:

```
AllOpenPosted    showStatus;
NoYes            showCurrentUser;
#define.CurrentVersion(1)
#localmacro.CurrentList
    showStatus,
    showCurrentUser
#endmacro
```

2. Create these additional form methods:

```
public void initParmDefault()
{;
    showStatus = AllOpenPosted::Open;
    showCurrentUser = true;
}

public container pack()
{
    return [#CurrentVersion,#CurrentList];
}

public boolean unpack(container packedClass)
{
    int version = RunBase::getVersion(packedClass);
    ;

    switch (version)
    {
        case #CurrentVersion:
            [version,#CurrentList] = packedClass;
            return true;
        default:
            return false;
    }
    return false;
}

public identifiername lastValueDesignName()
{
    return element.args().menuItemName();
}

public identifiername lastValueElementName()
{
    return this.name();
}

public UtilElementType lastValueType()
{
    return UtilElementType::Form;
```

```
}
public userId lastValueUserId()
{
    return curuserid();
}
public dataAreaId lastValueDataAreaId()
{
    return curext();
}
```

3. Add the following code to the bottom of the form's `run()`:

```
xSysLastValue::getLast(this);
AllOpenPostedField.selection(showStatus);
ShowUserCreatedOnly.value(showCurrentUser);
journalFormTable.designSelectionChangeAllOpenPosted();
journalFormTable.designSelectionChangeShowUserCreateOnly();
```

4. And the following code to the bottom of the form's `close()`:

```
showStatus      = AllOpenPostedField.selection();
showCurrentUser = ShowUserCreatedOnly.value();
xSysLastValue::saveLast(this);
```

5. Now to test the form, open **General ledger | Journals | General journal**, change filter values, close it, and run again. The latest filter selections should stay:

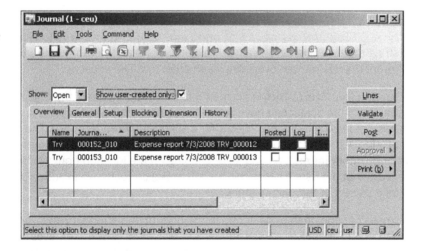

## How it works...

First of all, we define some variables. We will store the journal posting status filter value in `showStatus` and the current user filter value in `showCurrentUser`.

The macro `#CurrentList` is used to define a list of variables that we are going to store. Currently, we have two variables.

The macro `#CurrentVersion` defines a version of saved values. In other words, it says that the variables defined by the `#CurrentList`, which will be stored in system cache later, can be addressed using the number 1.

Normally, when implementing last value saving for the first time for particular object, `#CurrentVersion` is set to 1. Later on, if we decide to add new values or change existing ones, we have to change the value of `#CurrentVersion`, normally increasing it by 1. This ensures that the system addresses the correct list of variables in the cache and does not break existing functionality.

The `initParmDefault()` method specifies default values if nothing is found in the system cache. Normally, this happens if we run a form for the first time, we change `#CurrentVersion` or clean the cache. Later, this method is called automatically by the `xSysLastValue` object.

The methods `pack()` and `unpack()` are responsible for formatting a storage container from variables and extracting variables from a storage container respectively. In our case, `pack()` returns a container consisting of three values: version number, posting status, and current user toggle. Those values will be sent to the system cache after the form is closed. During an opening of the form, the `xSysLastValue` object uses `unpack()` to extract values from the stored container. It checks the container version from cache first, and if it matches the current version number, then the values from the cache are considered correct and are assigned to the form variables.

A combination of `lastValueDesignName()`, `lastValueElementName()`, `lastValueType()`, `lastValueUserId()`, and `lastValueDataAreaId()` return values form unique string representing saved values. This ensures that different users can store last values for different objects without overriding each other's values in cache.

The `lastValueDesignName()` method is meant to return the name of the object's current design in cases where the object can have several designs. In this recipe, there is only one design, so instead of leaving it empty, I used it for a slightly different purpose. The same **LedgerJournalTable** AOT form can represent different user forms like **Ledger journal**, **Periodic journal**, **Vendor payment journal**, and so on depending on the location from which it was opened. To ensure that the user's latest choices are saved correctly, we included the opening menu item name as part of the unique string.

The last two pieces of code need to be added to the bottom of the form's `run()` and `close()`. In the `run()` method, `xSysLastValue::getLast(this)` retrieves saved user values from cache and assigns them to the form's variables. The next two lines assign the same values to the respective form controls. `designSelectionChangeAllOpenPosted()` and `designSelectionChangeShowUserCreateOnly()` execute a form query to apply updated filters. Although both of those methods currently perform exactly the same action, we keep both for the future in case this functionality is updated. Code lines in `close()` are responsible for assigning user selections to variables and saving them to cache by calling `xSysLastValue::saveLast(this)`.

# Using tree controls

Frequent users should notice that some of the Dynamics AX forms have an option to switch to a tree layout. In some cases, especially when there are parent-child relations among records, it is a much clearer way to show the whole hierarchy as compared to a flat list. For example, projects and their subprojects displayed in the **Project Details** form give a much better overview when switched to a tree layout.

This recipe will discuss the principles of how to build tree-based forms. As an example, we will use the **Budget model** form, which can be opened from **General ledger | Setup | Budget | Budget model**. This form contains a list of budget models and their submodels. Although the data is organized using a parent-child structure, currently this form does not have a hierarchy layout. The goal of this recipe is to correct that problem.

## How to do it...

1.  In AOT, create a new class called **BudgetModelTree** with the following code:

```
class BudgetModelTree
{
    FormTreeControl tree;
    BudgetModelId   model;
}
void new(
    FormTreeControl _formTreeControl,
    BudgetModelId    _budgetModelId)
{;
    tree    = _formTreeControl;
    model   = _budgetModelId;
}
public static BudgetModelTree construct(
    FormTreeControl _formTreeControl,
    BudgetModelId    _budgetModelId = '')
{
    return new BudgetModelTree(
        _formTreeControl,
        _budgetModelId);
}
TreeItemIdx createNode(
    TreeItemIdx    _parentIdx,
    BudgetModelId _modelId,
```

```
    RecId           _recId)
{
    TreeItemIdx itemIdx;
    BudgetModel modelSub;
    ;

    itemIdx = SysFormTreeControl::addTreeItem(
        tree,
        _modelId,
        _parentIdx,
        _recId,
        0,
        true);
    if (model == _modelId)
    {
        tree.select(itemIdx);
    }
    while select modelSub
        where modelSub.ModelId == _modelId &&
            modelSub.Type      == HeadingSub::SubModel
    {
        this.createNode(
            itemIdx,
            modelSub.SubModelId,
            modelSub.RecId);
    }
    return itemIdx;
}
void buildTree()
{
    BudgetModel modelMain;
    BudgetModel modelSub;
    TreeItemIdx itemIdx;
    ;

    tree.deleteAll();
    tree.lock();
    while select modelMain
        where modelMain.Type == HeadingSub::Heading
        notexists join modelSub
```

```
            where modelSub.SubModelId == modelMain.ModelId &&
                  modelSub.Type        == HeadingSub::SubModel
        {
            itemIdx = this.createNode(
                FormTreeAdd::Root,
                modelMain.ModelId,
                modelMain.RecId);
            SysFormTreeControl::expandTree(tree, itemIdx);
        }
        tree.unLock(true);
    }
```

2. Open the **BudgetModel** form in AOT, and create a new tab page:

| Property | Value |
|----------|---------|
| Name | TabTree |
| Caption | Tree |

3. Add a new **Tree** control to the new tab page:

| Property | Value |
|----------|---------------|
| Name | ModelTree |
| Height | Column height |
| Width | Column width |

4. Add the following code to the bottom of the form's class declaration:

```
BudgetModelTree budgetModelTree;
```

5. Override the form's `init()` with the following code:

```
public void init()
{;
    super();
    budgetModelTree = BudgetModelTree::construct(ModelTree);
}
```

6. Override `pageActivated()` on the **TabTree** tab page with the following code:

```
public void pageActivated()
{;
    super();
    budgetModelTree.buildTree();
}
```

7. In AOT the **BudgetModel** form should look like the following screenshot:

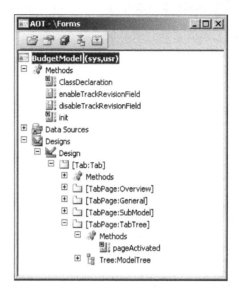

8. To test the tree control, open **General ledger | Setup | Budget | Budget model,** and select the **Tree** tab page. Notice how the ledger budget models are presented as a hierarchy:

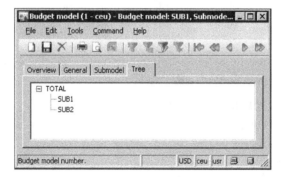

## How it works...

In order to separate the tree from the rest of the layout, we create a new tab page. Then, we add the actual tree control to the tab, which we use as a basis. Tree nodes are always generated from code. We also place all the tree-building logic into a separate class to make sure that it can be reused elsewhere, and the form itself does not get messy.

Besides the common `new()` and `construct()` methods, the class contains two methods, which actually generate the tree. The first method is `createNode()` and is used for creating a single budget model node or a whole branch. It is a recursive method, and it calls itself to generate the children of the current node. It accepts a parent node and a budget model as arguments. In this method, we create the node by calling the `addTreeItem()` method of the **SysFormTreeControl** class. The rest of the code loops through all submodels and creates subnodes (if there are any) for each of them.

Secondly, we create `buildTree()` where the whole tree is built. Before we actually start building it, we delete all nodes and lock the **Tree** control. Then, we add nodes by looping through all parent budget models and calling the previously mentioned `createNode()`. We call the `expandTree()` of the **SysFormTreeControl** class to show every parent budget model expanded. Once the hierarchy is ready, we unlock the **Tree** control.

Hierarchy generation might be time consuming, so we call it only when necessary, that is, when the tab page is actually opened. We override the tab page's `pageActivated()` and add a call to `buildTree()` there. Initially, to increase performance for bigger trees, only the first level of nodes has to be generated, and other nodes should be created only when the user clicks on the particular node. This could be achieved by placing the relevant code into the `expanding()` of the tree control in the form. Such an approach ensures that no time is spent on generating unused tree nodes.

## There's more...

Besides hierarchical layout, tree controls also allow users to use drag-and-drop functionality. This makes daily operations much quicker and more effective. Let's modify the previous example to support drag-and-drop. We are going to allow users to move ledger budget submodels to different parents within the tree. In order to do that, we need to make some changes to the **BudgetModelTree** class and the **BudgetModel** form.

Add the following code to the **BudgetModelTree** class declaration:

```
TreeItemIdx dragItemIdx;
TreeItemIdx lastItemIdx;
```

Create the following additional methods in this class:

```
boolean canMove()
{
    BudgetModel budgetModel;
    RecId       recId;
    ;

    recId = tree.getItem(dragItemIdx).data();
    select firstonly budgetModel
        where budgetModel.RecId == recId;
```

```
        return (budgetModel.Type == HeadingSub::SubModel);
    }
    void move(RecId _from, RecId _to)
    {
        BudgetModel modelFrom;
        BudgetModel modelTo;
        ;

        select firstonly modelTo
            where modelTo.RecId == _to;
        ttsbegin;
        select firstonly forupdate modelFrom
            where modelFrom.RecId == _from;
        modelFrom.ModelId = modelTo.SubModelId;
        if (modelFrom.validateWrite())
        {
            modelFrom.update();
        }
        ttscommit;
    }

    void stateDropHilite(TreeItemIdx _idx)
    {
        FormTreeItem item;
        ;

        if (lastItemIdx)
        {
            item = tree.getItem(lastItemIdx);
            item.stateDropHilited(false);
            tree.setItem(item);
            lastItemIdx  = 0;
        }
        if (_idx)
        {
            item = tree.getItem(_idx);
            item.stateDropHilited(true);
            tree.setItem(item);
            lastItemIdx = _idx;
        }
    }

    int beginDrag(int _x, int _y)
    {;
        [dragItemIdx] = tree.hitTest(_x, _y);
        return 1;
```

```
}
FormDrag dragOver(
    FormControl _dragSource,
    FormDrag    _dragMode,
    int         _x,
    int         _y)
{
    TreeItemIdx currItemIdx;
    ;

    if (!this.canMove())
    {
        return FormDrag::None;
    }

    [currItemIdx] = tree.hitTest(_x, _y);
    this.stateDropHilite(currItemIdx);
    return FormDrag::Move;
}
void drop(
    FormControl _dragSource,
    FormDrag    _dragMode,
    int         _x,
    int         _y)
{
    TreeItemIdx currItemIdx;
    ;

    if (!this.canMove())
    {
        return;
    }
    this.stateDropHilite(0);
    [currItemIdx] = tree.hitTest(_x,_y);
    if (!currItemIdx)
    {
        return;
    }
    this.move(
        tree.getItem(dragItemIdx).data(),
        tree.getItem(currItemIdx).data());
    tree.moveItem(dragItemIdx, currItemIdx);

}
```

Locate the **BudgetModel** form in AOT, find its **ModelTree** control, and change the following property:

| Property | Value |
|----------|-------|
| DragDrop | Manual |

Also, override the following methods of the **ModelTree** control:

```
public int beginDrag(int _x, int _y)
{
    return budgetModelTree.beginDrag(_x, _y);
}

FormDrag dragOver(
    FormControl  _dragSource,
    FormDrag     _dragMode,
    int          _x,
    int          _y)
{
    return budgetModelTree.dragOver(
        _dragSource,
        _dragMode,
        _x,
        _y);
}

void drop(
    FormControl  _dragSource,
    FormDrag     _dragMode,
    int          _x,
    int          _y)
{;
    budgetModelTree.drop(_dragSource, _dragMode, _x, _y);
}
```

Now when you open **General ledger | Setup | Budget | Budget model**, you should be able to move budget models within the tree with a mouse.

The main element in the latter modification is the **DragDrop** property of the tree control. It enables the drag-and-drop function, once we set its value to **Manual**. The next step is to override drag-and-drop events on the tree control. Tree controls could have a number of methods covering various drag-and-drop events. A good place to start investigating them is the **Tutorial_Form_TreeControl** class in the standard Dynamics AX application. In this example, we will cover only three of them:

▸ `beginDrag()` is executed when dragging begins. Here, we normally store the number of the item that is being dragged for later processing.

▸ `dragOver()` is executed once the dragged item is over another node. This method is responsible for highlighting nodes when the dragged item is over them. Its return value defines the mouse cursor icon once the item is being dragged.

▸ `drop()` is executed when the mouse button is released, i.e. dragged item is dropped over some node. Here, we normally place the code that does actual data modifications.

In this example, all logic is stored in the **BudgetModelTree** class. Each of the mentioned form methods calls the relevant method in the class. This is to reduce the amount of code placed on the form and allow the code to be reused on multiple forms. We added the following methods to the class:

▸ `canMove()` checks whether the currently selected node can be dragged. Although there might be more conditions, for this demonstration, we only disallow dragging of top nodes.

▸ `move()` is where the actual movement of the budget model is performed, i.e. submodel is assigned with another parent.

▸ `stateDropHilite()` is responsible for highlighting and removing highlight from relevant items. Using `stateDropHilited()`, we highlight the current item and we remove highlight from the previously highlighted one. This ensures that as we move the dragged item over the tree, items are highlighted once the dragged item is over them and the highlight is removed once dragged item leaves them. This method is called later from several places to make sure node highlighting works correctly.

▸ `beginDrag()` saves the item currently being dragged into a variable.

▸ `dragOver()` first checks if the currently selected item can be moved. If not, then it returns `FormDrag::None`, which changes the mouse cursor to the forbidden sign. Otherwise, the cursor is changed to an icon representing node movement. This method also calls `stateDropHilite()` to ensure correct node highlighting.

▸ `drop()` also checks if the item being dropped can be moved. If yes, then it uses `move()` to update the data and `moveItem()` to visually change the node's place in the tree. It also calls `stateDropHilite()` to update tree node highlighting.

Working with Data in Forms, Preloading images

Building Lookups, Building a tree lookup

# Building checklists

Anyone who preformed Dynamics AX application installation or upgrade has to be familiar with standard checklists. Normally, a checklist is a list of menu items displayed in logical sequence. Each item represents either mandatory or optional actions to be executed by the user in order to complete the whole procedure. In custom Dynamics AX implementations, checklists can be used as a convenient way to configure non standard settings. Checklists can also be implemented as a part of third-party modules for their initial setup.

In this recipe, we will create a checklist for user-friendly ledger budget setup. The checklist will consists of two mandatory and one optional item.

## How to do it...

1. Open AOT, and create a new class called `SysCheckListInterfaceBudget`:

```
interface SysCheckListInterfaceBudget
extends    SysCheckListInterface
{
}
```

2. Create three more classes—one for each checklist item, with the following code:

```
class       SysCheckListItem_BudgetModel
extends      SysCheckListItem
implements  SysCheckListInterfaceBudget
{
}

public str getCheckListGroup()
{
    return "Setup";
}

public str getHelpLink()
{
    #define.TopicId('AxShared.chm::/html/' +
        '84030522-0057-412C-BFC7-DBEB4D40E5A1.htm')
    ;

    return SysCheckListItem::sharedGuide(#TopicId);
```

```
}

public MenuItemName getMenuItemName()
{
    return menuitemdisplaystr(BudgetModel);
}

public MenuItemType getMenuItemType()
{
    return MenuItemType::Display;
}

str label()
{
    return "Models";
}

class     SysCheckListItem_BudgetRevision
extends    SysCheckListItem
implements SysCheckListInterfaceBudget
{
}

public void new()
{;
    super();
    this.placeAfter(classnum(SysCheckListItem_BudgetModel));
    this.indeterminate(true);
}

public str getCheckListGroup()
{
    return "Setup";
}

public str getHelpLink()
{
    #define.TopicId('AxShared.chm::/html/' +
        'AACC4353-C3EB-4982-BB7F-2B36D97FF25B.htm')
    ;

    return SysCheckListItem::sharedGuide(#TopicId);
}

public MenuItemName getMenuItemName()
{
    return menuitemdisplaystr(BudgetRevision);
}

public MenuItemType getMenuItemType()
```

```
{
    return MenuItemType::Display;
}
str label()
{
    return "Revisions";
}
class       SysCheckListItem_Budget
extends     SysCheckListItem
implements SysCheckListInterfaceBudget
{
}
public void new()
{;
    super();

    this.addDependency(
        classnum(SysCheckListItem_BudgetModel));

    this.placeAfter(
        classnum(SysCheckListItem_BudgetRevision));
}
public str getCheckListGroup()
{
    return "Create budgets";
}
public str getHelpLink()
{
    #define.TopicId('AxShared.chm::/html/' +
        '6A596E1E-6803-4410-B4E4-EDE4EF44AF6D.htm')
    ;

    return SysCheckListItem::sharedGuide(#TopicId);
}
public MenuItemName getMenuItemName()
{
    return menuitemdisplaystr(LedgerBudget);
}
public MenuItemType getMenuItemType()
{
    return MenuItemType::Display;
}
str label()
```

```
    {
        return "Budgets";
    }
```

3.  Create another class for the checklist itself:

```
    class SysCheckList_Budget extends SysCheckList
    {
        container log;
    }

    protected str getCheckListCaption()
    {
        return "Budget checklist";
    }

    protected str getHtmlHeader()
    {
        return "Budget checklist";
    }

    protected classId getInterfaceId()
    {
        return classnum(SysCheckListInterfaceBudget);
    }

    public void save(
        identifiername    _name,
        ClassDescription _description)
    {;
        if (!confind(log, _name))
        {
            log = conins(log, conlen(log)+1, _name);
        }
    }

    public boolean find(
        identifiername    _name,
        ClassDescription _description)
    {
        return confind(log, _name) ? true : false;
    }

    static void main(Args _args)
    {;
        SysCheckList::runCheckListSpecific(
            classnum(SysCheckList_Budget),
            true);
    }
```

4.  Open the **SysCheckList** class in AOT, and replace its checkListItemsHook() and checkListsHook() with the following code:

```
protected static container checkListsHook()
{
    return [classnum(SysCheckList_Budget)];
}

protected static container checkListItemsHook()
{
    return [classnum(SysCheckListItem_Budget),
            classnum(SysCheckListItem_BudgetRevision),
            classnum(SysCheckListItem_BudgetModel)];
}
```

5.  Open the **BudgetModel** form in AOT, and override its close() with the following code:

```
public void close()
{;
    super();

    SysCheckList::finished(
        classnum(SysCheckListItem_BudgetModel));
}
```

6.  Open the **BudgetRevision** form in AOT, and override its close() with the following code:

```
public void close()
{;
    super();

    SysCheckList::finished(
        classnum(SysCheckListItem_BudgetRevision));
}
```

7.  Open the **LedgerBudget** form in AOT, and override its close() with the following code:

```
public void close()
{;
    super();
    SysCheckList::finished(classnum(SysCheckListItem_Budget));
}
```

8. Create a new **Display** menu item **SysCheckList_Budget** with the following properties:

| Property | Value |
|---|---|
| Name | SysCheckList_Budget |
| Label | Budget checklist |
| ObjectType | Class |
| Object | SysCheckList_Budget |

9. To test the checklist, run the **SysCheckList_Budget** menu item from AOT. The following should appear on the right-hand side of the Dynamics AX window:

10. Click on the listed items to start and complete relevant actions. Notice how the status icons change upon completion of each task.

## How it works...

The main principle behind checklists is that we have to create a main class, which represents the checklist itself and a number of `SysCheckListItem` item classes, which act as list items. The relation between the main class and the items is made by the use of an interface, that is, each list item implements it, and the main class holds the reference to it.

In this example, we create an interface `SysCheckListInterfaceBudget` and specify it in the `getInterfaceId()` of the main checklist class `SysCheckList_Budget`. Next, we implement the interface in three `SysCheckListItem` classes, which correspond to **Models**, **Revisions**, and **Budgets** items in the checklist.

Each **SysCheckListItem** class contains a set of inherited methods, which allows us to define a number of different parameters for individual items:

> ▶ All initialization code can be added to the `new()` methods. In this example, we use `placeAfter()` to determine the position of the item in the list relative to other items, `indeterminate()` to make item optional and `addDependency()` to make an item inactive until another specified item is completed.

> ▶ `getCheckListGroup()` defines item dependency to a specific group. The Budget checklist has two groups, **Setup** and **Create budgets**.

> ▶ `getHelpLink()` is responsible for placing the relevant help link in the form of a question mark next to the item.

> ▶ `getMenuItemName()` and `getMenuItemType()` contain a name and a type of menu item, which is executed upon user request. Here, we have **Budget model**, **Budget revisions**, and **Ledger budget** forms respectively in each class.

> ▶ And finally custom labels can be set in `label()`.

Once the items are ready, we create the main checklist class `SysCheckList_Budget`, which extends the standard `SysCheckList`. We override some of the methods to add custom functionality to the checklist:

> ▶ `getCheckListCaption()` sets the title of the checklist.

> ▶ `getHtmlHeader()` could be used to add some descriptive text.

> ▶ As mentioned before, `getInterfaceId()` is the place where we specify the name of the checklist item interface.

> ▶ The methods `save()` and `find()` are used to store and retrieve respectively the status of each item in the list. In this example, we store statuses in the local variable `log` to make sure that statuses are reset every time we run the checklist.

> ▶ The static method `main()` runs the class. Here, we use `runCheckListSpecific()` of the system `SysCheckList` class to start the checklist.

The display menu item we created is pointing to the checklist class and may be used to add the checklist to a user menu.

When building checklists, it is necessary to add them and their items to the global checklist and checklist item list. the SysCheckList class contains two methods—checkLists() and checkListItems()—where all system checklists and their items are registered. The same class provides two more methods—checkListsHook() and checkListItemsHook()—where custom checklists should be added. As a part of this example, we also add our budget checklist and its items to the SysCheckList.

Final modifications have to be done in all checklist forms. We call the finished() of the SysCheckList class in the close() of each form to update the status of the corresponding checklist item. In other words, it means that item status will be set as completed when the user closes the form. This code does not affect the normal use of the form when it is opened from the regular menu. Of course, more logic could be added here if the completion of a specific item is not that straightforward.

Also notice that the system automatically adds a link called **Information**, which describes the checklist statuses:

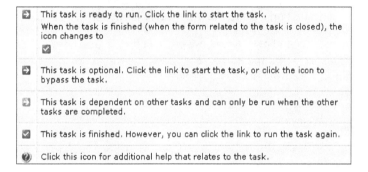

## There's more...

The checklist in this example stores item statuses per each run. This means that every time you close the checklist, its statuses are lost and are set to their initial states upon checklist start. By replacing save() and find() in SysCheckList_Budget with the following code, we can store statuses permanently in the **SysSetupLog** table:

```
public boolean find(
    identifiername    _name,
    ClassDescription _description)
{
    return SysSetupLog::find(_name, _description).RecId != 0;
}

public void save(
```

```
    identifiername    _name,
    ClassDescription _description)
{;
    SysSetupLog::save(_name, _description);
}
```

In this case, every time the checklist starts, the system will pick up its last status from the `SysSetupLog` table and allow the user to continue the checklist.

# Adding a "Go to the Main Table Form" link

**Go to the Main Table Form** is a feature of Dynamics AX, which allows users to jump to the main record just by right-clicking on the field and selecting the **Go to the Main Table Form** option. It is based on table relations and is available for those controls whose data fields have foreign key relationships with other tables.

Because of the data structure integrity, this feature works most of the time. However, when it comes to complex table relations, it does not work correctly or does not work at all. Another example of when this feature does not work automatically is when the form control is not bound to a table field. In such situations, **Go to the Main Table Form** has to be implemented manually.

In this recipe, to demonstrate how it works, we will modify the **Business relations** form in the **CRM** module to make sure that the **Employee** filter at the top of the form allows users to use the **Go to the Main Table Form** feature from the context menu.

## How to do it...

1. Open the **smmBusRelTable** form in AOT, and override `jumpRef()` of the **EmployeeFilter** control with:

```
public void jumpRef()
{
    EmplTable    emplTable;
    Args         args;
    MenuFunction menuFunction;
    ;

    emplTable = EmplTable::find(this.text());
    if (!emplTable)
    {
        return;
    }
    args = new Args();
    args.caller(element);
    args.record(emplTable);
    menuFunction = new MenuFunction(
```

```
          menuitemdisplaystr(EmplTable),
          MenuItemType::Display);
     menuFunction.run(args);
}
```

2. To test the result, open **CRM | Business Relation Details**, make sure an employee number is specified in the **Employee** filter, and right-click on the filter control. Notice that the **Go to the Main Table Form** option, which will open the **Employee** form, is now available:

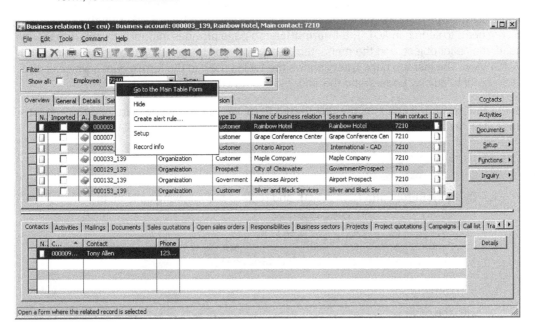

## How it works...

Normally, the **Go to the Main Table Form** feature is controlled by the relations between tables. If there are no relations or the form control is not bound to a table field, then this option is not available. But, we can force this option to appear by overriding the control's `jumpRef()` method.

In this method, we have to add code that opens the relevant form. This can be done by creating, initializing, and running a **FormRun** object, but the easier way is to simply run the relevant menu item. In this recipe, the code in `jumpRef()` does exactly that.

First, we check if the value in the control is a valid employee number. If yes, then we run the **Display** menu item **EmplTable** with an **Args** object containing the proper employee record. The rest is done automatically by the system, that is, the **Employee** form is opened with the employee information.

# Modifying the User setup form

The **User setup** form allows users to customize their most often used forms to fit their needs. Users can hide or move form controls, change labels, and so on. The setup is available for any Dynamics AX form and can be opened from the right-click context menu by selecting the **Setup** option.

As a developer, I also use this form very often. For example, it contains the very handy **System name** field, which displays the name of the currently selected table field or method, so you do not need to search in AOT. The **Information** tab page provides information about the form itself, the caller object, and the menu item used, and it allows opening those objects instantly in AOT view. The last tab page **Query** shows the tables used in the form's query, which is also very useful to quickly understand the underlying data structure.

In this recipe, we will enhance the **User setup** form. We will add a new button to the last tab page, which will open the selected table in AOT.

## How to do it...

1. Open **SysSetupForm** form in AOT, and replace the following code in its
   `fillQueryTreeQueryDatasource()`:

   ```
   formTreeItem = new FormTreeItem(
       nodeText,
       imagelist.image(#ImageDataSource),
       -1,
       null);
   ```

   with the code:

   ```
   formTreeItem = new FormTreeItem(
       nodeText,
       imagelist.image(#ImageDataSource),
       -1,
       queryBuildDataSource.table());
   ```

2. Add a new **ButtonGroup** to the **QueryPage** tab page:

   | Property | Value |
   | --- | --- |
   | Name | ButtonGroup1 |

3. Add a new **Button** to the created button group:

   | Property | Value |
   | --- | --- |
   | Name | EditTable |
   | Text | Edit |
   | AutoDeclaration | Yes |

4. Override the button's `clicked()` method:

```
void clicked()
{
    FormTreeItem formTreeItem;
    TableId      tableId;
    TreeNode     treeNode;
    #AOT
    ;

    formTreeItem = QueryTree.getItem(
        QueryTree.getSelection());
    tableId = formTreeItem.data();
    if (!tableId || !tableid2name(tableId))
    {
        return;
    }
    treeNode = infolog.findNode(
        #TablesPath +
        #AOTDelimiter +
        tableid2name(tableId));
    if (!treeNode)
    {
        return;
    }
    treeNode.AOTnewWindow();
}
```

5. Override `selectionChanged()` on the **QueryTree** control:

```
public void selectionChanged(
    FormTreeItem _oldItem,
    FormTreeItem _newItem,
    FormTreeSelect _how)
{;
    super(_oldItem, _newItem, _how);
    EditTable.enabled(
        tableid2name(_newItem.data())?true:false);
}
```

6. To test, open any form, for example, **Chart of Account Details** from the **General ledger**, and open **User setup** by right-clicking anywhere on the form and selecting the **Setup** option:

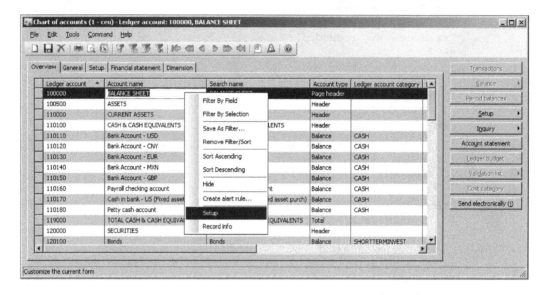

7. Go to the **Query** tab page, and select one of the tables in the query displayed:

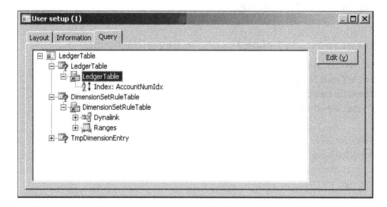

8. Click the **Edit** button to open this table in AOT:

## How it works...

First, we modify the creation of the query tree control. Normally, each tree node can hold some data. The tree in the **SysSetupForm** form does not have any data associated with nodes, so we have to modify the code and store the table number in each node representing a table.

Next, we add a new button and override its `clicked()`. In this method, we get the table number stored in the currently selected node—this is what we stored earlier—and search for that table in AOT. We display it in a new AOT window if found.

Finally, we override `selectionChanged()` on the **QueryTree** control to make sure the button's status is updated upon node selection. In other words, the **Edit** button is enabled if the current tree node contains some data, otherwise it is disabled.

In this way, we have modified the **User setup** form to provide us with a quick AOT access to the underlying tables.

# Modifying application version

Dynamics AX identifies its releases with two version numbers—kernel version and application version. For example, version number 5.0.593.0 means Dynamics AX 2009 RTM and 5.0.1000.52 is Dynamics AX 2009 Service Pack 1. Dynamics AX hotfix rollups are presented in a similar way by only updating the last version number digits. Version numbers an be viewed in the **About Microsoft** Dynamics AX dialog, which can be accessed from the **Help** menu.

Besides standard versioning, Dynamics AX allows adding additional versions for solution developers to control their releases. In this recipe, we will learn how to do that. We will modify standard application objects to incorporate our changes.

## Getting ready

Solution versions can be changed only in SL1, SL2, SL3, BUS (and BUP) layers.
SL1-SL3 layers are used for certified solutions and BUS—for business partner solutions.
To proceed further, we will need the BUS layer code in order to log in to the BUS and BUP
layers of the application.

## How to do it...

1. Log in to the BUS layer, and modify `sLxAppl()` of the **ApplicationVersion** class to:

```
private static client str sLxAppl()
{
    return '1.0.0';
}
```

2. Log in to the BUP layer, and modify the same method to:

```
private static client str sLxAppl()
{
    return '2.0.0';
}
```

3. The class in AOT should look like this:

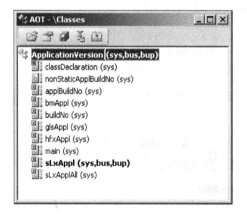

4.   Open **Help | About Microsoft** Dynamics AX, and notice the **Solution version** numbers:

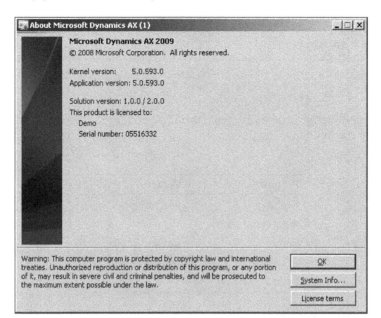

## How it works...

The **ApplicationVersion** class is the place where application version numbers are stored. For example, `applBuildNo()` returns the current application version. By modifying this class, Dynamics AX developers can modify original or custom version numbers. Later this class is called from the **SysAbout** form, which is actually the **About Microsoft** Dynamics AX dialog.

The class already contains a special method `sLxAppl()`, which should be used when defining a custom solution version. The interesting point is that different version numbers can be stored in different layers. In our example, first we set a version in BUS, and then we change that version in the BUP layer. And the result is that we can see both numbers separated by a slash in the **About Microsoft** Dynamics AX dialog. The text **Solution version** is added automatically, though it could be also changed.

## There's more...

Every Dynamics AX implementation project contains more or less customer-specific changes. Regardless of how big the modifications are, it is a good practice to use versioning. The modifications are normally stored in the VAR layer or any layer above it and are not included in automatic version display. However, if we look at the `run()` of the **SysAbout** form, we could notice that the information displayed on this form is actually formatted here. We can add our own code and relevant control to the form itself to display the custom name and version. So let's improve previous example and add an additional version called **VAR version**.

To follow existing practice, let's add one more method in the **ApplicationVersion** class first. (Do not forget to logout of BUP layer and log into your working layer). It will hold our version number:

```
static str varAppl()
{
    return '3.0.0';
}
```

In AOT, open **SysAbout** form and add a new **StaticText** control for displaying version-related information with the following properties:

| Property | Value |
| --- | --- |
| Name | VARVersion |
| AutoDeclaration | Yes |
| Width | Column width |
| BackStyle | Transparent |
| Text | |

The form in AOT should look like following:

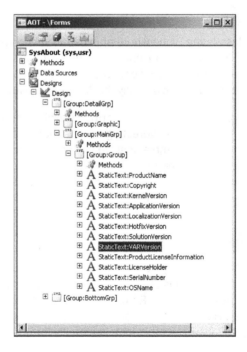

And finally, we modify the form's `run()`. Let's add:

```
str varVersionNumber = ApplicationVersion::varAppl();
```

right after:

```
str slxVersionNumber = ApplicationVersion::sLxApplAll();
```

and:

```
if (varVersionNumber)
{
    VARVersion.text('VAR version: ' + varVersionNumber);
}
```

right after:

```
if (slxVersionNumber)
{
    solutionVersion.text('Solution version: ' +
        slxVersionNumber);
}
```

Now, open **Help | About Microsoft** Dynamics AX again, and notice a new entry—**VAR version**:

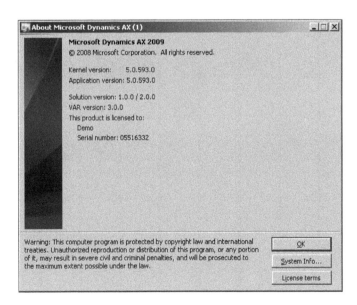

In this way, you can customize the display of the **About Microsoft** Dynamics AX dialog to ensure that any custom modification or module is listed here along with its version for user information.

# 3
# Working with Data in Forms

In this chapter, we will cover:

- ▸ Handling number sequences
- ▸ Creating custom filters
- ▸ Creating custom instant search filters
- ▸ Building selected/available lists
- ▸ Preloading images
- ▸ Creating wizards
- ▸ Creating default data wizards
- ▸ Processing multiple records
- ▸ Coloring records
- ▸ Adding images to records

## Introduction

This chapter basically supplements the previous one and explains about data organization in forms. It shows how to add custom filters to forms to allow users to filter data and how to create record lists for quick data manipulation.

This chapter also discusses how displaying data could be enhanced by adding icons to record lists and trees and how normal images could be stored along with the data, reusing existing Dynamics AX application objects.

A couple of recipes will show how to create wizards for guiding users through complex tasks. The chapter will also show several approaches to capturing user-selected records on forms for further processing and how to distinguish specific records by coloring them.

# Handling number sequences

As already discussed in the Creating a new number sequence recipe in Chapter 1, Processing Data, number sequences are widely used through the system as a part of the standard application. For using sequences in forms, Dynamics AX provides a special number sequence handler class. It is called **NumberSeqFormHandler** and its purpose is to simplify the usage of record numbering on Dynamics AX forms. Some of the standard Dynamics AX forms like **Customers** or **Vendors** already have this feature implemented.

This recipe will show how to use the number sequence handler on Dynamics AX forms. Although in this demonstration we will use an existing form, the same approach could be applied when creating new forms from scratch.

In the standard application, employee number has to be specified manually and in the Creating a new number sequence recipe, we have already created a new number sequence to be used for employees. In this recipe, we will go one step forward by starting to use this number sequence in the **Employee** form.

## How to do it...

1. In AOT, open **EmplTable** form and add the following code to the bottom of its class declaration:

```
NumberSeqFormHandler numberSeqFormHandler;
```

2. Also, create a new method called numberSeqFormHandler() in the same form:

```
NumberSeqFormHandler numberSeqFormHandler()
{;
    if (!numberSeqFormHandler)
    {
        numberSeqFormHandler = NumberSeqFormHandler::newForm(
            CompanyInfo::numRefEmplId().NumberSequence,
            element,
            EmplTable_ds,
            fieldnum(EmplTable, EmplId));
    }
    return numberSeqFormHandler;
}
```

3. In the same form, in the **EmplTable** data source's `create()`, add the following line before its `super()` method:

```
element.numberSeqFormHandler(
    ).formMethodDataSourceCreatePre();
```

4. And add the following code to the bottom of the same method:

```
if (!extern)
{
    element.numberSeqFormHandler(
        ).formMethodDataSourceCreate();
}
```

5. In the same data source in its `delete()`, add the following line right after `ttsbegin`:

```
element.numberSeqFormHandler(
    ).formMethodDataSourceDelete();
```

6. In the same data source in its `write()`, add the following line right after `super()`:

```
element.numberSeqFormHandler(
    ).formMethodDataSourceWrite();
```

7. In the same data source in its `validateWrite()`, add the following code right after `super()`:

```
ret = element.numberSeqFormHandler(
    ).formMethodDataSourceValidateWrite(ret) && ret;
```

8. In the same data source in its `linkActive()`, add the following line right after the variable declaration section:

```
element.numberSeqFormHandler(
    ).formMethodDataSourceLinkActive();
```

9. Finally, add the following code to the form's `close()` right before `super()`:

```
if (numberSeqFormHandler)
{
    numberSeqFormHandler.formMethodClose();
}
```

10. To test the employee numbering, open **Basic | Employee Details** and try to create several new records—the employee number has to be generated automatically:

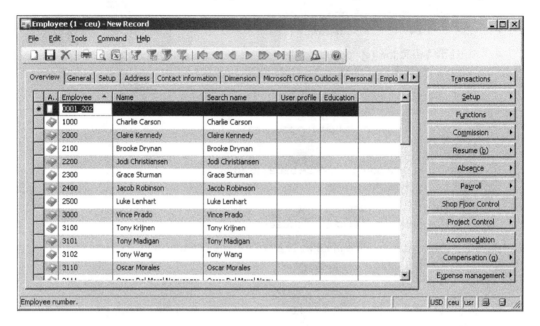

## How it works...

First, we declare the **NumberSeqFormHandler** object in the form's class declaration. Then, we create a new form method `numberSeqFormHandler()`, which creates an object of type **NumberSeqFormHandler** if it does not exist yet and returns it. This method allows us to store handler creation code in one place and reuse it as many times as we need.

We use the static constructor method `NumberSeqFormHandler::newForm()` to create a new number sequence handler. It accepts several arguments:

▶ The number sequence code, which was created in the prerequisite recipe. Here, we call the `numRefEmplId()` helper method from the `CompanyInfo` table to find which number sequence should be used when creating new employees. It was created earlier in the other recipe.

▶ The form object itself.

▶ The form data source where we need to apply the number sequence handler.

▶ The number of the field into which the number sequence will be populated.

The rest of the code in the various data source member methods ensures that the relevant **NumberSeqFormHandler** class methods are executed. The rest is done automatically inside the class.

**See also**

Processing Data, Creating a new number sequence

# Creating custom filters

Filtering on forms in Dynamics AX is implemented in a variety of ways. Dynamics AX provides generic filtering options like **Filter By Selection**, **Filter By Grid**, or **Advanced Filter/Sort** located in the toolbar as a part of the standard application and they are available for every form. Some of the existing application forms already have custom filters implemented, which normally are placed at the top of the form and represent the most often used search criteria. But nevertheless, I noticed that standard filtering is not always comfortable and user friendly and it is a very common request in every Dynamics AX implementation to add additional customized filters to some forms.

In this recipe, we will explore how to quickly add custom filters to a form. We will add three custom filters to the **Customers** form:

1.  **Stopped** will toggle between inactive and all customers.
2.  **Customer group** will allow displaying the customers belonging to a specific group.
3.  **Account statement** will allow displaying customers categorized by how often their account statement is being sent.

Each filter control is based on a different form control type—**CheckBox**, **StringEdit**, and **ComboBox** respectively.

## How to do it...

1.  In AOT, find the **CustAccountStatement** base enum. Duplicate it and rename it to **CustAccountStatementFilter**. Create a new element at the top of the exiting elements with the following properties:

| Property | Value |
|----------|-------|
| Name | None |
| Label | |
| Value | 99 |

2. In AOT, locate the **CustTable** form and add a new group at the top of the form's design with the following properties:

| Property | Value |
| --- | --- |
| Name | Filter |
| Caption | Filter |
| Columns | 3 |
| FrameType | Edged 3D |

3. Add a new **CheckBox** control to the created group with the following properties:

| Property | Value |
| --- | --- |
| Name | BlockedFilter |
| Label | Stopped |
| AutoDeclaration | Yes |

4. Add a new **StringEdit** control to the same group:

| Property | Value |
| --- | --- |
| Name | GroupFilter |
| ExtendedDataType | CustGroupId |
| AutoDeclaration | Yes |

5. Add a new **ComboBox** control to the same group:

| Property | Value |
| --- | --- |
| Name | StatementFilter |
| EnumType | CustAccountStatementFilter |
| AutoDeclaration | Yes |

6. Override the `modified()` methods for each control in the filter group with the following code:

```
public boolean modified()
{
    boolean ret;
    ;

    ret = super();
    if (ret)
    {
```

```
        CustTable_ds.executeQuery();
    }

    return ret;
}
```

7.  After all modifications, the **CustTable** form should look like this in AOT:

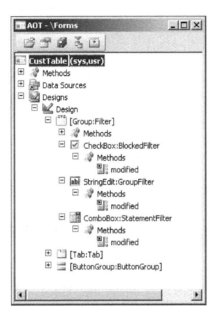

8.  In the same form, override `executeQuery()` of the **CustTable** data source with the following code:

```
public void executeQuery()
{
    QueryBuildRange rangeBlocked;
    QueryBuildRange rangeGroup;
    QueryBuildRange rangeStatement;
    ;

    rangeBlocked = SysQuery::findOrCreateRange(
        this.query().dataSourceTable(tablenum(CustTable)),
        fieldnum(CustTable, Blocked));

    rangeGroup = SysQuery::findOrCreateRange(
        this.query().dataSourceTable(tablenum(CustTable)),
        fieldnum(CustTable, CustGroup));

    rangeStatement = SysQuery::findOrCreateRange(
```

```
            this.query().dataSourceTable(tablenum(CustTable)),
            fieldnum(CustTable, AccountStatement));

        if (BlockedFilter.value())
        {
            rangeBlocked.value(
                SysQuery::valueNot(CustVendorBlocked::No));
        }
        else
        {
            rangeBlocked.value(SysQuery::valueUnlimited());
        }

        if (GroupFilter.text())
        {
            rangeGroup.value(queryvalue(GroupFilter.text()));
        }
        else
        {
            rangeGroup.value(SysQuery::valueUnlimited());
        }

        if (StatementFilter.selection() !=
                CustAccountStatementFilter::None)
        {
            rangeStatement.value(
                queryvalue(StatementFilter.selection()));
        }
        else
        {
            rangeStatement.value(SysQuery::valueUnlimited());
        }

        super();
    }
```

9. Finally, add the following line to the bottom of the form's `init()`:

   ```
   StatementFilter.selection(CustAccountStatementFilter::None);
   ```

10. To test the filter, open **Accounts receivable | Customer Details** and start changing the newly created filters—the customer list should match your criteria:

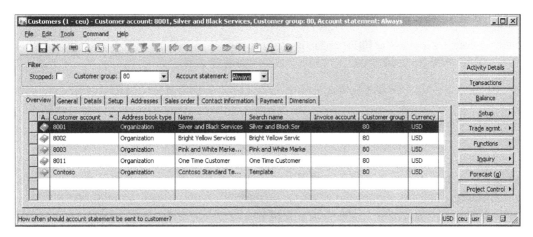

11. Click on the **Advanced Filter/Sort Open** button in the toolbar. You should see what filters are applied currently:

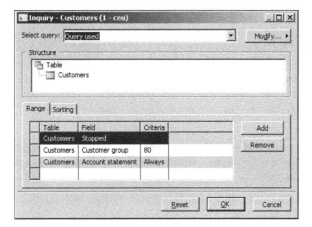

## How it works...

To make things tidy, we create a separate group called **Filter** for holding all custom filters. We set some properties to change the appearance of this group. The number of **Columns** is **3**, because there will be three controls inside it—one column for each control. **FrameType** is set to **Edged 3D**, so we have nice border around all the controls inside this group.

All three controls inside the **Filter** group must have the `AutoDeclaration` property set to `Yes`, which will allow accessing them from code later.

We are planning to place all filtering code in `executeQuery()` of the **CustTable** data source. So in each of the created filter controls, we override their `modified()` methods in order to call `executeQuery()` every time the user changes their value.

In `executeQuery()`, we place everything before its `super()`. This is because we have to apply the data source filters before the query is executed. We start this method with initializing a **QueryBuildRange** object for each of the filter controls. We use `finOrCreateRange()` of the **SysQuery** application class to get the range object. It is very useful, as we do not have to worry about existing ranges—if the range already exists, it will return it, if not then it will create a new one. It accepts two arguments a **QueryBuildDataSource** object and the field number.

Next, we check each filter control and pass its value to the relevant range:

- ▶ The first filter control is a **CheckBox**, so we check its value by using its `value()` method. Customer **Stopped** status could have three values: **No**, **Invoice**, and **All**. **No** means that the customer is active, **Invoice** means the customer is stopped for invoicing, and **All** means that the customer is stopped for all operations. If the control is checked, we set the range value to display everything that is not active, that is, it is stopped for invoicing or for all operations. Here we use `valueNot()` of the **SysQuery** application class to format the correct criteria for us. If the control is unchecked, we show all customers by clearing the range. We use `valueUnlimited()` of **SysQuery** for this purpose.

- ▶ The second filter is a **StringEdit** and is the simplest one. We check its value by calling its `text()` and if it is not empty we pass it to the range. Otherwise, we clear the range. Notice that here we use the global `queryvalue()` function, which is actually a shortcut to `value()` of the **SysQuery** application class, to let the application property format input text.

- ▶ The third filter is a **ComboBox**. We check the user-selected value by using its `selection()`. If it is not equal to **CustAccountStatementFilter::None**, we pass the value to the range, otherwise we clear the range.

Once again, the **SysQuery** helper class is very useful when working with queries as it does all kinds of data conversions to make sure they can be safely used. Here is a summary of the **SysQuery** methods used:

- ▸ `valueNot()` converts an argument to a safe string and adds a NOT statement in front of it.
- ▸ `valueUnlimited()` returns a string representing an unlimited query range value, i.e. not a range at all.
- ▸ `queryvalue()` is a shortcut to `value()` of **SysQuery**, which returns a safe string.

I would highly recommend using this class when building custom functionality and it is worth investigating the rest of the methods in it as they might be of use in other situations.

## There's more...

Normally, ranges added to **QueryBuildDataSource** use AND operators. Basically that means, in our example customers are filtered by stopped status AND by group AND by account statement sending period. But what if we need to show customers belonging to a specific group OR assigned to a specific account statement sending option?

Dynamics AX allows us to do that by passing more complex argument values to **QueryBuildRange** objects instead of simple ranges. Actually, **QueryBuildRange** accepts partial SQL statements representing the WHERE part of the statement.

To demonstrate that, let's edit the previous example to incorporate OR filtering between the customer group and account statement filters.

We only need to update `executeQuery()` with the following code:

```
public void executeQuery()
{
    QueryBuildRange rangeBlocked;
    QueryBuildRange rangeGroup;
    QueryBuildRange rangeStatement;
    str             sql;
    ;

    rangeBlocked = SysQuery::findOrCreateRange(
        this.query().dataSourceTable(tablenum(CustTable)),
        fieldnum(CustTable, Blocked));
    rangeGroup = SysQuery::findOrCreateRange(
        this.query().dataSourceTable(tablenum(CustTable)),
        fieldnum(CustTable, CustGroup));
    rangeStatement = SysQuery::findOrCreateRange(
        this.query().dataSourceTable(tablenum(CustTable)),
        fieldnum(CustTable, AccountStatement));
    if (BlockedFilter.value())
```

```
        {
            rangeBlocked.value(
                SysQuery::valueNot(CustVendorBlocked::No));
        }
        else
        {
            rangeBlocked.value(SysQuery::valueUnlimited());
        }
        if (GroupFilter.text() &&
            StatementFilter.selection() !=
                CustAccountStatementFilter::None)
        {
            sql = strfmt(
                '((%1 = "%2") || (%3 = %4))',
                fieldstr(CustTable,CustGroup),
                queryvalue(GroupFilter.text()),
                fieldstr(CustTable,AccountStatement),
                queryvalue(StatementFilter.selection()));
            rangeGroup.value(sql);
            rangeStatement.value(SysQuery::valueUnlimited());
        }
        else
        {
            if (GroupFilter.text())
            {
                rangeGroup.value(queryvalue(GroupFilter.text()));
            }
            else
            {
                rangeGroup.value(SysQuery::valueUnlimited());
            }
            if (StatementFilter.selection() !=
                    CustAccountStatementFilter::None)
            {
                rangeStatement.value(
                    queryvalue(StatementFilter.selection()));
            }
            else
            {
                rangeStatement.value(SysQuery::valueUnlimited());
            }
        }
        super();
    }
```

Here we made a couple of changes to this method. First, we added a new `sql` variable to the variable declaration section and second, we added an `if` statement right after processing the first range. The statement checks if both **Customer group** and **Account statement** controls contain values. If yes, new code is executed, otherwise the filters are processed as before.

In the new code, we are formatting the `WHERE` part of the SQL query. In SQL, it should be like this:

```
((CustGroup = "<value1>") || (AccountStatement = <value2>))
```

Field names and placeholders `<value1>` and `<value2>` are replaced with **Customer group** and **Account statement** values using global `strfmt()` function.

Using that kind of filter value it does not matter which range to use, as the system is picking up field names from the SQL and not the range. Here, we use the second range to pass the formatted SQL string and we clear the third range to make sure it does not interfere with the formatted SQL statement.

Now if we run the same form, **Customer Group** and **Account statement** filters should be applied using `OR`. Select some filter values and notice how the customer list changes:

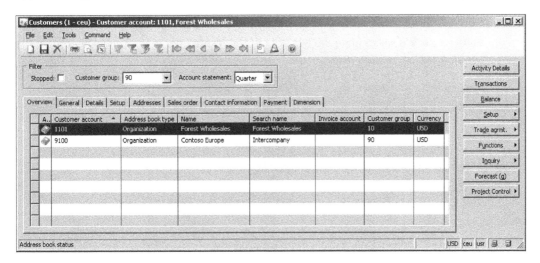

To double-check if the filter works correctly, open **Advanced Filter/Sort** from the toolbar. The customer group filter should be very similar to what we formatted in our code:

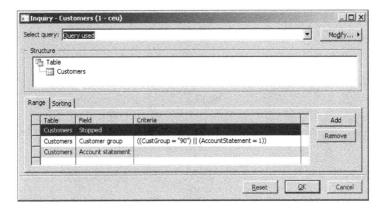

## See also

Processing Data, Building a query object

# Creating custom instant search filters

The majority of data search filters in Dynamics AX are not instant. Normally, the user types in search criteria and then has to press some button or the *Enter* key in order to execute the search and display the results.

This is acceptable for most people and in most circumstances. But, I have been asked couple of times to enhance the standard search filter to reflect user input instantly upon typing and display filtered data.

In this recipe, to demonstrate how this could be done, we will modify one of the standard Dynamics AX forms. We will change the behavior of the **Name** filter in the **Contacts** form in the **CRM** module to perform instant search upon the user typing.

## How to do it...

1. Open the **smmContactPerson** form in AOT, and find the **CtrlNameFilter** control inside the **Filter** group.

2. Override its `textChange()` with the following code:

```
public void textChange()
{;
    super();
    this.modified();
}
```

3. Edit its `modified()` method code by changing the following line:

```
nameFilter = this.text();
```

to:

```
nameFilter = '*'+this.text()+'*';
```

4. Override the control's `enter()` with the following code:

```
public void enter()
{;
    super();
    this.setSelection(
        strlen(this.text()),
        strlen(this.text()));
}
```

5.  To test the search, open **Basic | Setup | Addresses | Contact Details** or
    **CRM | Contact Details** and start typing into the **Name** filter. Notice how the contact
    list is being filtered:

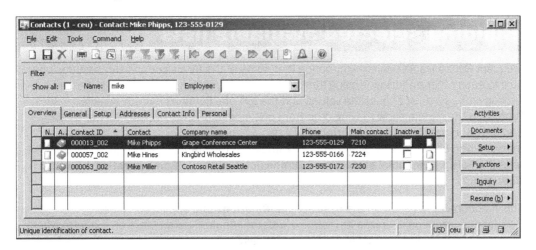

## How it works...

The user typing event triggers the `textChange()` method on the active control every time a
character is typed. So, we have to add search code to this method. However, because filtering
is already implemented on this form, we only need to call the control's `modified()` to start
the search. This way we ensure that the search is executed every time a character is typed.

We also modify the control's `modified()` by adding * to the beginning and the end of the
search string. This will make the search by partial string and will not require the user to type in
special search characters.

Finally, we have to correct cursor behavior. Currently, once the user types in the first character,
the search is executed and the focus is moved by the system out of the control and then
moved back selecting all the typed text. If the user continues typing, then the existing text will
be overwritten with the new character and the loop continues.

To fix this behavior, we have to override the control's `enter()`. This method is called every
time the control receives a focus whether it was done by a user's mouse, key, or by the
system. Here, we call `setSelection()`. Normally, the purpose of this method is to make
a text or a part of it selected. Its first argument specifies the beginning of the selection and
second one the end. In this recipe, we are using this method in a slightly different way. We
pass the length of the typed text as a first argument, which means the selection starts at
the end of the text. And we pass the same value as a second argument, which means that
selection ends at the end of the text. It does not make any sense from the selection point of
view, but it ensures that the cursor always stays at the end of the typed text allowing the user
to continue typing.

The last thing to note here is that system performance might be affected because a data search is executed every time the user types in a character. This is very important when working with large volumes of data.

# Building selected/available lists

Frequent Dynamics AX users might notice that some of the forms contain two sections placed next to each other and allow moving items from one side to the other. Normally, the right section contains a list of possible values and the left one contains already selected values. Buttons in the middle allow moving data from one side to another. Mouse double-clicking and drag-and-drop are also supported. Such design improves user experience as data manipulation becomes very user-friendly. Examples in the standard application are **General ledger | Setup | Financial statement | Dimension focuses** or **Administration | Setup | User groups**.

This functionality is based on the **SysListPanelRelationTable** application class. Developers only need to create its instance with the required parameters on the form where the list is required and the rest is done automatically.

This recipe will show the basic principle of how to create selected/available lists. We will add an option to the user to assign inventory items to buyer groups in the **Buyer groups** form in the **Inventory management** module setup.

## How to do it...

1.  In AOT, create a new table named **InventBuyerGroupList**. Accept the default properties as this table is only for demonstration.

2.  Add a new field to the table with the following properties:

    | Property | Value |
    | --- | --- |
    | Type | String |
    | Name | GroupId |
    | ExtendedDataType | ItemBuyerGroupId |

3.  Add another field to the table:

    | Property | Value |
    | --- | --- |
    | Type | String |
    | Name | ItemId |
    | ExtendedDataType | ItemId |

4. In AOT, open the **InventBuyerGroup** form and add a new **TabPage** control with the following properties to the end of the existing tab:

| Property | Value |
|---|---|
| Name | Items |
| Caption | Items |

5. Add the following line to the form's class declaration:

```
SysListPanelRelationTable sysListPanel;
```

6. Override the form's `init()` with the following code:

```
void init()
{
    container columns;
    #ResAppl
    ;

    columns = [fieldnum(InventTable, ItemId),
               fieldnum(InventTable, ItemName)];

    sysListPanel = SysListPanelRelationTable::newForm(
        element,
        control::Items,
        "Selected",
        "Available",
        #ImageItem,
        tablenum(InventBuyerGroupList),
        fieldnum(InventBuyerGroupList, ItemId),
        fieldnum(InventBuyerGroupList, GroupId),
        tablenum(InventTable),
        fieldnum(InventTable, ItemId),
        columns);

    super();

    sysListPanel.init();
}
```

7. Override `pageActivated()` on the created tab page:

```
public void pageActivated()
{;
    sysListPanel.parmRelationRangeValue(
        InventBuyerGroup.Group);

    sysListPanel.parmRelationRangeRecId(
        InventBuyerGroup.RecId);

    sysListPanel.fill();

    super();
}
```

8. The form should look like this in AOT:

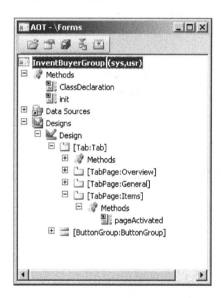

9. To test the list, open **Inventory management | Setup | Inventory | Buyer groups**, select any group, go to the **Items** tab page and use the buttons provided to move records from one side to the other. You could also double-click or drag-and-drop with your mouse:

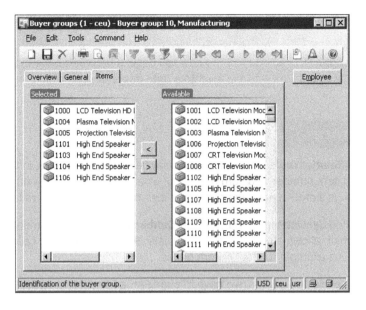

## How it works...

The table **InventBuyerGroupList** is used as a relation table between buyer groups and inventory items to support many-to-many relations. The **SysListPanelRelationTable** class will populate this table with the data automatically.

In terms of form design, the only thing that needs to be added is a new tab page called **Items**. **SysListPanelRelationTable** will add all the required controls to this page automatically.

In the form's class declaration, we declare a **SysListPanelRelationTable** object. The object is created in the form's `init()` using the static `newForm()` constructor. It accepts the following parameters:

1. The form object.
2. The name of the tab page.
3. The label of the left section.
4. The label of the right section.
5. The number of the image that is shown next to each record in the lists.
6. The relation table number.
7. The field number in the relation table representing the child table. In our case it is the item identification number—**ItemId**.
8. The field number in the relation table representing the parent table. In this case it is the buyer group number—**GroupId**.
9. The number of the table that is displayed in the lists.
10. A container of the field numbers displayed in each column.

We also have to initialize the list by calling it's member method `init()` in the form's `init()` right after `super()`.

The code in the `pageActivated()` of the new tab page is triggered once the user opens that tab page. It populates the lists with the inventory data depending on which buyer group is selected.

## There's more...

The **SysListPanelRelationTable** class can only display fields from one table. In the previous example, we used item number and item name. But what if we want to show other item related information, which is stored in a different table, for instance sales price or available quantity?

Another class called **SysListPanelRelationTableCallback** exists in the standard Dynamics AX application, which allows creating customized lists. To demonstrate its capabilities, we will expand the previous example to display item prices.

First in the form's class declaration, we have to change the list declaration to the following:

```
SysListPanelRelationTableCallback sysListPanel;
```

Next we need to create two methods—one for the left list, the other for the right, which generate and return data containers to be displayed in each section:

```
container selectedItems()
{
    container            ret;
    container            data;
    InventTable          inventTable;
    InventBuyerGroupList groupList;
    ;

    while select groupList
        join firstonly inventTable
            where inventTable.ItemId == groupList.ItemId
    {
        data = [inventTable.ItemId,
                inventTable.ItemId,
                inventTable.ItemName,
                inventTable.salesPcsPrice()];
        ret = conins(ret, conlen(ret)+1, data);
    }
    return ret;
}
container availableItems()
{
    container            ret;
    container            data;
```

```
InventTable            inventTable;
InventBuyerGroupList groupList;
;

while select inventTable
    notexists join firstonly groupList
        where groupList.ItemId == inventTable.ItemId
{
    data = [inventTable.ItemId,
            inventTable.ItemId,
            inventTable.ItemName,
            inventTable.salesPcsPrice()];
    ret = conins(ret, conlen(ret)+1, data);
}
    return ret;
}
```

Each method returns a container of containers. Each container in the main one represents one line in the section. It contains four items—the first is an identification number and the rest of them are the three columns.

Next, we replace the form's init() with the following code:

```
void init()
{
    container columns;
    #ResAppl
    ;

    columns = [0, 0, 0];
    sysListPanel = SysListPanelRelationTableCallback::newForm(
        element,
        control::Items,
        "Selected",
        "Available",
        #ImageItem,
        tablenum(InventBuyerGroupList),
        fieldnum(InventBuyerGroupList, ItemId),
        fieldnum(InventBuyerGroupList, GroupId),
        tablenum(InventTable),
        fieldnum(InventTable, ItemId),
        columns,
        0,
        '',
        '',
        identifierstr(selectedItems),
        identifierstr(availableItems));
    super();
    sysListPanel.init();
}
```

This time we used the static `newForm()` constructor of **SysListPanelRelationTableCallback**, which is very similar to the previous one, but accepts as arguments the names of methods, which will be used to populate the data in the right and left sections.

Also notice that the container that previously contained fields representing each list column now has three zeros. By doing that, we simply define that there will be three columns in each list and because the lists actually are generated outside **SysListPanelRelationTableCallback** class, we do not need to specify the field numbers of the columns anymore.

Now, when you run the **Buyer groups** form both sections contain additional column with item sales price:

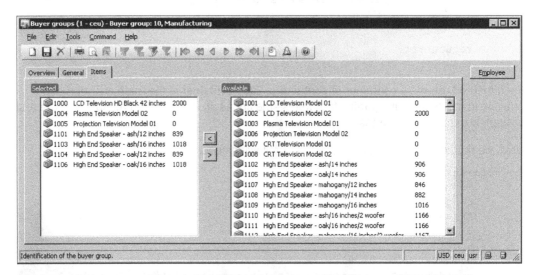

# Preloading images

Some of the Dynamics AX controls like trees or lists in most cases, to represent the data in a richer way, have small icon images in front of the text. Icons could represent a type, status, availability, or any other property of the current item in the control.

Images are binary data and their processing might be time consuming. The Dynamics AX application provides a way of handling images to increase application performance. Normally, on those forms with lists or trees all required images are preloaded during form initialization. This reduces image loading time when the image is actually displayed to the user.

For this purpose, Dynamics AX contains a set of **ImageListAppl** derivative classes, which holds a specific set of images required in specific circumstances. For example, the **ImageListAppl_Proj** class in the **Project** module preloads project-related images representing project and transaction types during project tree initialization. So virtually no time is consumed for displaying the images later, when the user starts browsing the project tree control.

In this recipe, we will create our own image list class for image preloading. As a base we will use the list created in the **There's more...** section for the Building selected/available lists recipe. We will add icons to both lists depending on the item type.

## How to do it...

1. In AOT, create a new class named **ImageListAppl_InventItem** with the following code:

```
public class ImageListAppl_InventItem extends ImageListAppl
{
}

protected void build()
{;
    super();
    this.add(#ImageItem);
    this.add(#ImageService);
    this.add(#ImageBOM);
}
```

2. In AOT, find the **SysListPanelRelationTableCallback** class and modify its `newForm()`:

```
static SysListPanelRelationTableCallback newForm(
        FormRun          formRun,
        int              parentId,
        str              captionLeft,
        str              captionRight,
        int              imageId,
        tableId          relationTable,
        fieldId          relationField,
        fieldId          relationRangeField,
        tableId          dataTable,
        fieldId          dataField,
        container        dataContainerFieldIds,
        fieldId          dataRangeField = 0,
        AnyType          dataRangeValue = '',
        identifiername   validateMethod = '',
        identifiername   leftMethod     = '',
```

```
        identifiername  rightMethod    = '',
        int             itemsNeeded    = 0,
        ImageListAppl    imageListAppl  = null)
    {
        SysListPanelRelationTableCallback sysListPanel =
            SysListPanelRelationTableCallback::construct();
        ;

        sysListPanel.parmFormRun(formRun);
        sysListPanel.parmParentId(parentId);
        sysListPanel.parmCaptionLeft(captionLeft);
        sysListPanel.parmCaptionRight(captionRight);
        sysListPanel.parmImageId(imageId);
        sysListPanel.parmRelationTable(relationTable);
        sysListPanel.parmRelationField(relationField);
        sysListPanel.parmRelationRangeField(relationRangeField);
        sysListPanel.parmDataTable(dataTable);
        sysListPanel.parmDataField(dataField);
        sysListPanel.parmDataContainerFieldIds(
            dataContainerFieldIds);
        sysListPanel.parmDataRangeField(dataRangeField);
        sysListPanel.parmDataRangeValue(dataRangeValue);
        sysListPanel.parmValidateMethod(validateMethod);
        sysListPanel.parmLeftMethod(leftMethod);
        sysListPanel.parmRightMethod(rightMethod);
        sysListPanel.parmItemsNeeded(itemsNeeded);
        sysListPanel.parmImageList(imageListAppl);
        sysListPanel.build();
        return sysListPanel;
    }
```

3. In AOT, fine the **InventBuyerGroup** form and replace its methods with the following code:

```
void init()
{
    container              columns;
    ImageListAppl_InventItem imageListAppl;
    ;

    columns = [0, 0, 0];
    imageListAppl = new ImageListAppl_InventItem(
        Imagelist::smallIconWidth(),
        Imagelist::smallIconHeight());
    sysListPanel = SysListPanelRelationTableCallback::newForm(
        element,
        control::Items,
        "Selected",
        "Available",
        0,
```

```
            tablenum(InventBuyerGroupList),
            fieldnum(InventBuyerGroupList, ItemId),
            fieldnum(InventBuyerGroupList, GroupId),
            tablenum(InventTable),
            fieldnum(InventTable, ItemId),
            columns,
            0,
            "",
            "",
            identifierstr(selectedItems),
            identifierstr(availableItems),
            0,
            imageListAppl);
        super();
        sysListPanel.init();
    }
    container selectedItems()
    {
        container             ret;
        container             data;
        InventTable           inventTable;
        InventBuyerGroupList groupList;
        ;

        while select groupList
            join firstonly inventTable
                where inventTable.ItemId == groupList.ItemId
        {
            data = [inventTable.ItemId,
                    inventTable.inventItemType().imageRessNo(),
                    inventTable.ItemId,
                    inventTable.ItemName,
                    inventTable.salesPcsPrice()];
            ret = conins(ret, conlen(ret)+1, data);
        }
        return ret;
    }
    container availableItems()
    {
        container             ret;
        container             data;
        InventTable           inventTable;
        InventBuyerGroupList groupList;
        ;

        while select inventTable
            notexists join firstonly groupList
                where groupList.ItemId == inventTable.ItemId
        {
```

```
data = [inventTable.ItemId,
        inventTable.inventItemType().imageRessNo(),
        inventTable.ItemId,
        inventTable.ItemName,
        inventTable.salesPcsPrice()];
    ret = conins(ret, conlen(ret)+1, data);
}
    return ret;
}
```

4. To test the results, open **Inventory management | Setup | Inventory | Buyer groups**, go to the **Items** tab page and notice that items, services, and bills of material in each section now have different icons:

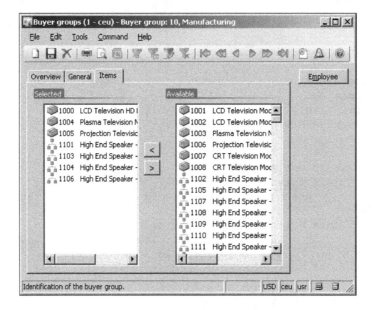

## How it works...

The first task in this recipe is to create a class that handles the required set of images. We only need three different images—one for each inventory item type: item, service, and BOM. I have to mention that there are several standard **ImageListAppl** classes like **ImageListAppl_Prod** or **ImageListAppl_BOMRouteTree** that already include the mentioned image resources along with other images. But those classes are used in other scenarios and for demonstration and it is more beneficial to create a new class.

Image resources are also already present in the system and so we do not have to do anything about this. We only need to include the relevant resources using add() in the build of the new **ImageListAppl_InventItem** class. The **ResAppl** macro could be explored if more images are required or custom macros could be created to custom images.

The second step is to slightly modify the **SysListPanelRelationTableCallback** class to make sure its `newForm()` accepts **ImageListAppl** as an argument and passes it to the class using the `parmImageList()` method. A new method could have been created here but I do not like the idea of copying that much code, especially when our changes are very small and do not affect class usage as the parameter is set to `null` by default.

The final step is to modify the form. First, we create a new `imageListAppl` object based on our class and pass it to the modified `newForm()` as a last argument. At this stage `sysListPanel` "knows" about the images we are going to use when displaying the lists. Then we modify the form's `selectedItems()` and `availableItems()` to include image resource numbers in the returned data. Here, we use standard functionality to identify the resource associated with the item type.

Now upon displaying the lists, `sysListPanel` reads preloaded image data from our class.

## There's more...

As mentioned earlier, images can be used on trees also. In this section, we will enhance the tree created in the Using tree controls recipe in Chapter 2, Working with Forms. We will add small icons in front of each node.

First in AOT, we create a new class called **ImageListAppl_LedgerBudget** with the following code:

```
class ImageListAppl_LedgerBudget extends ImageListAppl
{
}

protected void build()
{;
    super();
    this.add(#ImageFolder);
    this.add(#ImageLedgerBudget);
}
```

The class extends **ImageListAppl** and is responsible for preloading the images to be used on the tree. We will use only two different images a—folder icon for parent ledger budget models and a budget icon for submodels.

Next we need to modify the **BudgetModelTree** class created earlier in the book. Let's add the following line to the bottom of its class declaration:

```
ImageListAppl    imageListAppl;
```

Add the following code to `buildTree()` right after the variable declaration section:

```
imageListAppl = new ImageListAppl_LedgerBudget();
tree.setImagelist(imageListAppl.imageList());
```

This code creates the instance of **ImageListAppl_LedgerBudget** and passes it to the tree control.

Replace `createNode()` with the following code:

```
TreeItemIdx createNode(
    TreeItemIdx    _parentIdx,
    BudgetModelId _modelId,
    RecId          _recId)
{
    TreeItemIdx itemIdx;
    BudgetModel modelSub;
    ImageRes    imageRes;
    #ResAppl
    ;

    if (_parentIdx == FormTreeAdd::Root)
    {
        imageRes = imageListAppl.image(#ImageFolder);
    }
    else
    {
        imageRes = imageListAppl.image(#ImageLedgerBudget);
    }
    itemIdx = SysFormTreeControl::addTreeItem(
        tree,
        _modelId,
        _parentIdx,
        _recId,
        imageRes,
        true);
    if (model == _modelId)
    {
        tree.select(itemIdx);
    }
    while select modelSub
        where modelSub.ModelId == _modelId &&
              modelSub.Type     == HeadingSub::SubModel
    {
        this.createNode(
            itemIdx,
            modelSub.SubModelId,
            modelSub.RecId);
    }
    return itemIdx;
}
```

At the top of this method, we check whether the current node is a parent node. If yes, we set its image as the folder icon, otherwise—the budget icon. The rest of the code is the same.

To test the tree, open **General ledger | Setup | Budget | Budget model**, go to the **Tree** tab page and notice how the tree has changed:

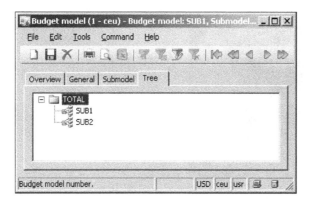

## See also

Working with Forms, Using tree controls

# Creating wizards

Wizards in Dynamics AX like everywhere else are used to help a user to perform a specific task. Some examples of standard Dynamics AX wizards are **Report wizard**, **Project wizard**, **Number sequence wizard**, and so on.

Normally, a wizard is presented to a user as a form with a series of steps. While running the wizard all user input is stored in temporary memory until the user presses the **Finish** button on the last wizard page.

In this recipe, we will create a new **Ledger account wizard**. First, we will use the standard Dynamics AX **Wizard Wizard** to create a framework and then we will add some additional user input controls manually.

## How to do it...

1. Open **Tools | Development tools | Wizards | Wizard Wizard**.

2. Click **Next** on the first page:

3. Select **Standard Wizard** and click **Next**:

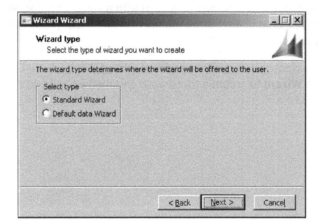

4. Specify **LedgerTable** as a name and click **Next**:

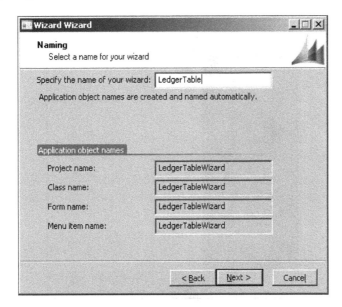

5. Accept the default number of steps and click **Next**:

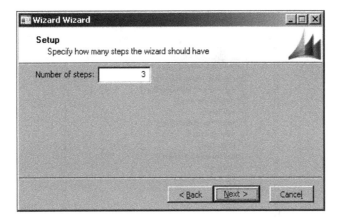

6.  Click **Finish** to complete the wizard:

7.  The wizard should have created an AOT development project with three objects:

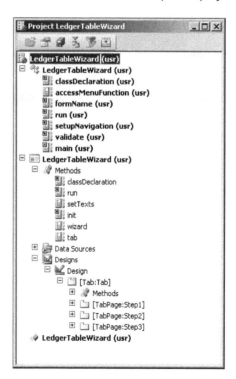

8. Modify the **LedgerTableWizard** class by adding the following line to its class declaration:

```
LedgerTable ledgerTable;
```

9. Create the following methods in the same class:

```
AccountNum parmAccount(
    AccountNum _account = ledgerTable.AccountNum)
{;
    ledgerTable.AccountNum = _account;
    return ledgerTable.AccountNum;
}

AccountName parmName(
    AccountName _name = ledgerTable.AccountName)
{;
    ledgerTable.AccountName = _name;
    return ledgerTable.AccountName;
}

LedgerAccountType parmType(
    LedgerAccountType _type = ledgerTable.AccountPlType)
{;
    ledgerTable.AccountPlType = _type;
    return ledgerTable.AccountPlType;
}

void setNext()
{;
    this.nextEnabled(
        ledgerTable.AccountNum && ledgerTable.AccountName);
}
```

10. Add the following line to the existing `setupNavigation()` method in the same class:

```
this.nextEnabled(false, 2);
```

11. Replace `validate()` of the same class with the following code:

```
boolean validate()
{;
    if (!ledgerTable.validateWrite())
    {
        return false;
    }
    return true;
}
```

12. Replace `run()` of the same class with the following code:

```
void run()
{;
    ledgerTable.insert();
    info(strfmt(
        "Ledger account '%1' was successfully created",
        ledgerTable.AccountNum));
}
```

13. In the **LedgerTableWizard** form create three `edit` methods with the following code:

```
edit AccountNum editAccount(
    boolean     _set,
    AccountNum  _account)
{;
    if (_set)
    {
        sysWizard.parmAccount(_account);
        sysWizard.setNext();
    }
    return sysWizard.parmAccount();
}
edit AccountName editName(
    boolean     _set,
    AccountName _name)
{;
    if (_set)
    {
        sysWizard.parmName(_name);
        sysWizard.setNext();
    }
    return sysWizard.parmName();
}
edit LedgerAccountType editType(
    boolean           _set,
    LedgerAccountType _type)
{;
    if (_set)
    {
        sysWizard.parmType(_type);
    }
    return sysWizard.parmType();
}
```

14. Change the form's design property:

| Property | Value |
| --- | --- |
| Caption | Ledger account wizard |

15. Modify the properties of the **Step1** tab page:

| Property | Value |
| --- | --- |
| Caption | Welcome |

16. Create a new **StaticText** control in this tab page with the following properties:

| Property | Value |
| --- | --- |
| Name | WelcomeTxt |
| Text | This wizard helps you to create a new ledger account. |

17. Modify the properties of the **Step2** tab page:

| Property | Value |
| --- | --- |
| Caption | Account setup |
| HelpText | Specify account number, name, and type. |

18. Create a new **StringEdit** control in this tab page with the following properties:

| Property | Value |
| --- | --- |
| Name | Account |
| DataMethod | editAccount |

19. Create another **StringEdit** control in this tab page with the following properties:

| Property | Value |
| --- | --- |
| Name | Name |
| DataMethod | editName |

20. Create a new **ComboBox** control in this tab page with the following properties:

| Property | Value |
| --- | --- |
| Name | Type |
| DataMethod | editType |

21. Modify the properties of the **Step3** tab page:

| Property | Value |
| --- | --- |
| Caption | Finish |

22. Create a new **StaticText** control in this tab page with the following properties:

| Property | Value |
| --- | --- |
| Name | FinishTxt |
| Text | This wizard is now ready to create new ledger account. |

23. Now the form should look like following in AOT:

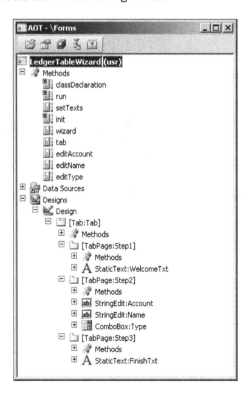

24. To test the newly created wizard, run the **LedgerTableWizard** menu item. The wizard should appear. On the first page click **Next**:

25. On the second page, specify **Account number**, **Account Name**, and **Account type**:

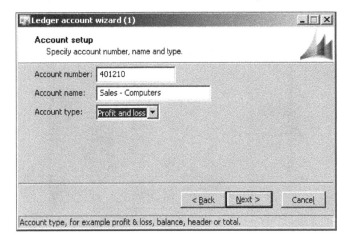

26. On the last page, click **Finish** to complete the wizard:

27. The **Infolog** should display a message that a new account was created successfully:

## How it works...

The **Wizard Wizard** creates three AOT objects for us:

1. The **LedgerTableWizard** class, which contains all the logic required to run a wizard.
2. The **LedgerTableWizard** form, which is the wizard layout.
3. And finally, the **LedgerTableWizard Display** menu item, which is used to start a wizard and could be added to a user menu.

In the **LedgerTableWizard** class, we declare the `ledgerTable` variable and create three parameter methods `parmAccount()`, `parmName()`, and `parmType()` for setting and retrieving account number, name, and type values from `ledgerTable` respectively.

All user input controls are placed on the second page. Here, we have to make sure that the user cannot pass this step without filling out the required information. For this purpose, we create `setNext()`, which controls the status of the **Next** button on the form. It calls `nextEnabled()` from the parent class to enable or disable the button. We pass the logical expression `ledgerTable.AccountNum && ledgerTable.AccountName` as an argument to ensure that **Next** is not enabled until the user specifies both account number and name. We do not have to worry about account type because it is set to **Profit & loss** by default and cannot be changed to empty.

Normally, `setNext()` should have a `switch` statement for performing different validations for different wizard steps, but it is not relevant here because we have only one step to validate.

`setupNavigation()` is used for defining initial button states. We use this method to disable the **Next** button on the second page by default. Note that, its second argument is a tab page number and although for demonstration purposes it is an integer, normally it should be defined as a macro.

All final validations has to go into `validate()`. This method is called right after user clicks **Finish** at the end of wizard and before main code is executed. Here we call `validateWrite()` on `ledgerTable` object to check if this object can accept user specified values.

Once the validation is done, the system executes all the code specified in `run()`. In our example, here we call `insert()` on the `ledgerTable` table and show an information message that a new account was successfully created.

On the **LedgerTableWizard** form, we create three `edit` methods and corresponding input controls on the second tab page for account number, name, and type respectively. Each edit method accepts a user input value, passes it to the `sysWizard` object, and calls `setNext()` to determine the status of the **Next** button.

The rest of the modifications are layout changes. We set the wizard caption and add some descriptive text on all wizard pages.

# Creating default data wizards

Default data wizards in Dynamics AX extend standard wizard functionality. Basically, both types of wizards do more or less the same task, but default data wizards are more oriented towards setting up initial data, which is not company specific. One of the examples in the standard application is the **Unit creation wizard** in **Basic | Setup | Units**. This wizard populates the table of units of measure with default data depending on the user selections during the running of the wizard.

Also it is good practice to provide default data wizards along with custom Dynamics AX modules. It can make the setup easier, saves the user's time, and makes a good impression about how user-friendly the software is.

In this recipe, we will create a new default data wizard. We will use the wizard for creating several new document types for document handling. If there are no document types initially, the standard application creates a number of basic types. Our wizard will be a supplement to this and will create two new document types for storing purchase documents.

## How to do it...

1. Run the **Wizard Wizard** from **Tools | Development tools | Wizards**. Click **Next** on the first page:

2. Select **Default data Wizard** on the second page and click **Next**:

3. Type **DocuType** in the **Specify the name of your wizard** input box and click **Next**:

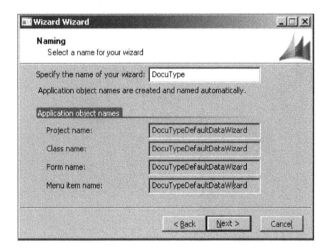

4. Click **Next** on the following page accepting the default value:

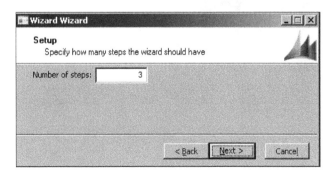

5.  Also accept the default on this page and click **Next**:

6.  Click **Finish** on the last page:

7. Once completed, **Wizard Wizard** creates a new development project containing a new class, form, and menu item:

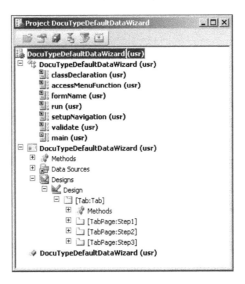

8. In AOT, find the existing **DocuTypeDefaultData** class, remove the `abstract` modifier from its class declaration, and add a **DocuType** variable:

```
class DocuTypeDefaultData extends SysDefaultData
{
    DocuType buffer;
}
```

9. Override following the methods in this class:

```
public Common buffer()
{
    return buffer;
}

protected fieldId keyFieldId()
{
    return fieldnum(DocuType, TypeId);
}

protected void setBuffer()
{;
    if (form_ds)
    {
        buffer = form_ds.cursor();
    }
```

```
    }

    protected void doTable(boolean useCurBuffer)
    {
        void insert()
        {
            if (!this.existDB())
            {
                buffer.insert();
            }
        }
        ;

        buffer.initValue();
        buffer.TypeId = "PO";
        buffer.Name   = "Purchase order";
        buffer.ActionClassId = classnum(DocuActionArchive);
        insert();

        buffer.initValue();
        buffer.TypeId = "PI";
        buffer.Name   = "Purchase invoice";
        buffer.ActionClassId = classnum(DocuActionArchive);
        insert();
    }

    protected boolean existTmp(DocuType _bufferToCheck)
    {
        DocuType   bufferExist;
        ;

        bufferExist = this.makeTmp();
        select firstOnly bufferExist
            index hint TypeIdx
            where bufferExist.TypeId == _bufferToCheck.TypeId
                && bufferExist.RecId  != _bufferToCheck.RecId;

        return bufferExist.RecId ? true : false;
    }

    public int64 createdNumDB()
    {
        return (select count(RecId) from DocuType).RecId;
    }
```

10. Create a class constructor:

```
public static DocuTypeDefaultData construct()
{
    return new DocuTypeDefaultData();
}
```

11. Find **SysDefaultData** in AOT and modify its constructVAR():

```
static SysDefaultData constructVAR(tableId tableId)
{;
    switch (tableId)
    {
        case tablenum(DocuType):
            return DocuTypeDefaultData::construct();
    }
    return null;
}
```

12. Add the following variable to the class declaration of the **DocuTypeDefaultDataWizard** class:

```
DocuTypeDefaultData docuTypeDefaultData;
```

13. Override its init():

```
boolean init()
{
    boolean ret;
    ;
    docuTypeDefaultData =
        SysDefaultData::newDefaultDataWizard(
            tablenum(DocuType),
            this);
    ret = super();
    return ret;
}
```

14. Create a new method:

```
DocuTypeDefaultData docuTypeDefaultData()
{
    return docuTypeDefaultData;
}
```

15. Delete its run().

16. Add a new data source to the **DocuTypeDefaultDataWizard** form:

| Property | Value |
|----------|-------|
| Name | DocuType |
| Table | DocuType |
| AllowEdit | No |
| AllowCreate | No |
| AllowDelete | No |

17. Override the table's method:

```
public void init()
{;
    super();
    DocuType.setTmp();
    DocuType.checkRecord(false);
}
```

18. Change the properties of the **Step1** tab page:

| Property | Value |
|----------|-------|
| Caption | Welcome |

19. Add a **StaticText** control to this tab page and set its properties:

| Property | Value |
|----------|-------|
| Name | WelcomeTxt |
| Text | This default data wizard creates two new document types. |
| Width | Column width |
| Height | Column height |

20. Change the properties of the **Step2** tab page:

| Property | Value |
|----------|-------|
| Caption | Document types |
| HelpText | Create document types |
| AutoDeclaration | Yes |

21. Add a **Grid** control to this tab page and change its properties:

| Property | Value |
|---|---|
| Name | Grid |
| DataSource | DocuType |

22. Add a new **StringEdit** control to the grid with the following properties:

| Property | Value |
|---|---|
| Name | TypeId |
| DataSource | DocuType |
| DataField | TypeId |

23. Add another **StringEdit** control to the grid with the following properties:

| Property | Value |
|---|---|
| Name | Name |
| DataSource | DocuType |
| DataField | Name |

24. Add one more **StringEdit** control to the grid with the following properties:

| Property | Value |
|---|---|
| Name | ActionClassName |
| DataSource | DocuType |
| DataMethod | ActionClassName |

25. Change the properties of the **Step3** tab page:

| Property | Value |
|---|---|
| Caption | Finish |
| AutoDeclaration | Yes |

26. Add a new **StringEdit** control to this tab page:

| Property | Value |
| --- | --- |
| Name | FinishTxt |
| AutoDeclaration | Yes |
| AllowEdit | No |
| Width | Column width |
| Border | None |

27. Add a new **ListView** control to the same tab page:

| Property | Value |
| --- | --- |
| Name | FinishListView |
| Width | Column width |
| Height | Column height |
| ViewType | Report |

28. Add the following code to the form's `init()`:

```
sysWizard.docuTypeDefaultData().parmForm_DS(DocuType_ds);
sysWizard.docuTypeDefaultData().init();
sysWizard.summaryInit(FinishListView);
```

right after this line:

```
sysWizard = element.Args().caller();
```

29. Create a new form method:

```
void initPage()
{;
    switch (true)
    {
        case Step2.isActivePage():
            sysWizard.docuTypeDefaultData().createTable();
            break;
        case Step3.isActivePage():
            sysWizard.summaryBuild(
                finishListView,
                FinishTxt);
            break;
    }
}
```

30. To test the results, run the **DocuTypeDefaultDataWizard** menu item. The wizard should appear. Click **Next** on the first page:

31. Review the document types to be created and click **Next**:

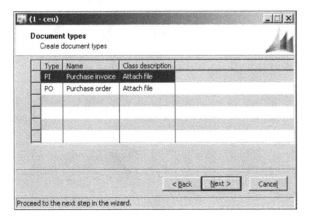

32. On the last page click **Finish** to create two new document types:

33. To check the results, open **Basic | Setup | Document management | Document types** and find the two types newly created by the wizard:

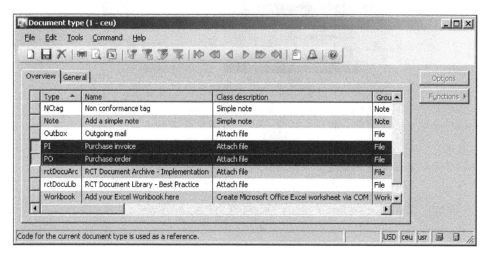

## How it works...

To create a framework for a new default data wizard we use the **Wizard Wizard** from the **Development tools** menu. On the second page, we have to select the **Default data Wizard** option, type in the wizard name on the third page, and accept the defaults on the rest of the pages. Of course, we could have created new wizard from scratch, but the **Wizard Wizard** saves a lot of time. The created menu item starts the wizard, the created class includes all the wizard logic, and created form presents the user with an interface. In this form each tab page corresponds to one wizard step.

Next, we need to create a new class derived from **SysDefaultData** for every type of default data we are going to use. In this example, we are populating a single table so it will be sufficient to create one class. The purpose of this class is to handle the data and table being updated. By following Dynamics AX naming conventions, the class name should be suffixed with the **DefaultData** string, that is, **DocuTypeDefaultData**. Such a class already exists in the application but it is empty and is not used—most likely it is reserved for future use. So no harm will be done if we use it for this demonstration, we just have to remove the `abstract` modifier from its class declaration.

The class should implement a number of methods, which are declared as abstract in the parent **SysDefaultData** class. Each abstract method in the latter class contains a brief developer comment on how to use each method. Here are the overridden methods:

- `buffer()`: returns the current record.
- `keyFieldId()`: returns the key field number of the table being updated.
- `setBuffer()`: sets the `buffer` variable.
- `doTable()`: inserts the data into a temporary table during the wizard run and into the actual table, once the wizard is completed.
- `existTmp()`: checks whether a record exists in the temporary table.
- `createdNumDB()`; returns how many records exist in a table being updated.

The created class should have its own `construct()` method and also has to be included into the `constructVAR()` method of **SysDefaultData** (`construct()` in **SysDefaultData** is used for system classes).

The following step is to modify the created **DocuTypeDefaultDataWizard** class. First, we add a variable of type **DocuTypeDefaultData** into its class declaration. Then, we initialize the variable in the class `init()` and create a method that returns that variable. Finally, we have to delete the `run()` created by the **Wizard Wizard**, because we do not have any specific logic to be implemented here and we can use the parent's `run()`.

The final step is to modify the form. We start with adding the **DocuType** table to the form and declaring this data source as temporary. On the first tab page (first wizard page) we add welcome text and description. On the second one, along with descriptive texts, we add a grid control with three fields from the **DocuType** table. This is where the user can review the data. Normally, here the user would be allowed to change the data. In such case, `validateWrite()` on the data source has to be overridden with a call to the wizard class to validate the data. The third page contains finishing text and a **ListView** control to show the existing number of records against how many will be created.

In the form's `init()`, we place the code that initializes the wizard handling class and in the `initPage()`, some logic to be executed on some wizard steps. On the second page, we initialize temporary data to be loaded and on the third page, we populate the **ListView** control with the summarized data.

## See also

Processing Data, Using a normal table a temporary table

# Processing multiple records

In my practice, I was asked a number of times to create various application functions that process user-selected records in a form grid. Regardless of what function is being created, the first step was always to determine what records were selected by the user.

In this recipe, we explore several ways of achieving this goal. We will modify the **Items** form in the **Inventory management** module by adding a new button to it, which lists currently selected records in the overview grid.

## How to do it...

1.  In AOT, open the **InventTable** form and create a new method with the following code:

```
void processSelectedItems()
{
    InventTable inventTableLocal;
    ;

    for (inventTableLocal = InventTable_ds.getFirst(true) ?
            InventTable_ds.getFirst(true) :
            InventTable;
        inventTableLocal;
        inventTableLocal = InventTable_ds.getNext())
    {
        info(strfmt(
```

```
            "You've selected item '%1'",
            inventTableLocal.ItemId));
    }
}
```

2.  Add a new **Button** to the form's **ButtonGroup** group:

| Property | Value |
| --- | --- |
| Name | ProcessSelectedItems |
| Text | Process |
| MultiSelect | Yes |

3.  Override its `clicked()` with the following code:

```
void clicked()
{;
    super();
    element.processSelectedItems();
}
```

4.  To test the record selection, open **Inventory management | Item Details**, select several records using *SHIFT* or *CTRL* and click the **Process** button. The selected items should be displayed in the **Infolog**:

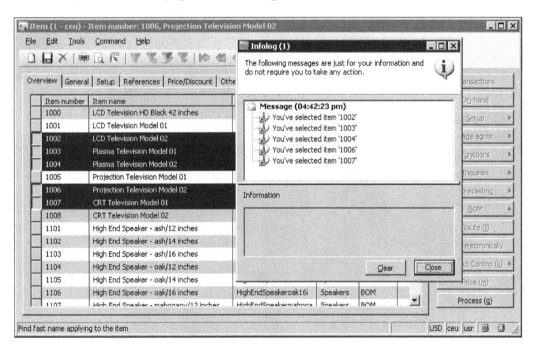

## How it works...

The key element in this recipe is a `for` statement in `processSelectedItems()`. First, it checks if more than one record is selected by calling `getFirst(true)` on the **InventTable** form data source. If yes, the `for` loops all the selected records from the data source, otherwise it uses the cursor, which corresponds to the currently selected single record. All selected records are then stored in the local variable `inventTableLocal`. In this example, we just output inventory item numbers into the **Infolog** using the global `info()` function.

The **ProcessSelectedItems** button is used to call the function above once the user clicks it. Notice that its property **MultiSelect** is set to **Yes** to ensure it is still enabled when multiple records are selected.

## There's more...

I have also experienced that sometimes Dynamics AX users struggle to select multiple records using *SHIFT* or *CTRL*. Sometimes, it is not clear that the form itself supports multiple record processing. In such cases a more convenient way of selecting multiple records could be to add a new checkbox in front of each record. This would remove all confusion and improve user experience. In order to implement that, we need to make few changes to the example above.

First, we add a new **Map** variable to the form's class declaration:

```
Map marked;
```

And in the form's `init()` right after the variable declaration section we create its instance:

```
marked = new Map(Types::Int64, Types::String);
```

Then, we create a new `edit` method on the **InventTable** data source with the following code:

```
edit boolean editMark(
    boolean     _set,
    InventTable _inventTable,
    boolean     _mark)
{;
    if (_set)
    {
        if (!_mark)
        {
            if (marked.exists(_inventTable.RecId))
            {
                marked.remove(_inventTable.RecId);
            }
        }
```

```
        else
        {
            marked.insert(
                _inventTable.RecId,
                _inventTable.ItemId);
        }
    }
    return marked.exists(_inventTable.RecId);
}
```

We also add a new **CheckBox** to the top of the form's **Grid** in the **Overview** tab page with the following properties:

| Property | Value |
|---|---|
| Name | Mark |
| Label | Select |
| DataSource | InventTable |
| DataMethod | editMark |

Finally, we have to modify `processSelectedItems()` to loop though the map. Replace the method with the following code:

```
void processSelectedItems()
{
    MapEnumerator     mapEnumerator;
    ;

    mapEnumerator = marked.getEnumerator();

    while (mapEnumerator.moveNext())
    {
        info(strfmt(
            "You've selected item '%1'",
            marked.lookup(mapEnumerator.currentKey())));
    }
}
```

Open the **Items** form again and notice that now it has a new checkbox **Select** in front of each record. Pick several records using it and click **Process**. The selected items should be displayed in the **Infolog**:

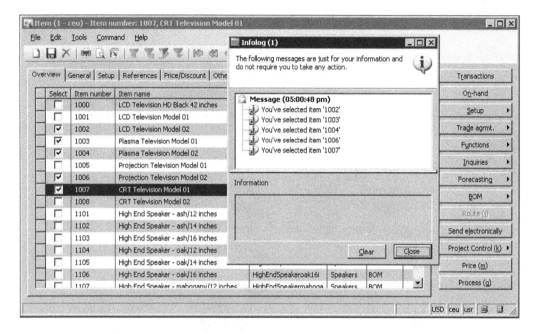

The principle of this technique is that we use a `Map` type object to store the list of selected item numbers. The `editMarked()` method is bound to the checkbox control and is responsible for adding a record to the map upon user selection and removing it from the map if the user deselects the checkbox.

We also use the `MapEnumerator` class to retrieve item numbers from the map for further processing.

# Coloring records

The possibility to color individual records is one Dynamics AX feature that can improve user experience. Normally, people like to see a reasonable number of colors in the interface they use. This makes their daily tasks not so boring.

One of the common requests is to emphasize the importance of disabled records, for example, terminated employees or stopped customers by displaying their records in a different color, normally red. An opposite example could be to show processed records like posted journals or invoices sales orders, let's say in green.

In this recipe, we will color locked-in-journal accounts in the **Chart of accounts** form.

## How to do it...

1. In AOT, open the **LedgerTableListPage** form and override the `displayOption()` method in its **LedgerTable** data source with the following code:

```
public void displayOption(
    Common                  _record,
    FormRowDisplayOption _options)
{;
    if (_record.(fieldnum(LedgerTable,BlockedInJournal)))
    {
        _options.backColor(WinAPI::RGB2int(255,100,100));
    }
    super(_record, _options);
}
```

2. To test the coloring, open **General ledger | Places | Chart of Accounts** and notice how locked-in-journal accounts are displayed now in a different color:

Chart of Accounts ▾

| Ledger account ▲ | Account name | Search name | Account type | Account category | Balance |
|---|---|---|---|---|---|
| 100000 | BALANCE SHEET | BALANCE SHEET | Page header | | 0.00 |
| 100500 | ASSETS | ASSETS | Header | | 0.00 |
| 110000 | CURRENT ASSETS | CURRENT ASSETS | Header | | 0.00 |
| 110100 | CASH & CASH EQUIVALENTS | CASH & CASH EQUIVALENTS | Header | | 0.00 |
| 110110 | Bank Account - USD | Bank Account - USD | Balance | CASH | 0.00 |
| 110120 | Bank Account - CNY | Bank Account - CAN | Balance | CASH | 0.00 |
| 110130 | Bank Account - EUR | Bank Account - EUR | Balance | CASH | 0.00 |
| 110140 | Bank Account - MXN | Bank Account - MXN | Balance | CASH | 0.00 |
| 110150 | Bank Account - GBP | Bank Account - GBP | Balance | CASH | 0.00 |
| 110160 | Payroll checking account | Payroll checking account | Balance | CASH | 0.00 |
| 110170 | Cash in bank - US (Fixed asset purch) | Cash in bank - US (Fixed asset purch) | Balance | CASH | 0.00 |
| 110180 | Petty cash account | Petty cash account | Balance | CASH | 0.00 |
| 119000 | TOTAL CASH & CASH EQUIVALENTS | TOTAL CASH & CASH EQUIVALENTS | Total | | 0.00 |
| 120000 | SECURITIES | SECURITIES | Header | | 0.00 |
| 120100 | Bonds | Bonds | Balance | SHORTTERMINVEST | 0.00 |
| 120200 | Other marketable securities | Other marketable securities | Balance | SHORTTERMINVEST | 0.00 |
| 120300 | Bill of Exchange (BOE) | Bill of Exchange (BOE) | Balance | CASHEQUIV | 0.00 |
| 120400 | BOE Remitted for Collection | BOE Remitted for Collection | Balance | CASHEQUIV | 0.00 |
| 120500 | BOE Remitted for Discount | BOE Remitted for Discount | Balance | CASHEQUIV | 0.00 |
| 120600 | Protested BOE | Protested BOE | Balance | CASHEQUIV | 0.00 |
| 129900 | TOTAL SECURITIES | TOTAL SECURITIES | Total | | 0.00 |

## How it works...

The method `displayOption()` on any form's data source can be used to change some of the visual options. Every time, before displaying the record, this method is called by the system with two arguments; the first is the current record and the second is a **FormRowDisplayOption** object, whose properties can be used to change record visual settings. In this example, we check if current ledger account record is locked in journal and if yes, we change the background property to light red by calling `backColor()`.

# Adding images to records

Dynamics AX can store images to be used along with data. Images could be used for various purposes, like a company logo that is displayed in every printed document, employee photos, inventory images, and so on. One of the most convenient ways to attach images to any record is to use the **Document handling** feature of Dynamics AX. This does not require any changes in the application. But **Document handling** is a very generic way of attaching files to any record and might not be suitable for specific circumstances.

Another way of attaching images to records could be to utilize standard application objects, though minor application changes are required. The company logo in the **Company information** form is one of the places where an image is stored in exactly this way.

In this recipe, we will explore the latter option. As an example, we will add the ability to store an image for each inventory item. Although inventory items already have a similar option, which is a part of the Enterprise Portal Framework, it is very inventory specific and unlike our example cannot be used anywhere else.

## How to do it...

1. Open the **InventTable** form in AOT and add a new **MenuItemButton** control to the bottom of its **ButtonGroup** with the following properties:

   | Property | Value |
   | --- | --- |
   | Name | CompanyImage |
   | MenuItemType | Display |
   | MenuItemName | CompanyImage |
   | Text | Item image |
   | DataSource | InventTable |

2.  Open **Inventory management | Item Details** and notice a new **Item image** button on the right:

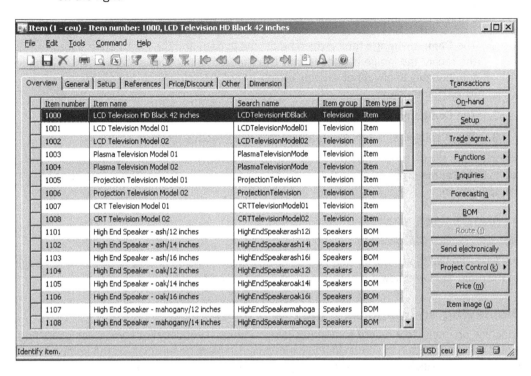

3.  Click on the button and then use the **Change** button to upload a new image for the selected item:

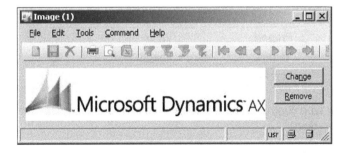

4.  The **Remove** button could be used to delete an existing image.

## How it works...

There are only three standard Dynamics AX objects involved here:

1. The **CompanyImage** table, which holds image data and the information about the record the image is attached to. The separate table allows easily hooking image functionality to any other existing table without modifying it or decreasing its performance.

2. The **CompanyImage** form, which shows an image and allows modifying it.

3. The **Display** menu item **CompanyImage**, which opens the form.

We only need to add the menu item to any form, like **InventTable** in our example and set its **DataSource** property against which we want to store an image. The rest is done by the application.

## There's more...

The following two topics will explain how a stored image could be displayed as a new tab page on the main form and how a stored image could be saved back to file.

### Displaying an image as a part of a form

Attaching an image to a record sometimes is not enough. I noticed that sometimes users find that clicking the button to see an image is not as convenient as having it on the same form. So here we will extend our recipe by displaying the stored image on a new tab page.

First, we need to add a new tab page to the end of the **InventTable** form's **Tab** control. This is where our image will be displayed. Set the **tab** page properties:

| Property | Value |
| --- | --- |
| Name | Image |
| Caption | Image |

Add a new **Window** type control to the tab page. This control will be used for displaying the image. Set its properties:

| Property | Value |
| --- | --- |
| Name | ItemImage |
| AutoDeclaration | Yes |
| Height | Column height |
| Width | Column width |

By setting **Height** and **Width** to **Column height** and **Column width** respectively, we ensure that the image control takes all possible space.

Add a new method to the **InventTable** form:

```
void loadImage()
{
    Image           img;
    CompanyImage companyImage;
    ;

    companyImage = CompanyImage::find(
        InventTable.dataAreaId,
        InventTable.TableId,
        InventTable.RecId);
    if (companyImage.Image)
    {
        img = new Image();
        img.setData(companyImage.Image);
        ItemImage.image(img);
    }
    else
    {
        ItemImage.image(null);
    }
}
```

This method first finds a **CompanyImage** record, which is attached to the current record and then displays the binary data using the **ItemImage** control. If no image is attached the **Window** control is cleared to display empty space.

Override pageActivated() of the newly created tab page with:

```
public void pageActivated()
{;
    super();
    element.loadImage();
}
```

In here, we simply call the previously created method once the user selects the image tab page.

The form should look like following in AOT:

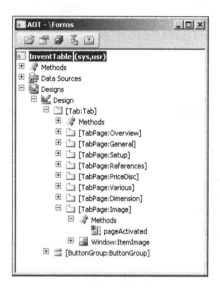

Now open **Item Details** from **Inventory management** and note the new tab page with the same image displayed:

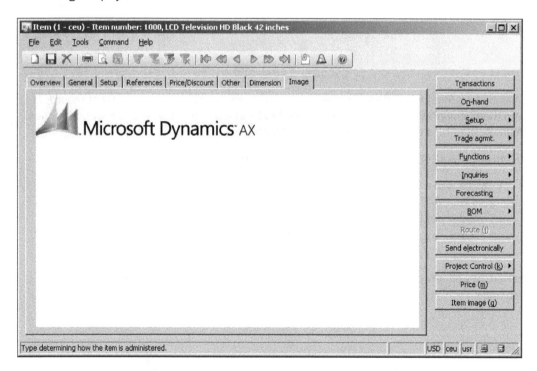

# Saving a stored image as a file

A couple of times in my practice it so happened that people lost images loaded into the system. Standard Dynamics AX does not provide a way of exporting loaded images. The images could be saved as files by creating and running a small job, which uses the **Image** class for image processing. In this topic, we will go a little beyond that and we will add a new button **Save as** to the **Image** form, which will allow us to save the loaded image as a file.

Let's add a new **Button** control to the **CompanyImage** form's **ButtonGroup** with the following properties:

| Property | Value |
| --- | --- |
| Name | SaveAs |
| Text | Save as |

Create a new method on the form:

```
void saveImage()
{
    Image    img;
    Filename name;
    str      type;
    #File
    ;

    if (!imageContainer)
    {
        return;
    }
    img = new Image();
    img.setData(imageContainer);
    type = '.'+strlwr(enum2value(img.saveType()));
    name = WinAPI::getSaveFileName(
        element.hWnd(),
        [WinAPI::fileType(type),#AllFilesName+type],
        '',
        '');
    if (name)
    {
        img.saveImage(name);
    }
}
```

This method will present the user with **Save As** dialog allowing choosing of the desired file name for saving the current image. Note that `imageContainer` is a form variable, which holds image data. If it is empty, it means there is no image attached and we do not run any of the code. We also check the loaded file type to make sure that our **Save As** dialog filters only files of that type.

Override the button's `clicked()` with the following code to make sure `saveImage()` is executed once the user clicks the button:

```
void clicked()
{;
    super();
    element.saveImage();
}
```

In AOT the form should look like this:

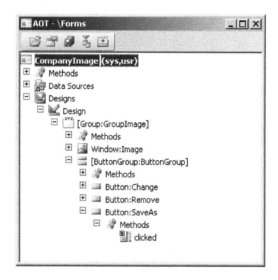

Now when you open the **Item image** form a new button **Save as** is available:

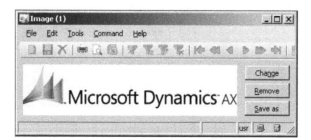

Use this button to save the item image as a file:

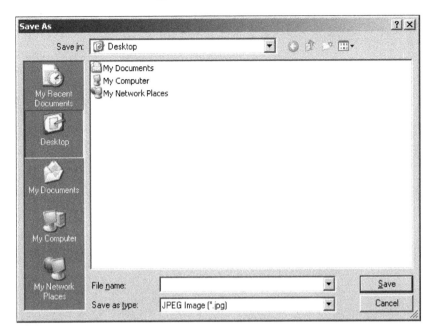

The **CompanyImage** form is used system wide, so note that this button is now available system wide too.

# 4
# Building Lookups

In this chapter, we will cover:

- ▸ Creating an automatic lookup
- ▸ Creating a lookup dynamically
- ▸ Using a form for lookup building
- ▸ Building a tree lookup
- ▸ Displaying a list of custom options
- ▸ Another way of displaying custom options
- ▸ Building a lookup based on record description
- ▸ Browsing for folders
- ▸ Selecting a file
- ▸ Picking a color
- ▸ Choosing a font

## Introduction

Lookups are the standard way to display a list of possible selection values to the user while editing or creating database records. Normally, standard lookups are created automatically by the system and are based on extended data types and table setup. It is also possible to override standard functionality by creating your own lookups from code or using Dynamics AX forms.

In this chapter, we will cover various lookup types like file selector, color picker, or tree lookup as well as the different approaches to create them.

# Creating an automatic lookup

Standard Dynamics AX lookups can be created in seconds without any programming knowledge. They are based on table or extended data type relations. If the relation is set on an extended data type, then all tables using this type will have automatic lookups based on extended data type. For example, if we look at the **ItemId** extended data type, we see that it is related to **ItemId** field in **InventTable** table. That means every control in the system bound to this extended data type will have automatic lookup to the **InventTable** table. It is also possible to override **extended data type** relations by specifying relations on the table itself. In this case, lookup will be based on the relations of the table. For example, we can create some relation on the **SalesLine** table and extend it to have an additional related fixed field **ItemType** equal to 2. In this case, all controls bound to the **ItemId** field in the **SalesLine** table will have a lookup showing only items of type 2, i.e. service.

This chapter will show how to create that very basic component using standard Dynamics AX table and extended data type relations.

As an example, we will create a default customer method of payment in the **Customer group** form.

## How to do it...

1. Open the **CustGroup** table in AOT, and add a new field:

| Property | Value |
|---|---|
| Type | String |
| Name | PaymMode |
| ExtendedDataType | CustPaymMode |

2. Add the newly created field to the end of the **Overview** field group of the table.

3.  To check the results, open **Accounts receivable | Setup | Customer groups**, and notice a new **Method of payment** column with the lookup:

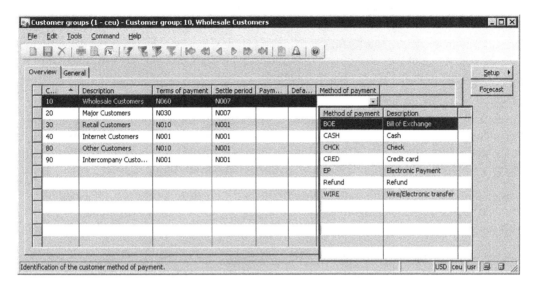

# How it works...

The newly created **PaymMode** field extends the **CustPaymMode** extended data type that has a defined relation to the **CustPaymModeTable** table. This relation ensures that our field and its form control have automatic lookup. By adding this field to the **Overview** field group, we make sure that it appears automatically in the **Customer group** form's grid in the **Overview** tab page.

# There's more...

The automatically generated lookup, in the example above, has only two columns—**Method of payment** and **Description**. Dynamics AX allows us to add more or change existing columns with minimum effort by changing various properties. Lookup columns can be controlled at several different places:

1.  Relation fields, either on an extended data type or a table itself, are always shown on lookups as columns. In our example, the extended data type **CustPaymMode** has a relation with **PaymMode** field in the **CustPaymModeTable** table and that's why it is displayed on the lookup.

2.  Fields defined in table **TitleField1** and **TitleField2** properties are also displayed as lookup columns. We can see that **Method of payment** is specified in **TitleField1** of the **CustPaymModeTable** table and **Description** is specified in **TitleField2**.

3. The first field of every table index is displayed as a column. If we look again in our example, we can see that the **CustPaymModeTable** table contains an index **CustPaymModeIdx**, which consists of the **PaymMode** field. This field is displayed as a lookup column.

4. The index fields, **TitleField1** and **TitleField2**, are in effect only when the **AutoLookup** field group of the table is empty. Otherwise, the fields defined in the **AutoLookup** group are displayed as lookup columns.

Duplicate fields are shown only once. In our example, we can see that **TitleField1** is set to **PaymMode** and **TitleField2** is set to **Name**. The extended data type relation is based on the **PaymMode** field, which is the same as **TitleField1**. The only index, **CustPaymModeIdx** also contains the **PaymMode** field. That means our lookup will have only two columns—**PaymMode** (labeled as **Method of payment**) and **Name** (labeled as **Description**).

Now, to demonstrate how the **AutoLookup** group can affect lookup columns, let's modify the previous example by adding another field to this group. Let's add the **PaymAccount** field to the **AutoLookup** group on the **CustPaymModeTable** table. Now, the lookup has one more column:

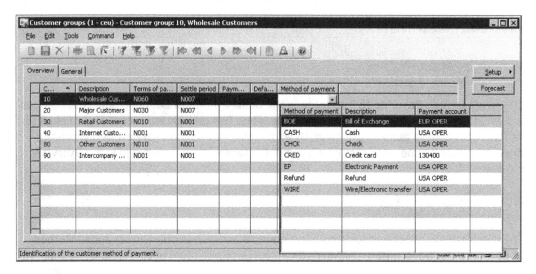

In this way we can quickly add more fields into lookups.

It is also possible to add **display** methods to the lookup's column list. We can extend our example by adding the `paymAccountName()` **display** method to the **AutoLookup** group on **CustPaymModeTable**. And here is the result:

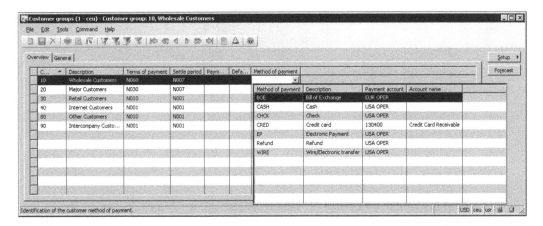

# Creating a lookup dynamically

Standard automatic lookups are widely used across the system, but sometimes it is required to show different fields from different data sources, apply various static or dynamics ranges, and so on. It is not possible to achieve such results by modifying or creating table relations, changing **TitleField1** or **TitleField2** properties, or editing the **AutoLookup** group. But Dynamics AX allows creating custom lookups either using AOT forms or dynamically generating them from X++ code. This recipe will demonstrate the latter option, which uses the `SysTableLookup` application class to build a runtime lookup from X++ code.

In standard Dynamics AX, every customer account can be assigned to a vendor account and vice versa. In this example, we will modify the **Vendor account** lookup on the **Customer Details** form to allow users to select only vendors that use the same currency as the customer.

## How to do it...

1. Open **VendTable** table in AOT, and create a new method:

```
public static void lookupVendorByCurrency(
    FormControl   _callingControl,
    CurrencyCode  _currency)
{
    Query                  query;
    QueryBuildDataSource   qbds;
    QueryBuildRange        qbr;
    SysTableLookup         lookup;
    ;

    query = new Query();

    qbds = query.addDataSource(tablenum(VendTable));

    qbr = qbds.addRange(fieldnum(VendTable, Currency));

    qbr.value(queryvalue(_currency));

    lookup = SysTableLookup::newParameters(
        tablenum(VendTable),
        _callingControl,
        true);

    lookup.parmQuery(query);

    lookup.addLookupField(
        fieldnum(VendTable, AccountNum),
        true);

    lookup.addLookupField(fieldnum(VendTable, Name));

    lookup.addLookupField(fieldnum(VendTable, Currency));

    lookup.performFormLookup();
}
```

2. Open the **CustTable** form in AOT, and override the `lookup()` method of the **VendAccount** field on the **CustTable** data source with the following code:

```
public void lookup(FormControl _formControl, str _filterStr)
{;
    VendTable::lookupVendorByCurrency(
        _formControl,
        CustTable.Currency);
}
```

3. In AOT, the form should look as shown below:

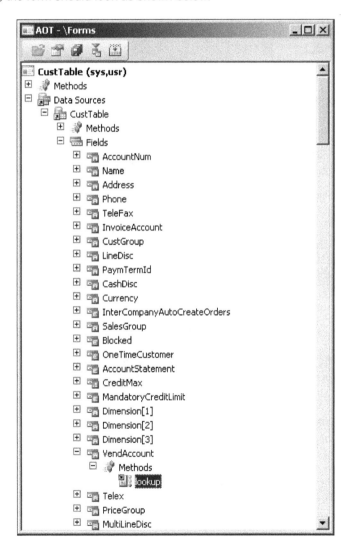

4. To test this, open **Accounts receivable | Customer Details**, and expand the **Vendor account** lookup located on the **General** tab page. The lookup is now different—it has the additional column **Currency** and vendors in the list match the customer currency:

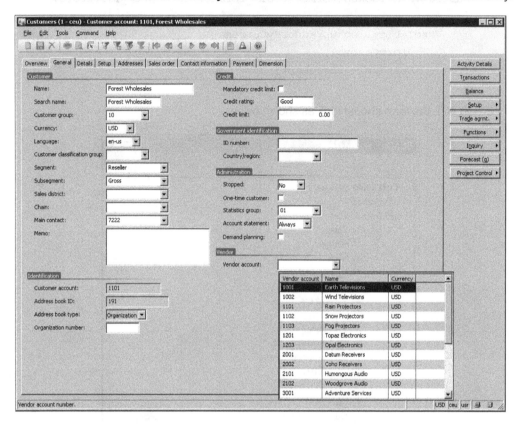

## How it works...

First, we create a method that generates the lookup on the **VendTable** table. That is a most convenient place for such a method, taking into consideration that it may be reused at a number of places.

In this method, we first create a new query, which will be the base for lookup records. We add a new **VendTable** data source to it, define a new **Currency** range, and set its value to the _currency argument.

Next, we create the actual lookup object and pass the query object through the parmQuery() member method. The lookup object is created by using the newParameters() constructor of SysTableLookup. This method accepts three parameters:

1. The Table ID, which is going to be displayed.
2. A reference to the form calling the control.

3.  An optional **Boolean** value, which specifies that the current control value should be highlighted in the lookup. The default is `true`.

Lookup columns are defined using the `addLookupField()` member method. We add three columns—**Vendor account**, **Name**, and **Currency**. This method accepts the following parameters:

1.  The field ID of the field that will be displayed as a column.

2.  An optional **Boolean** value that defines which column value is returned to the caller form upon user selection. The default is `false`.

And finally, we run the lookup by calling the `performFormLookup()` member method.

Now, we need to add some code to the `lookup()` of the **VendAccount** field of the **CustTable** data source in the **CustTable** form. Before the modification, **Vendor account** lookup was generated automatically by the system. We are changing this behavior by overriding the `super()` and calling the previously created method.

# Using a form for lookup building

In numerous situations, standard, automatic, or even dynamic runtime lookups cannot display the required data. For example, it might be a lookup with tab pages or a search field. In such cases, Dynamics AX offers the possibility to create an AOT form and use it as lookup.

In this recipe, we will demonstrate how to create a lookup using an AOT form. As an example, we will modify the standard customer account lookup to display only active customers.

## How to do it...

1.  In AOT, create a new form called **CustLookup**. Add a new data source with the following properties:

| Property | Value |
| --- | --- |
| Name | CustTable |
| Table | CustTable |
| AllowCreate | No |
| AllowEdit | No |
| AllowDelete | No |
| AllowCheck | No |
| OnlyFetchActive | Yes |
| Index | AccountIdx |

2. Change the form's following design properties:

| Property | Value |
| --- | --- |
| Frame | Border |
| WindowType | Popup |

3. Add a new **Grid** to the form's design:

| Property | Value |
| --- | --- |
| Name | Customers |
| ShowRowLabels | No |
| DataSource | CustTable |

4. Add a new **StringEdit** control to the grid:

| Property | Value |
| --- | --- |
| Name | AccountNum |
| DataSource | CustTable |
| DataField | AccountNum |
| AutoDeclaration | Yes |

5. Add another **StringEdit** control to the grid, right after **AccountNum**:

| Property | Value |
| --- | --- |
| Name | Name |
| DataSource | CustTable |
| DataField | Name |

6. Add one more **StringEdit** control to the grid, right after **Name**:

| Property | Value |
| --- | --- |
| Name | Phone |
| DataSource | CustTable |
| DataField | Phone |

7. Add a new **ComboBox** control to the end of the grid:

| Property | Value |
|---|---|
| Name | Blocked |
| DataSource | CustTable |
| DataField | Blocked |

8. Override the form's `init()` method with the following code:

```
public void init()
{;
    super();

    element.selectMode(AccountNum);
}
```

9. Override the form's `run()` with the following code:

```
public void run()
{
    FormStringControl callingControl;
    boolean          filterLookup;
    ;

    callingControl = SysTableLookup::getCallerStringControl(
        element.args());

    filterLookup = SysTableLookup::filterLookupPreRun(
        callingControl,
        AccountNum,
        CustTable_ds);

    super();

    SysTableLookup::filterLookupPostRun(
        filterLookup,
        callingControl.text(),
        AccountNum,
        CustTable_ds);
}
```

10. Finally, override `init()` of the **CustTable** data source with the following code:

```
public void init()
{
    Query               query;
    QueryBuildDataSource qbds;
    QueryBuildRange      qbr;
    ;

    query = new Query();

    qbds = query.addDataSource(tablenum(CustTable));

    qbr = qbds.addRange(fieldnum(CustTable, Blocked));

    qbr.value(queryvalue(CustVendorBlocked::No));

    this.query(query);
}
```

11. The form in AOT should look like this:

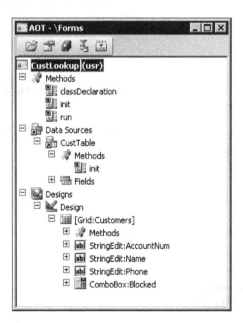

12. Locate the extended data type **CustAccount** in AOT, and change its property:

| Property | Value |
|----------|-------|
| FormHelp | CustLookup |

13. To test the results, open **Accounts receivable | Sales Order Details** and start creating a new sales order. Notice that now **Customer account** lookup is different, and it includes only active customers:

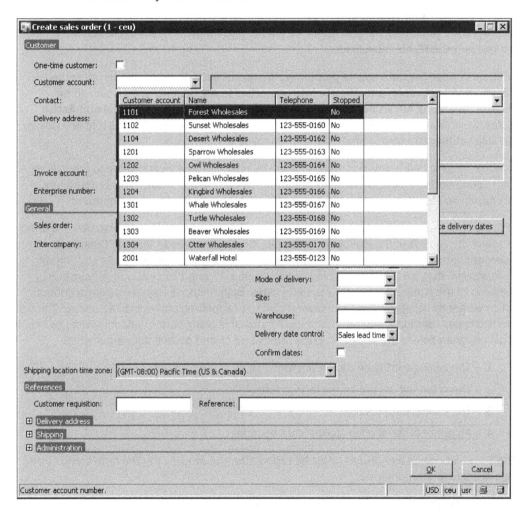

## How it works...

The newly created **CurrencyLookup** form will replace the automatically generated customer account lookup. It is recommended to append text **Lookup** to the end of the form name, so that lookups can be easily distinguished from other AOT forms.

In order to make our form lookup looks exactly like a standard lookup, we have to adjust its layout. So, we set form design **Frame** and **WindowType** properties respectively to **Border** and **Popup**. This removes form borders and makes the form lookup like a true lookup. By setting the grid property **ShowRowLabels** to **No**, we hide grid row labels, which are also not a part of automatically generated lookups. Then, we create a grid with four controls, which are bound to the relevant **CustTable** table fields.

Next, we change the data source properties. We do not allow any data change by setting **AllowEdit**, **AllowCreate**, and **AllowDelete** properties to **No**. Security checks should be disabled by setting **AllowCheck** to **No**. To increase performance, we set **OnlyFetchActive** to **Yes**, which will reduce the size of the database result set to only the fields that are visible. We also set the data source index to improve lookup performance.

Now, we need to define which form control will be returned as a lookup value to the calling form upon user selection. We need to specify it manually in the form's `init()` by calling `element.selectMode()` with the name of the **AccountNum** control as argument.

In the form's `run()`, we simulate standard lookup filtering, which allows user to user **\*** symbol to search for records in the lookup. For example, if the user types **1\*** into the **Customer account** control, the lookup will open automatically with all customer accounts starting with **1**. To achieve that, we use the `filterLookupPreRun()` and `filterLookupPostRun()` methods of the standard `SysTableLookup` class. Both methods requires calling a control, which we get by using `getCallerStringControl()` method of `SysTableLookup`. The first method reads user input and returns `true` if a search is being performed, otherwise, `false`. It must be called before the `super()` in the form's `run()` and accepts four arguments:

1. The calling control on the parent form.
2. The returning control on the lookup form.
3. The lookup data source.
4. An optional list of other lookup data sources.

The `filterLookupPostRun()` must be called after the `super()` in the form's `run()` and also accepts four arguments:

1. A result value from previously called `filterLookupPreRun()`.
2. The user text specified in the calling control.
3. The returning control on the lookup form.
4. The lookup data source.

The code in the **CustTable** data source's `init()` replaces the data source query created by its `super()` with the custom one. Basically, here we create a new `Query` object, add a range to show only active customers, and set this object as the new **CustTable** data source query. This ensures that there are no dynamic links from the caller form's data source.

The value **CustLookup** in the **FormHelp** property of the **CustAccount** extended data type will make sure that this form is opened every time the user opens **Customer account** lookup.

## See also

Processing Data, Building a query object

# Building a tree lookup

Form tree controls are a user-friendly way of displaying a hierarchy of related records like a company organizational structure, a bill of materials, projects, etc. Such a hierarchy can also be used in custom lookups allowing user to browse and select the required node in more convenient ways.

One of the previous recipes explained how to display the ledger budget model hierarchy in the **Budget model** form. In this recipe, we will reuse the previously created **BudgetModelTree** class to build a budget model tree lookup.

## How to do it...

1. Create a new form in AOT:

| Property | Value |
|----------|-------|
| Name | **BudgetModelLookup** |

2. Set its design properties to:

| Property | Value |
|----------|-------|
| Frame | Border |
| WindowType | Popup |

3. Add a new **Tree** control to the form's design.

| Property | Value |
|----------|-------|
| Name | ModelTree |

4. Add the following line to the form's class declaration:

```
BudgetModelTree    budgetModelTree;
```

5. Override the form's `init()` with:

```
public void init()
{
    FormStringControl callingControl;
    ;

    callingControl = SysTableLookup::getCallerStringControl(
        this.args());
    super();
    budgetModelTree = BudgetModelTree::construct(
        ModelTree,
        callingControl.text());
    budgetModelTree.buildTree();
}
```

6. Override `mouseDblClick()` and `mouseUp()` of the **ModelTree** control:

```
public int mouseDblClick(
    int      _x,
    int      _y,
    int      _button,
    boolean  _ctrl,
    boolean  _shift)
{
    int             ret;
    ;

    ret = super(_x, _y, _button, _ctrl, _shift);
    element.closeSelect(
        this.getItem(this.getSelection()).text());
    return ret;
}
public int mouseUp(
    int      _x,
    int      _y,
    int      _button,
    boolean  _ctrl,
    boolean  _shift)
{;
    super(_x, _y, _button, _ctrl, _shift);
    return 1;
}
```

7. The form should look like this in AOT:

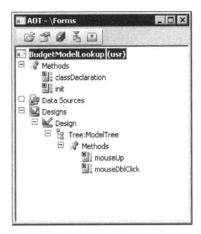

8. Open the extended data type **BudgetModelHeadId** in AOT, and set its **FormHelp** property:

| Property | Value |
|---|---|
| FormHelp | BudgetModelLookup |

9. To see the results, open **General ledger | Ledger budget**, and expand **Model** lookup:

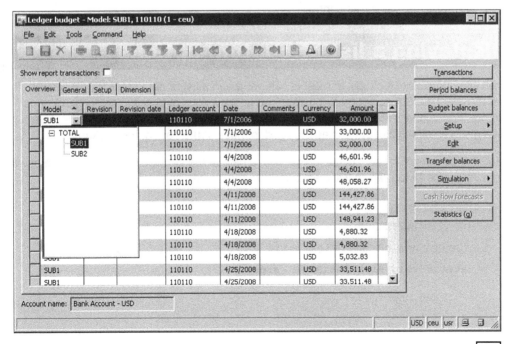

## How it works...

First, we create a new form called **BudgetModelLookup**, which is an actual lookup. We set the **Frame** and **WindowType** design properties to **Border** and **Popup** respectively to change the layout of the form to be like lookup.

In the form class declaration, we define the **BudgetModelTree** class which we have already created in one of the previous recipes.

The code in the form's `init()` builds the tree. Here, we create a new `budgetModelTree` object by calling the constructor `construct()`, which accepts two arguments:

1. A control of type **Tree**, which represents the actual tree.

2. Budget model, which is going to be preselected initially. Normally, it's a value of the calling control, which can be detected by using `getCallerStringControl()` method of `SysTableLookup` application class..

The code in `mouseDblClick()` returns the user-selected value from the tree back to the calling control and closes the lookup.

`mouseUp()` has to be overridden to return 1 to make sure that the lookup does not close while the user expands or collapses tree nodes.

## See also

Working with Forms, Using tree controls

# Displaying a list of custom options

When speaking about lookups, in most cases, we mean a list of data records presented to the user for selection. But sometimes, it is required to show a list of possible selection options that are "hardcoded" into the application or retrieved from an external system or file. Normally, it is a much smaller list of options as opposed to those of the data-driven lookups.

In this recipe, we will create such a lookup with a help of the global `pickList()` function. We use a Dynamics AX job, which will create and run the lookup.

## How to do it...

1. Create a new job called `PickList`:

```
static void PickList(Args _args)
{
    Map choices;
    str ret;
```

```
    ;

    choices = new Map(
        Types::Integer,
        Types::String);
    choices.insert(1, "Dynamics AX 2009");
    choices.insert(2, "Dynamics AX 4.0");

    ret = pickList(choices, "", "Choose version");
    if (ret)
    {
        info(strfmt("You've selected option No. %1", ret));
    }
}
```

2. Run the job for the results:

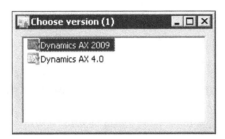

3. Double-click on one of the options:

## How it works...

The lookups created using the global `pickList()` function are based on values stored in a map. In our example, we define a new map called `choices` and initialize it. The map keys are of type **integer** and values of type **string**.

Next we insert "Dynamics AX 2009" as the first option and "Dynamics AX 4.0" as the second. At this stage, the map is ready to pass it to `pickList()`.

This function accepts three parameters:

1. A map, which contains lookup values. Here, we pass our `choices` variable.
2. A column header, which is not used.
3. A lookup title, which in our case is "**Choose version**".

The function returns a key value from the map, which could be used for further processing.

## There's more...

The global `pickList()` function is a way of displaying generic custom data in the lookup. Besides that, standard Dynamics AX contains a number of other global lookup functions, which can be used for different purposes.

### Companies

The global `pickDataArea()` function can be used to allow a user to select one of the Dynamics AX companies. But in order to use it, we first need to correct the function itself. In my version of Dynamics AX, it returns a `DataArea` type. However, it should return `DataAreaId`. Open the `Global` class in AOT, find `pickDataArea()`, and make sure the first line is:

```
static DataAreaId pickDataArea()
{
    . . .
```

Restart the Dynamics AX client in order to apply the changes.

Next, create a new job called `PickDataArea()`:

```
static void PickDataArea(Args _args)
{
    DataAreaId dataAreaId;
    ;

    dataAreaId = pickDataArea();
    if (dataAreaId)
    {
```

```
            info(strfmt("You've selected %1", dataAreaId));
        }
    }
```

And run it:

Upon user selection, the function returns the selected company account number.

## Domains

Another global method called `pickDomain()` can be used for choosing Dynamics AX domains. It is very similar to the previous example, and it also contains a mistake in its code. We need to change the line `args.parm(' 10')` to `args.parm(' 9')` in the `pickDomain()` function of the `Global` class in order to make it work. The modified method should look like this:

```
static domainId pickDomain()
{
    Object  formRun;
    Args    args;
    ;

    args = new Args(formstr(SysPick));
    args.parm(' 9');
    ...
```

Do not forget to restart the Dynamics AX client again. Once this is done, we can create a new job called `PickDomain()`:

```
static void PickDomain(Args _args)
{
    DomainId domainId;
    ;

    domainId = pickDomain();
    if (domainId)
    {
        info(strfmt("You've selected %1", domainId));
    }
}
```

You should get the following result after the job is started:

The return value of the lookup is the Dynamics AX Domain ID.

## User groups

The global `pickUserGroup()` allows us to present the user with a list of Dynamics AX user groups. It accepts a user ID as an optional argument. If this argument is present, the lookup will display only groups that this user belongs to, otherwise all groups. In the job code below, we list all the groups of the user who is currently logged in:

```
static void PickUserGroup(Args _args)
{
    UserGroupId userGroupId;
    ;

    userGroupId = pickUserGroup(curuserid());
    if (userGroupId)
    {
        info(strfmt("You've selected %1", userGroupId));
    }
}
```

And here is the result:

## Users

Another global function called `pickUser()` shows a list of Dynamics AX users. The job below is used to demonstrate how it works:

```
static void PickUser(Args _args)
{
    UserId userId;
    ;

    userId = pickUser();
    if (userId)
    {
        info(strfmt("You've selected %1", userId));
    }
}
```

The result is a lookup with a list of all Dynamics AX users:

The `pickUser()` function can accept one optional argument of type **Map**, which contains a custom list of users. This might be useful when the lookup must show only some of the system users.

## Tables

More advanced pieces of custom Dynamics AX functionality may require a user to select one of the application tables directly. An example in standard Dynamics AX can be **Definition groups**, which can be accessed in Administration/Periodic/Data export/import.

The global function `pickTable()` is the key element of this functionality. The following job demonstrates how it works:

```
static void PickTable(Args _args)
{
    TableId tableId;
    ;
```

```
        tableId = pickTable(false, true, true, false, false);

        if (tableId)
        {
            info(strfmt(
                "You've selected %1",
                tableid2name(tableId)));
        }
    }
}
```

The result is a lookup with a list of Dynamics AX tables, which returns a table ID upon user selection:

`pickTable()` accepts five optional arguments, which drives the number of tables being listed:

1. Include data dictionary maps?
2. Include temporary tables?
3. Include system tables?
4. Include views?
5. Show only tables to which the user has access rights?

## Table fields

A list of table fields can be displayed by using the global `pickField()` function. This function accepts a table ID as argument and presents the user with the list of fields of that table. The following job displays a list of fields of the **LedgerTable** table:

```
static void PickField(Args _args)
{
    FieldId fieldId;
    ;

    fieldId = pickField(tablenum(LedgerTable));
```

```
        if (fieldId)
        {
            info(strfmt(
                "You've selected %1",
                fieldid2name(tablenum(LedgerTable),fieldId)));
        }
    }
```

The result is a list of **LedgerTable** table fields:

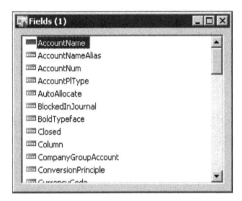

The lookup returns the selected field ID.

## Classes

In even complex custom functionality, sometimes it is necessary to allow the user to specify a Dynamics AX AOT class directly. We allow helper functions here too. The following job demonstrates how the global PickClass() function can present a list of classes to the user for selection:

```
static void pickClass(Args _args)
{
    ClassId classId;
    ;

    classId = pickClass(false);

    if (classId)
    {
        info(strfmt(
            "You've selected %1",
            classid2name(classId)));
    }
}
```

And the job's result is a list of Dynamics AX classes:

The function accepts one optional argument, which allows us to include/exclude system classes. In the previous example, we exclude system classes by passing `false` as an argument.

## Interfaces

The global function `pickInterface()` is very similar to the previous function, except that it shows a list of Dynamics AX interfaces. The job below demonstrates the usage of this function:

```
static void PickInterface(Args _args)
{
    ClassId classId;
    ;

    classId = pickInterface(false);
    if (classId)
    {
        info(strfmt(
            "You've selected %1",
            classid2name(classId)));
    }
}
```

And the result is a list of Dynamics AX interfaces:

This function also accepts one optional argument to include or exclude system interfaces.

# Another way of displaying custom options

Global system functions like `pickList()`, `pickUser()` and similar in Dynamics AX allow developers to build various lookups displaying a list of custom options. Besides that, the standard Dynamics AX application contains several additional global lookup functions, which have a slightly richer user interface.

One of the functions is called `selectSingle()` and presents the user with a list of selectable options created using a **container** type variable.

In this recipe for demonstration purposes, we will create a job that shows the principle of how to use this function. As sample data, we will use different versions of Dynamics AX.

## How to do it...

1. Create a new job called `SysListSelect`:

```
static void SysListSelectSingle(Args _args)
{
    container choices;
    container sel;
    boolean   ok;
    ;

    choices = [
```

```
        ["2009\nDynamics AX 2009",1,true],
        ["4.0\nDynamics AX 4.0",2,false]];
    sel = selectSingle(
        "Choose version",
        "Please select Dynamics AX version",
        choices,
        ["Version","Description"]);
    ok = conpeek(sel,1);
    if (ok)
    {
        info(strfmt(
            "You've selected option No. %1",
            conpeek(sel,2)));
    }
}
```

2.  Run the job to start the lookup:

3.  Select one of the options, and click the **OK** button. The information message displays the selected option:

## How it works...

In this recipe, we first fill in the `choices` variable with values. Basically, here we build a container of containers. Each container inside the parent container is made of three elements and represents one selectable option in the list:

1. The first element is a selection text. Normally, it is displayed as one column, but in this example, we can use `\n` inside the text to create more columns.
2. The second element is the number of the list item. This value is returned upon user choice.
3. And the third value specifies whether the option is preselected by default.

Once list values are ready, we call `selectSingle()` to build the actual lookup. This function accepts five arguments:

1. Window title.
2. Lookup description.
3. A container of list values, in our case, `choices`.
4. A container representing column headings, in our case, **Version** and **Description**.
5. A reference to a caller object, normally a Dynamics AX form or control. In this example, we do not use this parameter.

`singleSelect()` returns a container of two elements:

1. `true` or `false` depending if the lookup was closed using the **OK** button.
2. The key value of the user-selected option.

## There's more...

You may have noticed that the lookup, which is created using `singleSelect()`, allows choosing of only one option from the list. There is another similar global function called `selectMultiple()`, which is exactly the same except that the user can select multiple options from the list. The following code demonstrates its usage:

```
static void SysListSelectMultiple(Args _args)
{
    container choices;
    container sel;
    boolean   ok;
    int       i;
    ;

    choices = [
        ["2009\nDynamics AX 2009",1,true],
        ["4.0\nDynamics AX 4.0",2,false]];
    sel = selectMultiple(
```

```
        "Choose version",
        "Please select Dynamics AX version",
        choices,
        ["Version","Description"]);
ok = conpeek(sel,1);
if (ok)
{
    for (i=1; i <= conlen(conpeek(sel,2)); i++)
    {
        info(strfmt(
            "You've selected option No. %1",
            conpeek(conpeek(sel,2),i)));
    }
}
}
```

Once the lookup is opened, you can select multiple options:

After clicking **OK** button, the information message shows selected options:

Note that here the second value of the returned container is a container of selected key values.

# Building a lookup based on record description

Most of Dynamics AX data lookups display a list of records where the first column always contains a value, which is returned to a calling form. The first column in the lookup normally contains a unique record identification value, which is used to build relations between tables.

For example, customer lookup displays customer account number, customer name, and some other fields; inventory item lookup displays item number, item name, and other fields. In these examples and most other cases, it is OK because unique record identification value is self explanatory.

But in some cases, the record identifier can be not so user-friendly and may require showing additional information on the parent form. One of the ways of solving such issues is to create a lookup, which is actually based on the record identifier, but upon user selection returns the record description or other more explanatory field. In the standard Dynamics AX application, you can find a number of places where the contact person is displayed as a person name, even though the actual table relation is based on contact person ID.

In this recipe, we will replace language selection lookup on **Vendors** form to show language description instead of language ID.

## How to do it...

1.  Create a new `String` extended data type:

    | Property | Value |
    | --- | --- |
    | Name | LanguageDescriptionExt |
    | Extends | LanguageDescription |
    | Label | Language |

2.  Open the `VendTable` table in AOT, and add a new `edit` method:

    ```
    client server edit LanguageDescriptionExt editLanguage (
        boolean                 _set,
        LanguageDescriptionExt _languageDescription)
    {;
        if (_set)
        {
            this.LanguageId = _languageDescription;
        }
        return LanguageTable::languageId2Description(
            this.LanguageId);
    }
    ```

3. Open the `VendTable` form in AOT, and modify the `LanguageId` control properties in the following way:

| Property | Value |
|----------|-------|
| Visible | No |

4. Create a new control of type **StringEdit** right below the **LanguageId** control with properties as shown below:

| Property | Value |
|----------|-------|
| Name | editLanguage |
| DataSource | VendTable |
| DataMethod | editLanguage |

5. Override the `editLanguage` contol's `lookup()` method with:

```
public void lookup()
{;
    this.performTypeLookup(extendedtypenum(LanguageId));
}
```

6. After all modifications, the `VendTable` form should look like this in AOT:

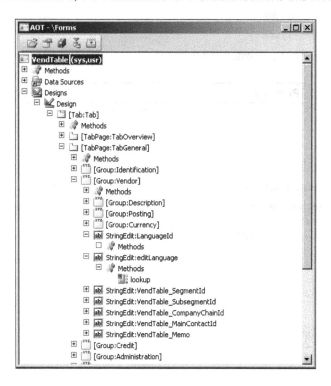

Next open **Accounts payable | Vendor Details**, go to the **General** tab page, and check the newly created **Language** lookup:

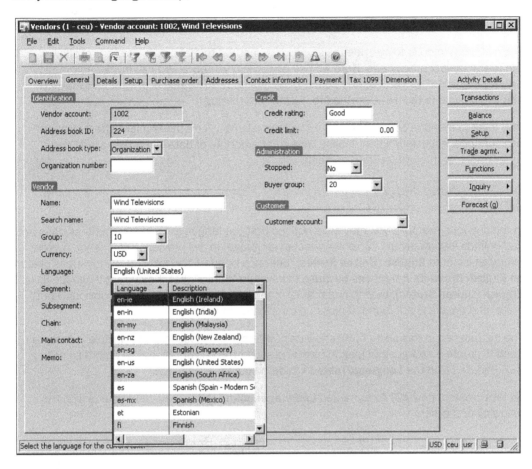

## How it works...

In this recipe, we are using the `edit` method to display a language description instead of the language ID. The language description is based on the extended data type **LanguageDescription**, which has the label **Description**. In order to change that label, we create a new extended data type called **LanguageDescriptionExt** with the right label—**Language**.

The edit method is created on **VendTable** and uses the newly created extended data type. This ensures that the label of the user control stays the same. Note that this method accepts a **LanguageDescriptionExt** extended data type as its second argument, but actually it receives a **LanguageId** returned from the lookup. This is totally fine, because both types are based on the `string` basic type and **LanguageId** is less in size. The method returns a language description based on the language ID.

We have almost everything ready, and now we need to adjust the `VendTable` form to show the new field. First, we hide the existing `LanguageId` control by setting its `Visible` property to `No`. Then we create a new control that points to the `edit` method on the `VendTable` table. This ensures that the language description is shown on the control.

The last thing to do is to override the `lookup()` method to make sure the control allows the user to select a language. Here we use `performTypeLookup()` to invoke automatic `LanguageId` lookup. As described earlier, the lookup return value is of type `LanguageId`, and it is passed to the `edit` method for further processing.

One thing to mention here is that the `edit` (and `display`) methods might affect system performance, especially when dealing with great amounts of data when they are added, for example, to the form overview screen.

## There's more...

In the previous example, you may have noticed that the language lookup sometimes does not find or finds incorrectly the currently selected language. In the previous screenshot, current language is set to **English (United States)**, but once opened, the focus of the lookup is placed on **English (Ireland)**. It happens because the system "thinks" that the current language ID is **English (United States)**, tries to find that ID in the list of languages, which is obviously not there, and once it is not found, it picks up the closest match.

The instructions in this section will show us how to solve this issue. The principle is that we need to create a new custom lookup form and select the current language record by calling `findValue()` on the **LanguageTable** form data source.

So let's create a new AOT form named **LanguageLookup**. Add a new data source with the following properties:

| Property | Value |
| --- | --- |
| Name | LanguageTable |
| Table | LanguageTable |
| Index | Key |
| AllowCreate | No |
| AllowDelete | No |
| AllowEdit | No |
| AllowCheck | No |

Add a new grid to the form's design:

| Property | Value |
| --- | --- |
| Name | Languages |
| ShowRowLabels | No |
| DataSource | LanguageTable |
| DataGroup | Languages |

Once the form is saved, two new controls should appear in the grid automatically. Change the properties of `Languages_LanguageId`:

| Property | Value |
| --- | --- |
| AutoDeclaration | Yes |

Override the form's `init()` and `run()` with the following code:

```
public void init()
{;
    super();
    element.selectMode(Languages_LanguageId);
}
public void run()
{
    LanguageId languageId;
    ;

    languageId = element.args().lookupValue();
    super();
    LanguageTable_ds.findValue(
        fieldnum(LanguageTable,LanguageId), languageId);
}
```

The key element is `LanguageTable_ds.findValue()` in the form's `run()`, which sets the cursor on the currently selected language record. Language ID is retrieved from the arguments object by using `lookupValue()`.

In AOT, the form should look like this:

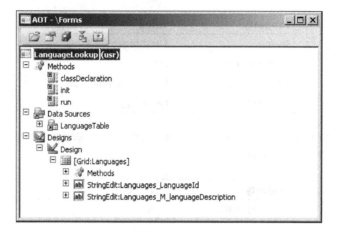

Next, we need to create a new static method in the **LanguageTable** table, which opens the new lookup form:

```
public client static void lookupLanguage(
    FormStringControl _callingControl,
    LanguageId _languageId)
{
    FormRun formRun;
    Args     args;
    ;

    args = new Args();
    args.name(formstr(LanguageLookup));
    args.lookupValue(_languageId);

    formRun = classfactory.formRunClass(args);
    formRun.init();

    _callingControl.performFormLookup(formRun);
}
```

Here, we use the `formRunClass()` method of global `classfactory` object. Note that the second argument of this method is of type `LanguageId`, and it is passed to the newly created form by using `lookupValue()` via the `args` argument object.

The final touch is to change the code in the `lookup()` of **editLanguge** on the **VendTable** form, which invokes the new lookup form:

```
public void lookup()
{;
    LanguageTable::lookupLanguage(this, VendTable.LanguageId);
}
```

Now, when you open **Accounts receivable | Vendor Details**, the currently set vendor language in the **Language** lookup will be preselected correctly:

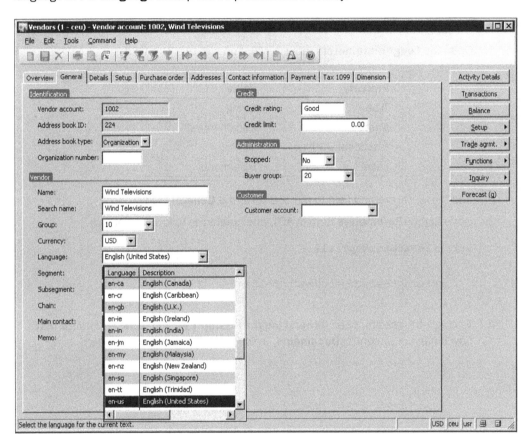

# Browsing for folders

Folder browsing lookups are used when the user is required to specify a local or network folder for storing or retrieving Dynamics AX data. In this recipe, we will see how such lookups could be built using various techniques.

As an example, we will create a new control called **Documents** in the **Ledger parameters** form, which will store a folder path.

## How to do it...

1. Open the **LedgerParameters** table in AOT, and create a new field:

   | Property | Value |
   | --- | --- |
   | Type | String |
   | Name | DocumentPath |
   | ExtendedDataType | FilePath |
   | Label | Documents |

2. Add the newly created field to the bottom of the **General** field group.

3. Open **LedgerParameters** form in AOT, and create the following method:

   ```
   str filePathLookupTitle()
   {
       return "Select document folder";
   }
   ```

4. To check the results, open **General ledger | Setup | Parameters**, and notice that now it has a new control **Documents**, which allows you to select a folder:

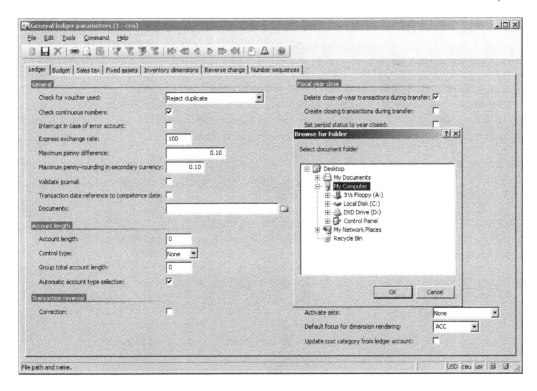

## How it works...

The folder browsing lookup is bound to the **FilePath** extended data type, and it appears automatically near every control that is based on that type. In this recipe, we add a new **DocumentPath** field, which extends **FilePath** and consequently inherits the lookup.

We also add the **DocumentPath** field to the **General** field group in order for it to appear on the form automatically.

Browsing for folder lookup requires the `filePathLookupTitle()` method on a caller form. This method returns a lookup description text. Dynamics AX will show an error, if this method is not present on a caller.

## There's more...

In this section, we will explore other enhancements to the previous example. Firstly, we will build exactly the same lookup but using different approach and secondly, we will enable **Make New Folder** button on the lookup.

## Manual folder browsing lookup

The described technique works fine in most cases. But personally, I prefer the other way of creating such lookups for two main reasons.

First is that standard folder browsing lookup requires the `filePathLookupTitle()` method to be present on a caller form. The name of this method has to be exactly like this and cannot be prefixed with a three letter code, as per best practice recommendations, and it might lead to confusions when performing system changes in the future.

Another reason is that a single form cannot have two or more folder browsing lookups unless they share the same description. Every lookup calls the same `filePathLookupTitle()` and will obviously have the same descriptions.

The standard browse-for-folder lookup form internally uses `WinAPI::browseForPath()` to invoke the standard Windows folder browsing dialog. We can reuse this method to create a folder browsing lookup manually.

We have to modify our previous example by deleting `filePathLookupTitle()` from the **LedgerParameters** form and overriding the `lookup()` method of the **DocumentPath** field in the **LedgerParameters** form data source:

```
public void lookup(FormControl _formControl, str _filterStr)
{
    FilePath path;
    ;

    path = WinAPI::browseForPath(
        element.hWnd(),
        "Select document folder extended");
    LedgerParameters.DocumentPath = path;
    LedgerParameters_ds.refresh();
}
```

Now, if you open the lookup, you may notice that it looks exactly the same as before apart from its description. Using this technique, we can create more than one folder browsing lookup on the same form without adding additional methods to the form itself.

## Adding a Make New Folder button

Standard Dynamics AX contains one more `WinAPI` method called `browseForFolderDialog()`. Besides selecting a folder, it allows us to create a new one. It accepts three optional arguments:

1. The lookup description.
2. The preselected folder path.
3. `true` to show and `false` to hide the **Make New Folder** button. This button is shown by default, if this argument is omitted.

Let's override the `lookup()` method of the **DocumentPath** field in the **LedgerParameters** form data source with:

```
public void lookup(FormControl _formControl, str _filterStr)
{
    FilePath path;
    ;

    path = WinAPI::browseForFolderDialog(
        "Select document folder extended",
        LedgerParameters.DocumentPath,
        true);
    LedgerParameters.DocumentPath = path;
    LedgerParameters_ds.refresh();
}
```

Note that now, the folder browsing lookup has a **Make New Folder** button, which allows the user to create a new folder straight away:

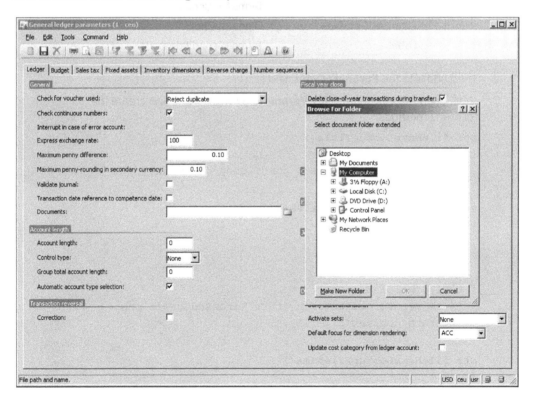

# Selecting a file

The previous recipe explained how to create a folder browsing lookup. This recipe will show several approaches to create a file lookup using standard Dynamics AX.

As an example, we will create a **Terms & conditions** control in the **Form setup** form in Account payable, which allows storing a path to the text document.

## How to do it...

1. Open **VendFormLetterParameters** table in AOT, and create a new field with properties:

   | Property | Value |
   | --- | --- |
   | Type | String |
   | Name | TermsAndConditions |
   | ExtendedDataType | FilenameOpen |
   | Label | Terms & conditions |

2. Then add it to the **PurchaseOrder** field group.

3. Next, open the **VendFormletterParameters** form in AOT, and create the following methods:

```
str fileNameLookupTitle()
{
    return "Select Terms & conditions document";
}
str fileNameLookupInitialPath()
{
    container file;
    ;

    file = fileNameSplit(
        VendFormletterParameters.TermsAndConditions);
    return conpeek(file ,1);
}
str fileNameLookupFilename()
{
    Filename    path;
    Filename    name;
    Filename    type;
    ;
```

```
    [path, name, type] = fileNameSplit(
        VendFormletterParameters.TermsAndConditions);

    return name + type;
}

container fileNameLookupFilter()
{
    #File
    ;

    return [WinAPI::fileType(#txt),#AllFilesName+#txt];
}
```

4. As a result, we should be able to select and store a text file in the **Account payable | Setup | Forms | Form setup** form under the **Purchase order** tab page:

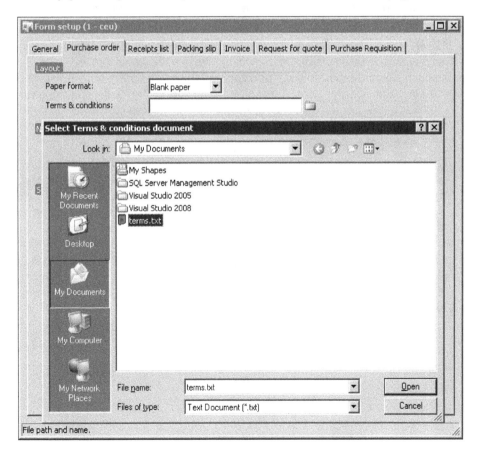

## How it works...

The extended data type **FilenameOpen** of the newly created table field is bound to a standard Dynamics AX file lookup form, which presents the user with the file selection dialog.

By adding this field to the **PurchaseOrder** field group in the **VendFormLetterParameters** table, we ensure that it is displayed on the **Form setup** form in the **Layout** group under the **Purchase order** tab.

The following four form methods are called by the lookup and must be present on the caller form:

1.  `fileNameLookupTitle()` contains text to be displayed as a lookup title.

2.  `fileNameLookupInitialPath()` is used to identify the initial directory. If there is a value in the **Terms & conditions** field, this method strips the filename part and returns a directory path to the lookup to be opened as the starting browsing point. Here, we use the global function `filenamesplit()` to process the stored file path. If the field is empty, the lookup starting point is the last used folder.

3.  `fileNameLookupFilename()` detects the current value in the field and extracts the filename to be displayed on the lookup. We use the global `fileNameSplit()` function again to separate given directory path into three parts—directory path, filename, and file extension. For example, if the current **Terms & conditions** value is `\\LONDON\Documents\terms.txt`, once the user clicks on the lookup button, the method returns only the filename `terms.txt` (file name + file extension) separated from the rest of the directory path.

4.  `fileNameLookupFilter()` is responsible for displaying a list of allowed file extensions. It returns a container of allowed extensions in pairs of two. The first, third, fifth, etc value is the name of the file extension and the second, fourth, sixth, etc is an extension filter. In this example, only text files are allowed and the method returns two values in the container. The first value is a string **Text Document** and the second one is `*.txt`. In order to avoid literals in X++ code, we use the #File macro definitions `#txt` and `#AllFileName`, which respectively contain the string `.txt` and `*`, which are concatenated by the lookup to present the user with the **Text Document** (`*.txt`) filter. `WinAPI::fileType()` according to current Windows registry settings converts file extensions to textual representation.

## There's more...

The previous technique requires creating a number of methods on the caller form and will not work with multiple file lookups on the same form. A different approach could be used to avoid those issues. Let's modify the previous example by removing all four methods from the form itself and overriding the `lookup()` method on the **TermAndConditions** field of the **VendFormLetterParameters** data source:

```
public void lookup(FormControl _formControl, str _filterStr)
{
    FilenameOpen file;
    Filename     path;
    Filename     name;
    Filename     type
    #File
    ;

    [path, name, type] = filenamesplit(
        VendFormLetterParameters.TermsAndConditions);
    file  = WinAPI::getOpenFileName(
        element.hWnd(),
        [WinAPI::fileType(#txt),#AllFilesName+#txt],
        path,
        "Select Terms & conditions document",
        "",
        name + type
        );
    if (file)
    {
        VendFormLetterParameters.TermsAndConditions = file;
        VendFormLetterParameters_ds.refresh();
    }
}
```

This method calls `getOpenFileName()` method of **WinAPI** application class, which opens the standard Windows file selection dialog. The method accepts a number of arguments:

1. A handler to the calling window.
2. A container of allowed file extensions. It is exactly what `fileNameLookupFilter()` returns.
3. The lookup title.
4. The default file extension.
5. The preselected file path.

After all those modifications, the appearance of the lookup stays the same.

## Picking a color

In this recipe, we will be creating a color lookup. As an example, we will create the possibility to choose a color in the **Company information** form, which might be used to define different colors for each Dynamics AX company. That's one of my favorites and is very useful in Dynamics AX multi-company installations. Normally, I use additional code, which reads the user setting and changes the background color of all forms in the same company. This allows users to easily identify in which company they are and prevents incorrect postings.

### How to do it...

1. Open the **CompanyInfo** table in AOT, and create a new field with properties:

   | Property | Value |
   | --- | --- |
   | Type | Integer |
   | Name | CompanyColor |
   | ExtendedDataType | CCColor |

2. Open the **CompanyInfo** form in AOT, and add a new **IntEdit** control into the **TopPanel** group right after the **GroupName** group. Set the following properties:

   | Property | Value |
   | --- | --- |
   | Name | CompanyColor |
   | AutoDeclaration | Yes |
   | Label | Company color |
   | LookupButton | Always |
   | ShowZero | No |
   | ColorScheme | RGB |

3. Create a new **edit** method in the **CompanyInfo** form data source:

```
edit CCColor editCompanyColor(
    boolean     _set,
    CompanyInfo _companyInfo,
    CCColor     _color)
{;
    if (_companyInfo.CompanyColor)
    {
        CompanyColor.backgroundColor(
            _companyInfo.CompanyColor);
    }
    else
    {
```

```
            CompanyColor.backgroundColor(
                WinAPI::RGB2int(255,255,255));
    }
    return 0;
}
```

4. Set the name of the newly created method in the **DataMethod** property of the previously created **CompanyColor** control:

| Property | Value |
|----------|-------|
| DataSource | CompanyInfo |
| DataMethod | editCompanyColor |

5. And override its `lookup()` method with:

```
public void lookup()
{
    int        red;
    int        green;
    int        blue;
    container color;
    ;

    [red, green, blue] = WinApi::RGBint2Con(
        CompanyColor.backgroundColor());
    color = WinAPI::chooseColor(
        element.hWnd(),
        red,
        green,
        blue,
        null,
        true);
    if (color)
    {
        [red, green, blue] = color;
        CompanyInfo.CompanyColor = WinAPI::RGB2int(
            red,
            green,
            blue);
        CompanyColor.backgroundColor(
            CompanyInfo.CompanyColor);
    }
}
```

6.  In the end the form should look like this in AOT:

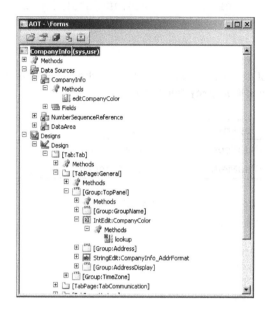

7.  To test the results, open **Basic | Setup | Company information**, and click on the **Company color** lookup:

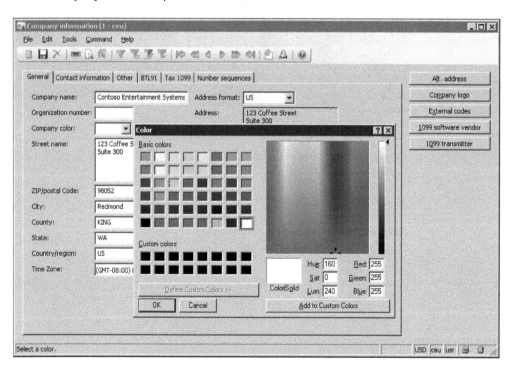

## How it works...

Colors in Dynamics AX are stored as integers, so first we create a new **Integer** field. The rest of the code needs to be added to the form itself.

On the form we create the **IntEdit** control, which represents the company color selection. We have to force the appearance of the lookup button by setting the **LookupButton** property to **Always**. We also need to set **ColorScheme** to **RGB** to make sure the control allows us to set its color as an integer.

Next, we create the **edit** method, which is bound to the created control. It is only responsible for setting the control's background to match the stored color. The background is set to white, if no value is present. The method always returns 0, because we do not want to show color code in it. The control's **ShowZero** property is set to **No** to ensure that even 0 is not displayed. In this way, we create a control that looks like a real color selection control although Dynamics AX does not have a standard one. The method is bound to the control by specifying its name in the control's **DataMethod** property.

The last thing to do is to override the control's `lookup()` method with the code that invokes the color picker. Here we use `RGBint2Con()` method of **WinAPI** application class to retrieve the current control's background color, which is passed to `chooseColor()` of **WinAPI** to make sure that current color is preselected on the lookup. Note that numeric color representation here is converted into red, green, and blue color components by the use of `RGBint2Con()`. The `chooseColor()` is the main method, which builds the lookup. It accepts the following arguments:

1. Current window handle.
2. Red color component.
3. Green color component.
4. Blue color component.
5. A binary object representing up to 16 custom colors.
6. Defining if the lookup is initially expanded.

This method returns a container of red, green, and blue color components, which has to be converted to a numeric value in order to store it in the table field.

## There's more...

You probably have noticed that the fifth argument in the example above is set to `null`. This is because we did not use custom colors. This feature is not that important but may be used in some circumstances.

We will update the `lookup()` method with additional code to implement custom colors:

```
public void lookup()
{
    int        red;
    int        green;
    int        blue;
    container color;
    Binary     customColors;
    ;

    customColors = new Binary(64);

    customColors.byte(0,255);
    customColors.byte(1,255);
    customColors.byte(2,0);

    customColors.byte(4,0);
    customColors.byte(5,255);
    customColors.byte(6,0);

    customColors.byte(8,255);
    customColors.byte(9,0);
    customColors.byte(10,0);

    [red, green, blue] = WinApi::RGBint2Con(
        CompanyColor.backgroundColor());

    color = WinAPI::chooseColor(
        element.hWnd(),
        red,
        green,
        blue,
        customColors,
        true);

    if (color)
    {
        [red, green, blue] = color;
        CompanyInfo.CompanyColor = WinAPI::RGB2int(
            red,
            green,
            blue);

        CompanyColor.backgroundColor(
            CompanyInfo.CompanyColor);
    }
}
```

Here, we define the variable `customColors` as a `Binary` object for storing initial custom colors. The object structure contains 64 elements for storing color codes. The set of red, green, and blue color components are stored to every three object elements in sequence with a single space between each set. In the previous code, we store yellow (red = 255, green = 255, and blue = 0) in elements from 0 to 2, green (red = 0, green, = 255, blue = 0) from 4 to 6, and red (red = 255, green = 0, blue = 0) from 8 to 10. The system allows creating up to 16 custom colors. Note that the color lookup now looks a bit different:

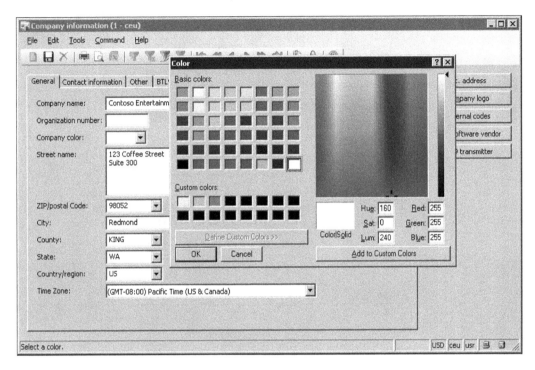

Custom colors can be modified by the user and can be stored in the table field or cache for later use by storing the whole binary `customColors` object.

## See also

Working with Forms, Changing common form appearance

# Choosing a font

The Dynamics AX **Options** from **Tools** menu allows users to define their preferred fonts and sizes for various application areas. In custom functionality, it might also be necessary to add similar options allowing configuring font properties.

In this recipe, we will add an option to select a font in the **Form setup** form in the **Accounts receivable** module for sales invoice layout. The code in this recipe could be used in conjunction with the code that reads this parameter and actually changes invoice font.

## How to do it...

1. Open the **CustFormLetterParameters** table in AOT.
2. Add a new field:

| Property | Value |
| --- | --- |
| Type | String |
| Name | InvoiceFontName |
| ExtendedDataType | FontName |

3. Add one more field:

| Property | Value |
| --- | --- |
| Type | Integer |
| Name | InvoiceFontSize |
| ExtendedDataType | FontSize |

4. Open the **CustFormLetterParameters** form in AOT, and add a new display method to the **CustFormLetterParameters** data source:

```
display Name displayInvoiceFont(
    CustFormLetterParameters _custFormLetterParameters)
{;
    if (CustFormLetterParameters.InvoiceFontName)
    {
        return strfmt(
            "%1, %2",
            _custFormLetterParameters.InvoiceFontName,
            _custFormLetterParameters.InvoiceFontSize);
```

```
    }
    return "";
}
```

5.  Add a new group to the **Invoice** tab page right after the **GroupInvoice** group:

| Property | Value |
|----------|-------|
| Name | GroupFont |
| Caption | Font |
| Columns | 2 |
| Columnspace | 0 |

6.  Add a **StringEdit** control to the newly created group:

| Property | Value |
|----------|-------|
| Name | InvoiceFont |
| AutoDeclaration | Yes |
| Label | Font name & size |
| DataSource | CustFormLetterParameters |
| DataMethod | displayInvoiceFont |

7.  Add a new **Button** to the same group:

| Property | Value |
|----------|-------|
| Name | InvoiceFontLookup |
| ButtonDisplay | Image only |
| NormalResource | 2633 |

8.  Override `clicked()` on the **InvoiceFontLookup** button with the following code:

```
void clicked()
{
    container font;
    ;

    font = WinAPI::chooseFont(
        element.hWnd(),
        SysFontType::ScreenFont,
        CustFormLetterParameters.InvoiceFontName,
        CustFormLetterParameters.invoiceFontSize);
```

```
    if (conlen(font))
    {
        CustFormLetterParameters.InvoiceFontName =
            conpeek(font,1);
        CustFormLetterParameters.InvoiceFontSize =
            conpeek(font,2);
        InvoiceFont.update();
    }
}
```

9.  Here is how it looks in AOT after all the modifications have been done:

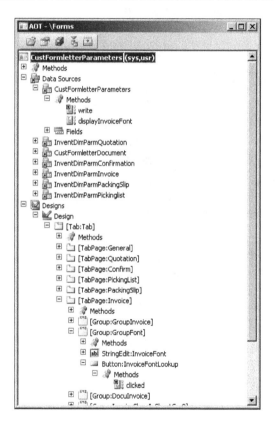

10. To test the results, open **Accounts receivable | Setup | Forms | Form Setup**, and click on the **Font** lookup button on the **Invoice** tab page:

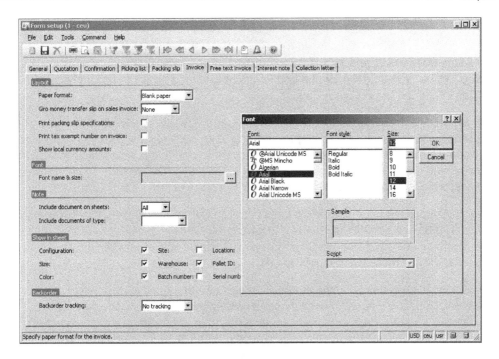

11. Upon its closure, the lookup fills in the **Font name & size** field with the selected values:

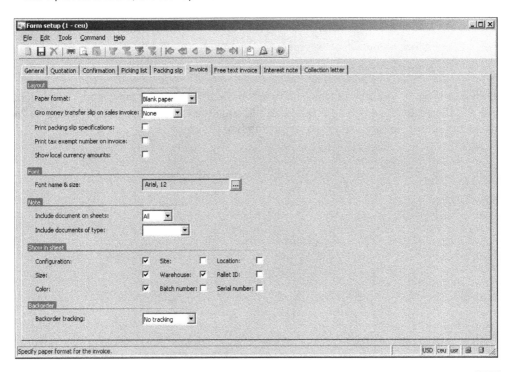

## How it works...

First, we create two new fields in the **CustFormLetterParameters** table for storing font name and size. We use standard **FontName** and **FontSize** extended data types to make sure that the fields inherit the correct properties.

Next, we modify the **CustFormLetterParameters** form. We will be adding the **Font name & size** control, which is bound to the **display** method `displayInvoiceFont()`. The method resides on the **CustFormLetterParameters** form data source and is responsible for displaying font name and size in one line separated by a comma. In this way, we save some form layout space instead of displaying font name and size in separate fields.

Dynamics AX does not have a standard font control so we "fake" it by placing a **StringEdit** field followed by a **Button** control together in one form group. We need to set few of the group's properties to make sure it has two columns, and there is no space between group elements, so the user will see those two controls as one.

The last thing to do is to modify the button. To make sure that it looks exactly like existing Dynamics AX font controls, we change its properties so that the appearance changes to a small three dot button. The `clicked()` method has to be overridden with the code that calls the lookup. Here, we use `chooseFont()` method of **WinAPI** application class to display the standard Windows font selection dialog. This method accepts four arguments:

1. Current window handler.
2. Selection between screen or printer font.
3. Current font name, which will be preselected in the lookup.
4. Current font size, which will be preselected in the lookup.

The `chooseFont()` method returns a container of two elements, where the first one is font name and the second one is a size. Note that although the font selection dialog contains **Font style** section, the style is not returned by this method.

# 5
# Processing Business Tasks

In this chapter, we will cover:

- ▸ Creating new general journals
- ▸ Posting general journals
- ▸ Processing project journals
- ▸ Creating and posting ledger vouchers
- ▸ Changing automatic transaction text
- ▸ Creating purchase orders
- ▸ Posting purchase orders
- ▸ Creating sales orders
- ▸ Posting sales orders
- ▸ Creating company-specific document layout
- ▸ Creating electronic payment format
- ▸ Building a "Display dimensions" dialog

## Introduction

This chapter explains how to process various business operations in Dynamics AX. We will discuss how to create and post various journals. This chapter also explains how to work with the ledger voucher object and how to enhance the setup of automatically generated transaction texts. Posting purchase and sales orders and changing business document layout per company are also discussed here. The chapter includes other features like creating a new electronic payment format and controlling the display of inventory dimensions.

# Creating new general journals

Journals in Dynamics AX are manual worksheets that can be posted into the system. One of the frequently used journals for financial operations is the **General journal**. Sometimes, I call it the father of all other financial journals as it allows processing virtually all types of postings: ledger account transfers, fixed asset operations, customer/vendor payments, bank operations, project expenses, and similar. Other derived journals like the **Fixed assets** journal or **Payment journal** in **Accounts receivable** or **Accounts payable** are optimized for specific business tasks but, basically, they do the same job.

Dynamics AX also contains other types of journals, for example, in the **Inventory management** or **Production** modules. Although those journals are more connected to their specific area, they still share the same principles.

In this recipe, we will demonstrate how to create a new general journal from X++ code. This is often required when developing custom functionality, which automatically creates journals on the user's behalf in order to save time. To demonstrate the principle, we will create a journal with a single line. A similar approach could be applied when creating other journals types.

## How to do it...

1.  Open AOT and create a new class called **LedgerJournalTransData** with the following code:

```
class LedgerJournalTransData extends JournalTransData
{
}

void create(
    boolean _doInsert       = false,
    boolean _initVoucherList = true)
{;
    lastLineNum++;

    journalTrans.LineNum = lastLineNum;

    if (journalTableData.journalVoucherNum())
    {
        this.initVoucher(
            lastVoucher,
            false,
            _initVoucherList);
    }

    this.addTotal(false, false);
```

```
       if (_doInsert)
       {
            journalTrans.doInsert();
       }
       else
       {
            journalTrans.insert();
       }

       if (journalTableData.journalVoucherNum())
       {
            lastVoucher = journalTrans.Voucher;
       }
   }
}
```

2. Open the **LedgerJournalStatic** class in AOT and replace its `newJournalTransData()` with the following code:

```
LedgerJournalTransData newJournalTransData(
    JournalTransMap    _journalTrans,
    JournalTableData _journalTableData)
{
    return new LedgerJournalTransData(
        _journalTrans,
        _journalTableData);
}
```

3. In AOT, create a new class called **JournalCreate** with the following code:

```
class JournalCreate
{
}

void create()
{
    LedgerJournalTable      jourTable;
    LedgerJournalTrans      jourTrans;
    LedgerJournalTableData jourTableData;
    LedgerJournalTransData jourTransData;
    LedgerJournalStatic     jourStatic;
    ;

    jourTableData = JournalTableData::newTable(jourTable);

    jourTable.JournalNum   = jourTableData.nextJournalId();
```

```
        jourTable.JournalType = LedgerJournalType::Daily;

        jourTable.JournalName = 'GenJrn';

        jourTableData.initFromJournalName(
            LedgerJournalName::find(jourTable.JournalName));

        jourStatic    = jourTableData.journalStatic();

        jourTransData = jourStatic.newJournalTransData(
            jourTrans,
            jourTableData);

        jourTransData.initFromJournalTable();

        jourTrans.CurrencyCode    = 'USD';
        jourTrans.initValue();
        jourTrans.TransDate          = systemdateget();
        jourTrans.AccountNum         = '110180';
        jourTrans.OffsetAccount      = '170150';
        jourTrans.AmountCurDebit     = 1000;

        jourTransData.create();

        jourTable.insert();
    }

    void run()
    {;
        try
        {
            ttsbegin;

            this.create();

            ttscommit;
        }
        catch (Exception::Deadlock)
        {
            retry;
        }
    }

    public static void main(Args _args)
    {
        JournalCreate journalCreate;
        ;

        journalCreate = new JournalCreate();

        journalCreate.run();
    }
```

4.  Run the class and check the results by opening **General ledger | Journals | General journal**:

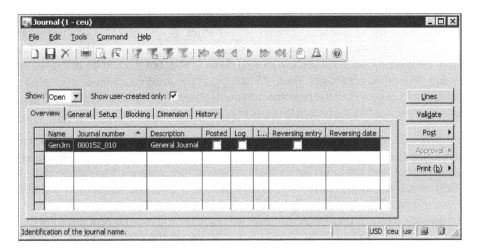

5.  Click the **Lines** button to open journal lines and notice the created line:

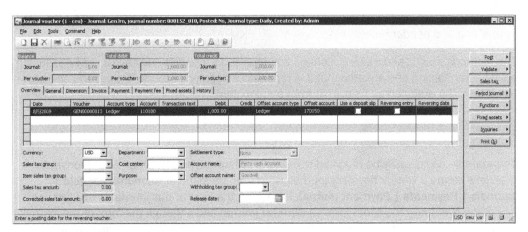

## How it works...

First we create the **LedgerJournalTransData** class, which will handle the creation of journal lines. Basically, it is the same as **JournalTransData** and extends all of its methods apart from create(). This method is also a copy of the same method in **JournalTransData** with the exception that it does not check the **VoucherDraw** field on the **LedgerJournalTable** table. Although this checking is valid for other journals, it has to be excluded here, because the **LedgerJournalTable** table does not contain this field.

Next, we modify `newJournalTransData()` of **LedgerJournalStatic** to use our newly created class.

The new **JournalCreate** class will be used to demonstrate the journal creation. All logic is placed in its `create()`. Here, we create a new `jourTableData` object used for journal record handling. Then, we initialize journal number, type, and the name of the actual journal record. For demonstration purposes the journal name is text, but it could be easily replaced with a value from some parameter. Next, we call `initFromJournalName()` on the `jourTableData` object to initialize some additional values from journal name settings. At this stage, the journal header record is ready to be created.

Next, we create a journal line. Here we first create a new `jourTransData` object for handling the journal line, then we call `initFromJournalTable()` to initialize additional values from the journal header, and finally we set journal line values like currency, transaction date, and so on. Normally, those values have to be taken from user input, external data, or any other source depending on the functionality being built. In this example, we simply specify the values manually. Replace them with your own values matching your current environment. Also note that we call `initValue()` on `jourTrans` after we set the currency value. This ensures that exchange rate and some other values are initialized correctly. `initValue()` can also be called without setting the currency value first. In this case, the company currency will be used.

And finally, we call `create()` on `jourTransData` and `insert()` on `jourTable` to create journal line and header records respectively.

The methods `run()` and `main()` contain common code. The first one calls `create()` inside a single transaction and ensures that it is repeated if deadlock occurs. The second one allows the class to be executed on its own or from a menu item.

## There's more

The example could easily be modified to create a different type of journal. To demonstrate that, let's create a vendor payment journal, which can be found at **Accounts payable | Journals | Payments | Payment journal**. If we open the form of this journal in AOT, we can see that it is actually the same form as **General journal** and although the form of the journal lines is different from that of **General journal** lines it still uses the same **LedgerJournalTrans** data source.

1. Let's replace `create()` in **JournalCreate** class with the following code:

```
void create()
{
    LedgerJournalTable      jourTable;
    LedgerJournalTrans      jourTrans;
    LedgerJournalTableData  jourTableData;
    LedgerJournalTransData  jourTransData;
    LedgerJournalStatic     jourStatic;
    ;
```

```
jourTableData = JournalTableData::newTable(jourTable);
jourTable.JournalNum  = jourTableData.nextJournalId();
jourTable.JournalType = LedgerJournalType::Payment;
jourTable.JournalName = 'APPay';
jourTableData.initFromJournalName(
    LedgerJournalName::find(jourTable.JournalName));
jourStatic    = jourTableData.journalStatic();
jourTransData = jourStatic.newJournalTransData(
    jourTrans,
    jourTableData);
jourTransData.initFromJournalTable();
jourTrans.CurrencyCode    = 'USD';
jourTrans.initValue();
jourTrans.TransDate       = systemdateget();
jourTrans.AccountType     = LedgerJournalACType::Vend;
jourTrans.AccountNum      = '1001';
jourTrans.OffsetAccountType = LedgerJournalACType::Bank;
jourTrans.OffsetAccount   = 'USA OPER';
jourTrans.AmountCurDebit  = 1000;
jourTransData.create();
jourTable.insert();
}
```

2. Run the class now and open **Accounts payable | Journals | Payments | Payment journal** to check the results:

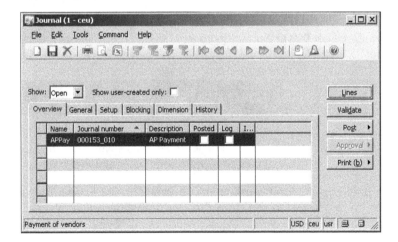

3. Click the **Lines** button to view journal lines:

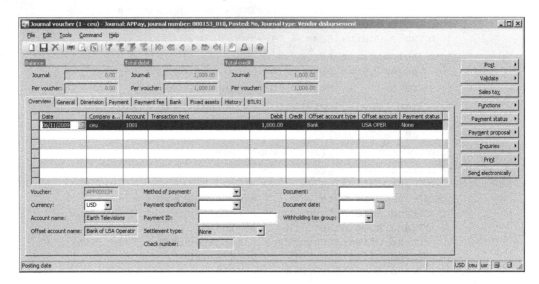

The code in this section has only slight differences compared to the previous example:

▶ We changed the journal type to be vendor disbursement, that is, **LedgerJournalType::Payment**.

▶ We set a different journal name, which matches payment journal configuration.

▶ We changed the journal line account type to vendor and account to vendor number.

▶ And finally, we set **Offset account type** to be bank and **Offset account** to bank account ID.

# Posting general journals

Posting journals from X++ code on the user's behalf is an inseparable supplement to journal creation explained in the Creating new general journals recipe. Normally, this operation is done right after the journal is created or later when some user action is triggered.

In this recipe, we will explore how to post general journals from X++ code. The journal we are going to process is the one we created in the Creating new general journals recipe.

## How to do it...

1. Open AOT and create a new class called **JournalPost** with the following code (replace `000152_010` with your journal number):

```
class JournalPost
{
}

public static void main(Args _args)
{
    LedgerJournalCheckPost jourPost;
    LedgerJournalTable      jourTable;
    ;

    jourTable = LedgerJournalTable::find('000152_010');

    jourPost = LedgerJournalCheckPost::newLedgerJournalTable(
        jourTable,
        NoYes::Yes);

    jourPost.run();
}
```

2. Run the class and notice the **Infolog** confirming that the journal was successfully posted:

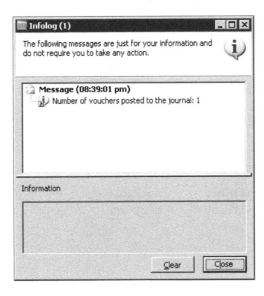

3. Optionally, open **General ledger | Journals | General journal** and find the processed journal to make sure it was posted.

## How it works...

We create a new class called **JournalPost**, which will post the journal. Here, we use the system **LedgerJournalCheckPost** class, which does all the work. This class ensures that all necessary validations are performed. It also locks the journal so no other user can process it.

All code is located in `main()` of **JournalPost**. First, we find the journal **000152_010** created in the previous recipe.

Next, we create a new `jourPost` object by calling `newLedgerJournalTable()` on **LedgerJournalCheckPost**. This method accepts a journal header record to be processed and a **boolean** argument defining that the journal should be validated and posted or validated only. In this recipe, we set `NoYes::Yes`, which means that the journal will be validated and posted.

Finally, we post the journal by calling `run()`.

# Processing project journals

The **Project** module in Dynamics AX is tightly integrated with the **General ledger**. It also contains four journals—**Hour**, **Expense**, **Item**, and **Fee**, which are used in a similar way to other journals. For example, the **Expense** journal is actually based on the same data sources as the **General journal**.

In this recipe, we will create a journal from X++ code in the **Project** module. We will create the **Hour** journal, which is very specific to the **Project** module.

## How to do it...

1. In AOT, create a new class called **ProjJournalCreate** with the following code:

```
class ProjJournalCreate
{
}

void create()
{
    ProjJournalTable      jourTable;
    ProjJournalTrans      jourTrans;
```

```
        ProjJournalTableData jourTableData;
        ProjJournalTransData jourTransData;
        ProjJournalStatic    jourStatic;
        ;

        jourTableData = JournalTableData::newTable(jourTable);

        jourTable.JournalId     = jourTableData.nextJournalId();
        jourTable.JournalType   = ProjJournalType::Hour;
        jourTable.JournalNameId = 'Hours';

        jourTableData.initFromJournalName(
            ProjJournalName::find(jourTable.JournalNameId));

        jourStatic = jourTableData.journalStatic();

        jourTransData = jourStatic.newJournalTransData(
            jourTrans,
            jourTableData);

        jourTransData.initFromJournalTable();

        jourTrans.initValue();

        jourTrans.ProjId        = '10001';
        jourTrans.initFromProjTable(
            ProjTable::find(jourTrans.ProjId));

        jourTrans.TransDate     = systemdateget();
        jourTrans.ProjTransDate = jourTrans.TransDate;

        jourTrans.CategoryId    = 'Design';
        jourTrans.setHourCostPrice();
        jourTrans.setHourSalesPrice();
        jourTrans.TaxItemGroupId =
          ProjCategory::find(jourTrans.CategoryId).TaxItemGroupId;

        jourTrans.EmplId        = '1000';
        jourTrans.Txt           = 'Design documentation';
        jourTrans.Qty           = 8;

        jourTransData.create();

        jourTable.insert();
    }

void run()
{;
    try
```

```
    {
        ttsbegin;

        this.create();

        ttscommit;
    }
    catch (Exception::Deadlock)
    {
        retry;
    }
}

public static void main(Args _args)
{
    ProjJournalCreate journalCreate;
    ;

    journalCreate = new ProjJournalCreate();

    journalCreate.run();
}
```

2. Run the class and check the results by going to **Project | Journals | Hours | Hour**:

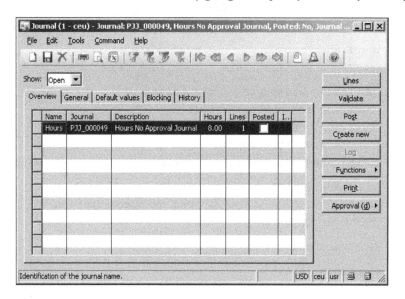

3. Click the **Lines** button to open journal lines and notice the created line:

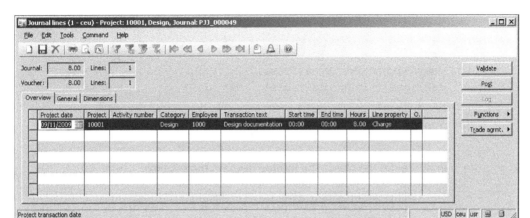

## How it works...

In this recipe we have created a very similar class in the way we already created one in the Creating new general journals recipe. Its create() is slightly modified to match project-related classes and values. Notice in its variable declaration section that all classes are prefixed with **Proj**. The following aspects were changed (Replace PJJ_000049 with your journal number):

▶ Journal type is set to **ProjJournalType::Hour**, which corresponds to the hour journal.

▶ Journal name is set to match **Project** journal setup parameters.

▶ Journal line jourTrans field values are set to fulfill hour journal requirements, that is, we set project number, project date, category, initialize cost and sales prices, and so on.

The methods run() and main() are identical to those of the previous recipe with the only difference being that run() uses the **ProjJournalCreate** class instead of **JournalCreate**.

## There's more...

The journal is created and it is ready to be posted. This procedure again is very similar to that in the Posting general journals recipe. In AOT, we create another class called **ProjJournalPost** with the following code (replace PJJ_000049 with your journal number):

```
class ProjJournalPost
{
}
public static void main(Args _args)
{
    ProjJournalCheckPost jourPost;
```

```
    ;

    jourPost = ProjJournalCheckPost::newJournalCheckPost(
        true,
        true,
        JournalCheckPostType::Post,
        tablenum(ProjJournalTable),
        'PJJ_000049');

    jourPost.run();
}
```

To post the journal, we run the class. The **Infolog** displays the results:

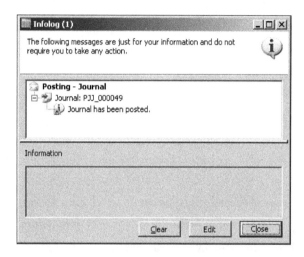

Here we use **ProjJournalCheckPost** to process the journal. This class is specially designed for the Project module. It extends **JournalCheckPostLedger**, which is also a parent class for other specific journal processing classes in other Dynamics AX modules. A new instance is created using newJournalCheckPost(), which accepts the following arguments:

- ▸ boolean whether to block the journal while it is being posted. It is good practice to set it to true as this ensures that no one modifies this journal while it is being posted.

- ▸ boolean whether to display results if the journal was posted successfully.

- ▸ The type of action being performed. Possible values for this class are either **Post** or **Check**. The latter one only validates the journal and the first one validates and posts the journal at once.

- ▸ The table ID of the journal being posted.

- ▸ The journal number to be posted.

And finally, run() contains the rest of the code, which processes the journal.

# Creating and posting ledger vouchers

All financial transactions regardless of where they are originated end up in the **General ledger** module. When it comes to customized functionality, developers should use Dynamics AX APIs to create the required system entries. No transactions can be created directly as this is a very critical step and it may impact on the accuracy of financial data.

To ensure system data consistency, Dynamics AX provides numerous APIs for developers to use. One of them is ledger voucher processing. It is a very basic interface and all other interfaces are based on it if they require financial transaction posting. Vouchers in Dynamics AX are balancing financial entries representing an operation. They include two or more ledger transactions. The ledger voucher API ensures that all required criteria like voucher numbers, financial periods, ledger accounts, financial dimensions, balances, and others are valid.

In this recipe, we will demonstrate how to process ledger vouchers. We will create code that posts a single voucher.

## How to do it...

1.  In AOT, create a new class called **VoucherPost** with the following code:

```
class VoucherPost
{
}
public static void main(Args _args)
{
    LedgerVoucher             voucher;
    LedgerVoucherObject       voucherObj;
    LedgerVoucherTransObject  voucherTrObj1;
    LedgerVoucherTransObject  voucherTrObj2;
    Dimension                 dim;
    ;

    voucher = LedgerVoucher::newLedgerPost(
        DetailSummary::Detail,
        SysModule::Ledger,
        '');
    voucherObj = LedgerVoucherObject::newVoucher('SYS00001');
    voucher.addVoucher(voucherObj);
    voucherTrObj1 = LedgerVoucherTransObject::newCreateTrans(
```

```
            voucherObj,
            LedgerPostingType::LedgerJournal,
            '110180',
            dim,
            'USD',
            1000,
            0,
            0);
        voucherTrObj2 = LedgerVoucherTransObject::newCreateTrans(
            voucherObj,
            LedgerPostingType::LedgerJournal,
            '170150',
            dim,
            'USD',
            -1000,
            0,
            0);
        voucher.addTrans(voucherTrObj1);
        voucher.addTrans(voucherTrObj2);
        voucher.end();
    }
```

2. Run the class to post a new voucher to the ledger.

3. To check what has been posted, open **General Ledger | Inquiries | Voucher transactions** and type in the voucher number used in the code:

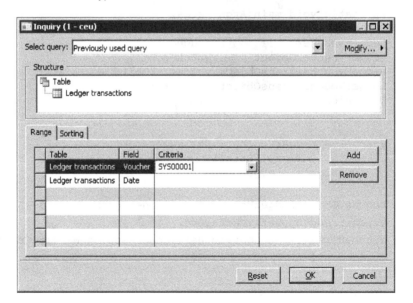

4. Click **OK** to display the posted voucher:

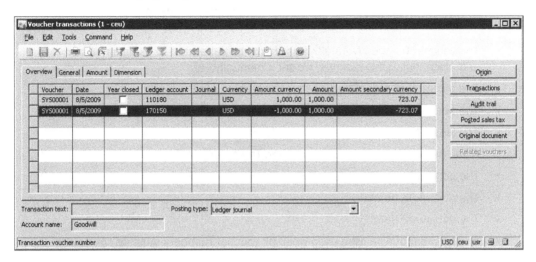

## How it works...

To demonstrate the usage of ledger vouchers, we create a new class and place all the code in its `main()` to make sure we can run this class from AOT.

The first step is to create a `voucher` object of type **LedgerVoucher**. It should be created for each posting per each company. Here, we call `newLedgerPost()` on `LedgerVoucher`. It accepts three mandatory and four optional arguments:

▶ Post detailed or summarized ledger transactions.

▶ The system module from which the transactions are originating.

▶ A number sequence code, which is used to generate the voucher number. In this example, we will set the voucher number manually, so this argument can be set to empty.

▶ The transaction type that will appear in the transaction log.

▶ The transaction text.

▶ A `boolean` value specifying whether this voucher should meet approval requirements.

▶ A `boolean` value defining whether the voucher could be posted without a posting type when posting inventory transactions.

The second step is to create `voucherObj` of type **LedgerVoucherObject**. This object represents a single voucher. We call the `newVoucher()` method of the **LedgerVoucherObject**. It accepts one mandatory and a number of optional parameters:

- ▸ The voucher number. Normally, this should be generated by using a number sequence, but in this example we set it manually.
- ▸ The transaction date. The default is the session date.
- ▸ The system module from which the transactions are originating.
- ▸ The ledger transaction type.
- ▸ A flag that defines a correcting voucher. The default is **No**.
- ▸ The posting layer. The default is **Current**.
- ▸ The document number.
- ▸ The document date.
- ▸ An argument of type **Map** used when all voucher numbers must be continuous.
- ▸ The acknowledgement date.

The method `addVoucher()` adds the created voucher object to the voucher.

Third step is to create voucher transactions. Transactions are handled by the **LedgerVoucherTransObject** class. They are created by calling its static `newCreateTrans()` with eight mandatory and seven optional arguments:

- ▸ The ledger voucher object.
- ▸ The ledger posting type.
- ▸ The ledger account number.
- ▸ The financial dimension. In this example, we create a voucher with no dimensions by passing an empty **Dimension** type variable.
- ▸ The currency code.
- ▸ The amount in currency.
- ▸ The related table number.
- ▸ The related record number.
- ▸ The quantity if used.
- ▸ The exchange rate.
- ▸ The exchange rate of the secondary currency.

- Is triangulation used?
- Is the transaction marked for bridging?
- A **ProjectLedger** object for **Project** module specific postings.
- The amount in the company currency.

In this demonstration, we call this method twice to create sample transactions.

The fourth step is to add the created transaction objects to the voucher by calling its addTrans().

And finally we call end() on the voucher, which posts the transactions to the ledger.

# Changing automatic transaction text

Every financial transaction in Dynamics AX can (and normally should) have a descriptive transaction text. Some texts are entered by user, some are generated by the system. The latter option happens for automatically generated transactions where the user cannot interact with the process.

Dynamics AX provides a way to define texts for automatically generated transactions. The setup can be found in **Basic | Setup | Transaction text**. Here the user can create custom transaction texts for various automatic transaction types and languages. The text itself can have a number of placeholders—digits with percent sign in front of them, which are replaced with actual values during the process. Placeholders can be from **%1** to **%6** and they are replaced with the following values:

- %1: the transaction date
- %2: a relevant number like invoice, delivery note, etc.
- %3: the voucher number
- %4-%6: custom; depends on the module

Although most of the time the existing values are enough, I was still requested a number of times to add additional ones. One of the latest requests was to include the vendor name into vendor payment journal lines automatically generated by payment proposals. We will use this case as an example in this recipe.

## Getting ready

First we need to make sure the vendor payment transaction text is set up properly. Open **Basic | Setup | Transaction text**, find a line with **Vendor - Payment, Vendor** and change the text to **Payment to %5** like the following:

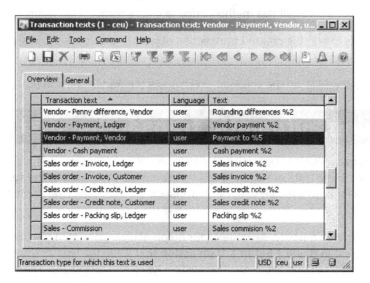

## How to do it...

1. Open AOT, find the **CustVendPaymProposalTransferToJournal** class and add the following code to its `getTransactionText()`:

```
transactionTxt.setKey2(
    _custVendPaymProposalLine.custVendTable().Name);
```

right after:

```
transactionTxt = new TransactionTxt(
    LedgerTransTxt::VendPaymentVend);
```

2. Open **Accounts payable | Journals | Payments | Payment journal** and create a new journal. Then create payment lines using the **Create payment proposal** function. Notice that now the transaction texts include vendor name:

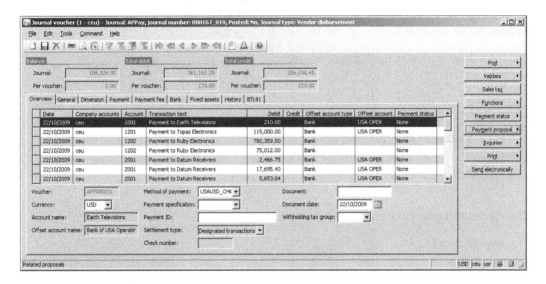

## How it works...

The lines generated by vendor payment proposals are transferred into the journal by using the **CustVendPaymProposalTransferToJournal** class. Its getTransactionText() method is responsible for formatting transaction texts. If we look inside it we can see that the **TransactionTxt** class is used for this purpose. The following methods are used for each placeholder:

▶ **%1**: setDate()

▶ **%2**: setFormLetter()

▶ **%3**: setVoucher()

▶ **%4**: setKey1()

▶ **%5**: setKey2()

▶ **%6**: setKey3()

By looking at the code we can see that only **%4** (setKey1()) is used, so we can occupy **%5** and fill it with the vendor name. To achieve that, we have to call setKey2() with the vendor name as an argument. We place the code in the **ModuleCustVend::Vend** section of the switch statement to make sure it is executed only when generating vendor payments.

If more than 3 custom placeholders are required it is always possible to add an additional one by creating a new `setKey()` method in the **TransactionTxt** class. For example, if we want to add placeholder **%7** we have to do the following:

Add the following code to the class declaration:

```
str 20 key4;
```

Create a new method:

```
void setKey4(str 20 _key4)
{;
    key4 = _key4;
}
```

Change the last line of the `txt()` method to:

```
return strfmt(
    txt,
    transDate,
    formLetterNum,
    voucherNum,
    key1,
    key2,
    key3,
    key4);
```

After those modifications we can use `setKey4()` when generating transactions.

Although even more placeholders could be added, it should be considered that the transaction text field has a finite number of characters and excessive text will be simply truncated.

# Creating purchase orders

Creating purchase orders from code is one of the many things that are required when building custom functionality. Normally, the user selects only a few bits of information like vendor account, item number, delivery date, etc. and the rest is created by the system. It is also possible that purchase orders may be created as part of some process in custom modules.

In this recipe, we will learn how to create a purchase order from X++ code. We will use a standard method provided by the application.

## How to do it...

1. In AOT, create a new class called **PurchaseOrderCreate** with the following code:

```
class PurchaseOrderCreate
{
}

public static void main(Args _args)
{
    NumberSeq   numberSeq;
    PurchTable  purchTable;
    PurchLine   purchLine;
    ;

    ttsbegin;
    numberSeq = NumberSeq::newGetNumFromCode(
        PurchParameters::numRefPurchId().numberSequence,
        true);
    purchTable.PurchId = numberSeq.num();
    purchTable.initValue();
    purchTable.initFromVendTable(VendTable::find('1001'));
    if (!purchTable.validateWrite())
    {
        throw Exception::Error;
    }
    purchTable.insert();
    purchLine.PurchId = purchTable.PurchId;
    purchLine.ItemId  = '1205';
    purchLine.createLine(true, true, true, true, true, true);
    ttscommit;
}
```

2. Run the class to create a new purchase order.

3. Open **Accounts payable | Purchase Order Details** to view the created purchase order:

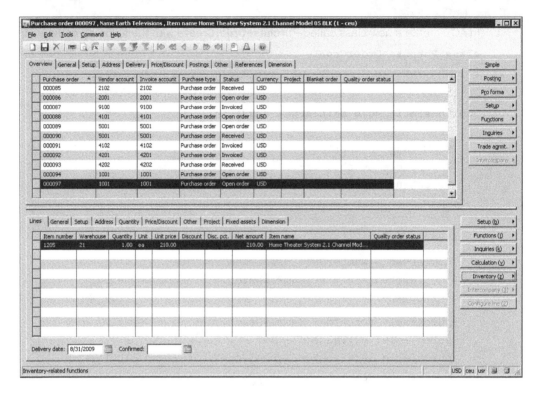

## How it works...

First we create a new class, which will run our code using its `main()`. Here we place all the code into a `ttsbegin/ttscommit` pair to make sure everything is rolled back if something goes wrong.

The method starts with generating the next number for a new purchase order.

Next, we call `initValue()` and `initFromVendTable()` to initialize various `purchTable` fields. Normally, the argument of `initFromVendTable()` should come from a user selection screen or other source. For demonstration purposes, here we simply use the first vendor number from the list.

If we pass validation of `validateWrite()` successfully, we create a purchase order header by calling `purchTable.insert()`.

The next thing to do is to create purchase order lines. Here we need minimal information. First, we assign a purchase order number and then we set the item number. As previously the item number should come from user input or some other source. For demonstration purposes, we use item **1205** from the inventory list.

And finally, we call `createLine()` on the `purchLine` table to create a line. This method could be called a number of times depending on the number lines that need to be created. This method accepts a number of optional `boolean` arguments:

▸ Perform data validations before saving? The default is `false`.

▸ Initialize from **PurchTable** table? The default is `false`.

▸ Initialize from **InventTable** table? The default is `false`.

▸ Calculate inventory quantity? The default is `false`.

▸ Add miscellaneous charges? The default is `true`.

▸ Use trade agreements to calculate item price? The default is `false`.

# Posting purchase orders

Purchase order posting is the next logical step after creating a purchase order. Normally, in the application, users use the **Posting** button on the **Purchase Order Details** form to post purchase orders. This function can also be executed from code and can be integrated into various customizations.

In this recipe, we will use a standard Dynamics AX API to post a purchase order and print the relevant document from code. As an example we will post and print the previously created purchase order.

## How to do it...

1. In AOT, create a new class called **PurchaseOrderPost** with the following code (replace 000097 with your number):

```
class PurchaseOrderPost
{
}
public static void main(Args _args)
{
    PurchFormLetter purchFormLetter;
    PurchTable      purchTable;
    ;

    purchTable = PurchTable::find('000097');
    purchFormLetter = PurchFormLetter::construct(
        DocumentStatus::PurchaseOrder);
    purchFormLetter.update(
        purchTable,
        '',
        systemdateget(),
        PurchUpdate::All,
```

```
        AccountOrder::None,
        NoYes::No,
        NoYes::Yes);
}
```

2. Run the class to post the specified purchase order and display the **Purchase order** document:

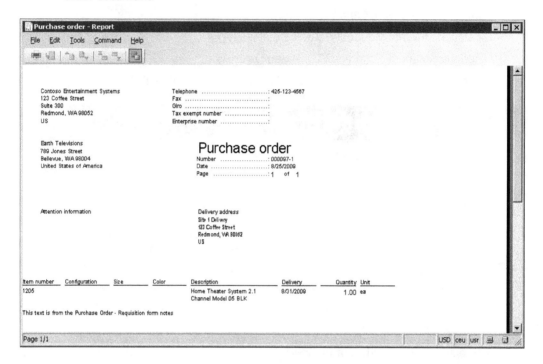

3. Open **Accounts payable | Purchase Order Details**, select the previously specified purchase order, click the **Inquiries** button, and choose **Purchase order** to view the results:

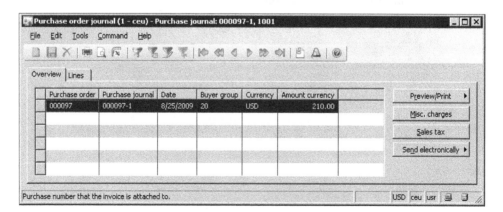

## How it works...

To demonstrate purchase order posting, we start with creating a new class named **PurchOrderPost** with a `main()` method.

The method starts with finding purchase order **000097**, which we created in the previous recipe. Here, we normally would replace this code with user input or an output from some other function.

Next, we call `construct()` on the **PurchFormLetter** class to create a new `purchFormLetter` object. The method accepts an argument of type **DocumentStatus**, which defines the type of posting to be done. Here we are doing a posting of type purchase order, so we use `DocumentStatus::PurchaseOrder` as a value. `construct()` also accepts a second optional `boolean` argument, which controls whether a new **PurchParmUpdate** record used for purchase order posting grouping should be created. The default is `true`.

The last thing to do is to call `update()` on `purchFormLetter`, which does the actual posting. It accepts a number of arguments:

- The purchase order header record, that is, **PurchTable**.
- An external document number, not used when posting a purchase order.
- The transaction date. The default is system date.
- The quantity to be posted. The default is `PurchUpdate::All`. Other options like `PurchUpdate::PackingSlip` or `PurchUpdate::ReceiveNow` are not relevant when posting a Purchase order.
- Order summary update. This argument is not relevant in this example. The default is `AccountOrder::None`.
- A `boolean` value defining whether a preview or actual posting should be done.
- A `boolean` value defining whether the document should be printed.
- A `boolean` value specifying whether printing management should be used. The default is `false`.
- A container of a number of **TmpFrmVirtual** records. This argument is optional and is used only when posting purchase invoices.

## There's more...

The same technique could be used to post a purchase packing slip or invoice. We will replace the code from the example above:

```
purchFormLetter = PurchFormLetter::construct(
    DocumentStatus::PurchaseOrder);
```

with:

```
purchFormLetter = PurchFormLetter::construct(
    DocumentStatus::Invoice);
```

and:

```
purchFormLetter.update(
    purchTable,
    '',
    systemdateget(),
    PurchUpdate::All,
    AccountOrder::None,
    NoYes::No,
    NoYes::Yes);
```

with:

```
purchFormLetter.update(
    purchTable,
    '8001',
    systemdateget(),
    PurchUpdate::All,
    AccountOrder::None,
    NoYes::No,
    NoYes::Yes);
```

Now when you run the class, the purchase order should be updated to an invoice and the invoice document should be printed:

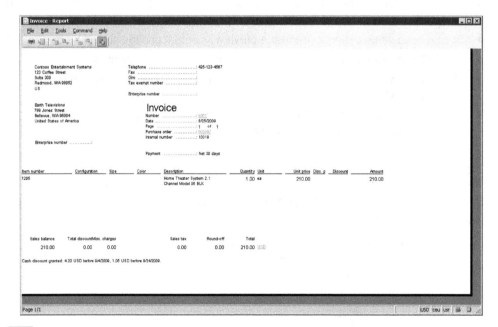

Check the purchase order by opening **Accounts payable | Purchase Order Details**, selecting the previously specified purchase order, clicking the **Inquiries** button, and choosing **Invoice** to view the results:

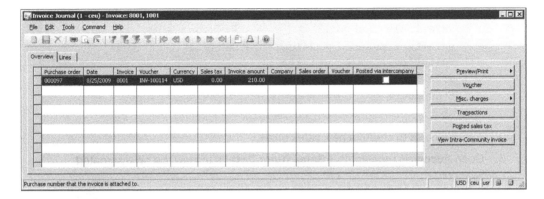

# Creating sales orders

Creating sales orders in Dynamics AX is very similar to creating purchase orders both in the application and from code.

In this recipe, we will create a new sales order from code. We will use a similar approach to that which we used in the Creating purchase orders recipe.

## How to do it...

1.  Open AOT and create a new class called **SalesOrderCreate** with the following code:

```
class SalesOrderCreate
{
}
public static void main(Args _args)
{
    NumberSeq  numberSeq;
    SalesTable salesTable;
    SalesLine  salesLine;
    ;

    ttsbegin;
    numberSeq = NumberSeq::newGetNumFromCode(
        SalesParameters::numRefSalesId().numberSequence,
        true);
    salesTable.SalesId = numberSeq.num();
    salesTable.initValue();
    salesTable.CustAccount = '1101';
```

```
salesTable.initFromCustTable();
if (!salesTable.validateWrite())
{
    throw Exception::Error;
}
salesTable.insert();
salesLine.SalesId = salesTable.SalesId;
salesLine.ItemId  = '1205';
salesLine.createLine(true, true, true, true, true, true);
ttscommit;
}
```

2. Run the class to create a new sales order.

3. Open **Accounts receivable | Sales Order Details** to view the newly created sales order:

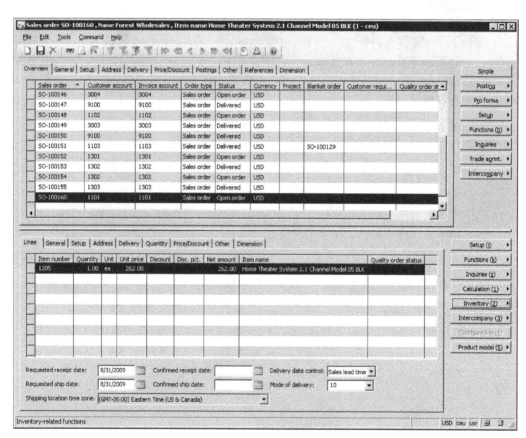

## How it works...

First we create a new class, which will run our code using its `main()`. Here, we place all the code into a `ttsbegin/ttscommit` pair to make sure everything is rolled back if something goes wrong.

The method starts with generating the next number for a new sales order.

Next, we call `initValue()` and `initFromCustTable()` to initialize various `purchTable` fields. Note that `initFromCustTable()` works slightly different from `initFromVendTable()`, i.e. we set `CustAccount` first and call the method afterwards instead of passing **CustTable** as an argument. Normally, the customer account should come from a user selection screen or some other source. For demonstration purposes, we simply use customer **1101** from the list.

Once validation is completed successfully by using `validateWrite()`, we create a sales order header record by calling `salseTable.insert()`.

Next, we create sales order lines. First, we assign the sales order number and then we specify the item number. As before, the item number should come from user input or some other source. For demonstration purposes, we use item **1205** from the inventory list.

And finally, we call `createLine()` on the `salesLine` table to create a line. This method could be called a number of times depending on how many lines need to be created. The method accepts a number of optional `boolean` arguments:

- ▸ Perform data validations before saving? The default is `false`.
- ▸ Initialize from **SalesTable** table? The default is `false`.
- ▸ Initialize from **InventTable** table? The default is `false`.
- ▸ Calculate inventory quantity? The default is `false`.
- ▸ Add miscellaneous charges? The default is `true`.
- ▸ Use trade agreements to calculate item price? The default is `false`.
- ▸ Reserve the item? The default is `false`.
- ▸ Ignore customer credit limit? The default is `false`.
- ▸ An inventory transaction number used to copy product model information. This argument is used only when the **Product Builder** module is active. The default is empty.

# Posting sales orders

Sales order posting is also done in a very similar way to posting a purchase order. The posting function can be executed from code and can be integrated into various customizations.

In this recipe, we will use a standard Dynamics AX API to post and print a sales packing slip document from code. As an example, we will post and print a packing slip for the sales order created in the previous recipe.

## How to do it...

1.  In AOT, create a new class called **SalesOrderPost** with the following code (replace SO-100160 with your number):

```
class SalesOrderPost
{
}

public static void main(Args _args)
{
    SalesFormLetter salesFormLetter;
    salesTable      salesTable;
    ;

    salesTable = SalesTable::find('SO-100160');

    salesFormLetter = SalesFormLetter::construct(
        DocumentStatus::PackingSlip);

    salesFormLetter.update(
        salesTable,
        systemdateget(),
        SalesUpdate::All,
        AccountOrder::None,
        NoYes::No,
        NoYes::Yes);
}
```

2. Run the class to create a packing slip for the specified sales order and display the **Packing slip** document on the screen:

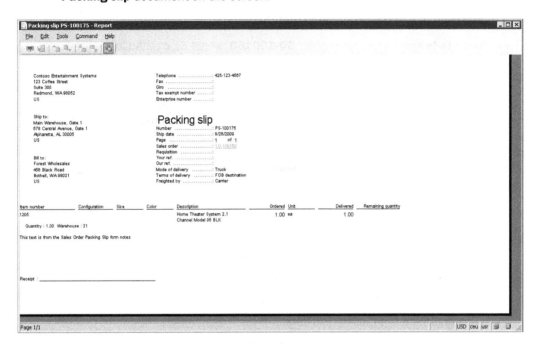

3. Open **Accounts receivable | Sales Order Details**, select the previously specified sales order, the click **Inquiries** button, and choose **Packing slip** to view results:

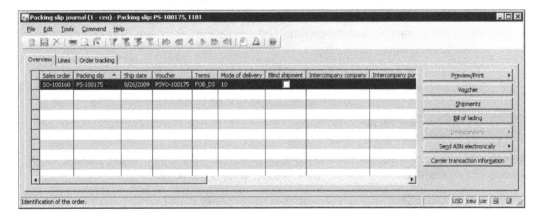

## How it works...

First, we create a new class named **SalesOrderPost** with a `main()` method.

The method starts with finding sales order **SO-100160**, which we created in the previous recipe. Here, we would normally replace this code with user input or an output from another source.

Next, we call `construct()` on the **SalesFormLetter** class to create a new `salesFormLetter` instance. The method accepts an argument of type **DocumentStatus**, which defines the type of posting. Here, we use `DocumentStatus::PackingSlip` for sales packing slip posting. `construct()` also accepts a second optional `boolean` argument, which controls whether a new **SalesParmUpdate** record, used for sales order posting grouping, should be created. The default is `true`.

And finally, we call `update()` on `salesFormLetter`, which does actual posting. It accepts a number of arguments:

- The sales order header record, i.e. **SalesTable**.
- The transaction date. The default is system date.
- The quantity to be posted. The default is `SalesUpdate::All`.
- This argument is not used. The default is `AccountOrder::None`.
- A `boolean` value defining should preview or actual posting be done.
- A `boolean` value defining should document be printed.
- A `boolean` value specifying should printing management be used. The default is `false`.
- Keep the remaining quantity on order; otherwise it is set to zero. This argument is used when posting credit notes.
- A container of a number of **TmpFrmVirtual** records. This argument is optional and is used only when posting sales invoices.

## There's more...

**SalesFormLetter** could also do other types of posting, like order confirmation, picking list, or invoice. For example, to invoice for the sales order, replace the code:

```
salesFormLetter = SalesFormLetter::construct(
    DocumentStatus::PackingSlip);
```

with:

```
salesFormLetter = SalesFormLetter::construct(
    DocumentStatus::Invoice);
```

Run the class and notice that now the sales order was invoiced:

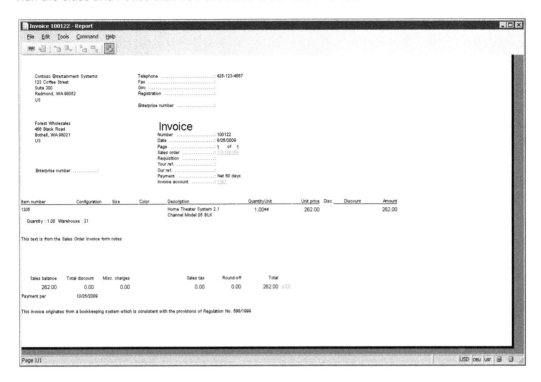

Open **Accounts receivable | Sales Order Details**, select the previously specified sales order, click the **Inquiries** button, and choose **Invoice** to view the results:

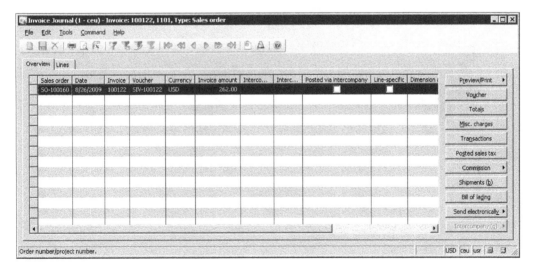

# Creating company-specific document layout

In most of the multi-company projects on which I have worked on, I was asked to created separate layouts for documents like **Purchase order** or **Sales invoice** for each Dynamics AX company. One of the approaches was to create several Dynamics AX report designs and switch them by calling the report member method `design()` depending on the company the user is. But this method proved to be too complicated, especially when the report logic is different for each company and it is much more difficult to control changes if the same report is used in more than two companies.

Another more convenient approach, which I used for a number of implementations, was to use a separate report for each company and switch them depending on in which company it is being printed.

In this recipe, we will demonstrate the latter technique to print different reports per company. As an example we will use a **Purchase Order** document.

## How to do it...

1. In AOT make a duplicate of the **PurchPurchaseOrder** report. Name it **PurchPurchaseOrder2** and change its `purchaseOrderTxt()` method found in the **PurchaseOrder** section to:

```
display str purchaseOrderTxt()
{
    return "PurchPurchaseOrder2";
}
```

2. In AOT, create a new class called `PurchPurchaseOrder` with the following code (replace CEU with one of your company codes):

```
class PurchPurchaseOrder
{
}
public static void main(Args _args)
{
    ReportRun    reportRun;
    ReportName   reportName;
    ;

    switch (curext())
    {
        case 'CEU':
            reportName = reportstr(PurchPurchaseOrder2);
            break;
        default:
            reportName = reportstr(PurchPurchaseOrder);
```

```
            break;
    }
    _args.name(reportName);
    reportRun = new ReportRun(_args);
    reportRun.init();
    reportRun.run();
}
```

3. Modify the properties of the `PurchPurchaseOrder`, `PurchPurchaseOrderCopy`, and `PurchPurchaseOrderOriginal` **Output** menu items as following:

| Property | Value |
| --- | --- |
| ObjectType | Class |
| Object | PurchPurchaseOrder |

4. To test, open **Accounts payable | Purchase Order Details**, select any open purchase order and post it using the **Post | Purchase order** button. If the current company matches the company defined earlier, i.e. **CEU**, the report title should look like the following:

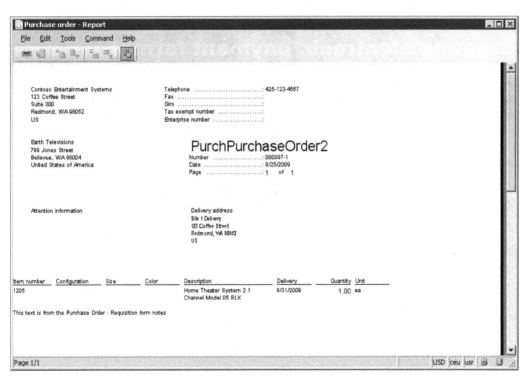

## How it works...

In this recipe, first we make a copy of the existing purchase order report and change its title. This is done only to make sure we can distinguish which report is printed. Normally, **PurchPurchaseOrder2** should be a valid report for one of the companies.

**PurchPurchaseOrder** is the main place where report switching is done. It is like a thin layer between the report caller and the report itself. All the code is placed in its `main()`. Here we are using a `switch` statement to define rules determining which report is printed. For demonstration purposes we print the standard purchase order report in all cases except when the current company is **CEU**. In this case, we print a newly created **PurchPurchaseOrder2**. In real environments this code has to be modified, so that it reads the report name from some parameters table, for example **VendFormletterParameters**, which is a data source of **Accounts payable | Setup | Forms | Form setup**. The rest of the code runs the report from code.

The final bit is to modify all menu items that are used to run the report. For a purchase order there are three menu items—**PurchPurchaseOrder**, **PurchPurchaseOrderCopy**, and **PurchPurchaseOrderOriginal** —that allow opening the purchase order document report. We need to make sure that our class is called here. Same principle could be applied for other purchase and sales business documents.

# Creating electronic payment format

Electronic payments these days are being used more often. They save time and reduce paperwork. Although Dynamics AX provides a number of standard out-of-the-box electronic payment formats for various countries, there is always the case when the required format is not present or does not exactly match customer bank requirements. In such cases, we either modify the existing format that is the closest match to the required one or even create a totally new format from scratch.

In this recipe, we will create a custom electronic payment format and will process a vendor payment using it. We will learn the general principles of building such functionality.

## How to do it...

1.  Open AOT and create a new class called **VendOutPaymRecord_Test** with the following code:

```
class VendOutPaymRecord_Test extends VendOutPaymRecord
{
}
void output()
{
    str         outRecord;
    Name        companyName;
```

```
        BankAccount bankAccount;
        ;

        outRecord = strrep(' ', 50);
        companyName = substr(
            custVendPaym.recieversCompanyName(), 1, 40);
        bankAccount = substr(
            custVendPaym.recieversBankAccount(), 1, 8);
        outRecord = strpoke(outRecord, companyName, 1);
        outRecord = strpoke(outRecord, bankAccount, 43);
        file.write(outRecord);
    }
```

2. Create another class named **VendOutPaym_Test** with the following code:

```
class VendOutPaym_Test extends VendOutPaym
{
}
public PaymInterfaceName interfaceName()
{
    return "Test payment format";
}
public classId custVendOutPaymRecordRootClassId()
{
    return classnum(VendOutPaymRecord_Test);
}
protected Object dialog(
    DialogRunbase _dialog,
    boolean _forceOnClient)
{
    DialogRunbase dialog;
    ;

    dialog = super(dialog, _forceOnClient);
    this.dialogAddFileName(dialog);
    return dialog;
}
boolean validate()
{
    return true;
}
void open()
{
    #LocalCodePage
    ;

    file = CustVendOutPaym::newFile(filename, #cp_1252);
    if (!file || file.status() != IO_Status::Ok)
    {
```

```
        throw error(
            strfmt("File %1 could not be opened.", filename));
    }
    file.outFieldDelimiter('');
    file.outRecordDelimiter('\r\n');

    file.write("Starting file:");
}

public void close()
{;
    file.write("Closing file.");
}
```

3.  Open **Accounts payable | Setup | Payment | Methods of payment** and create a new record as follows:

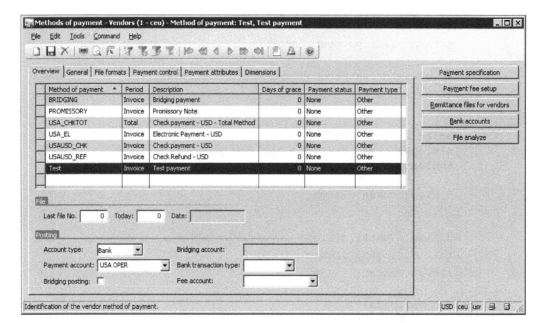

4. Open the **File formats** tab page, click on the **Setup** button and move **Test payment format** from the right to the left:

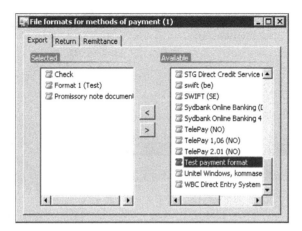

5. Then go back to the **Methods of payment** form and select this format as **Export format**:

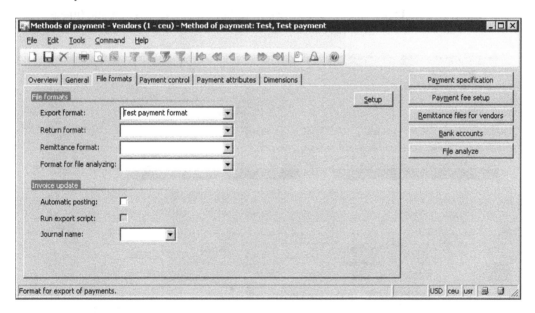

6. Open **Accounts payable |Journals | Payments | Payment journal** and create a new journal:

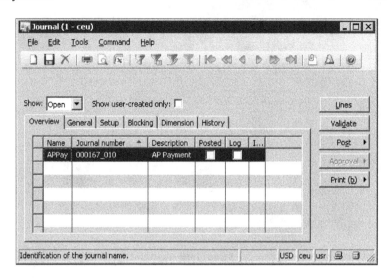

7. Click on the **Lines** button to open the journal lines and create a new line (make sure you set Method of payment to Test):

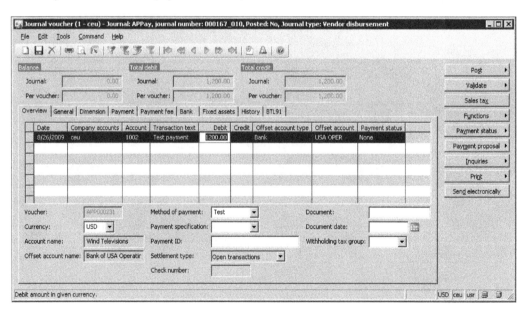

8. Next, click **Functions | Generate payments**. Fill in the dialog fields as below:

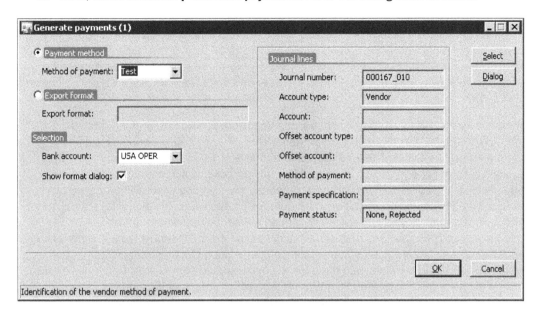

9. Click **OK** and choose the export file name:

10. Click **OK** to complete the process and notice that the journal line's **Payment status** changed from **None** to **Sent**. That means payment was generated successfully.

11. Open the created file with any text editor, for example **Notepad** to check its content:

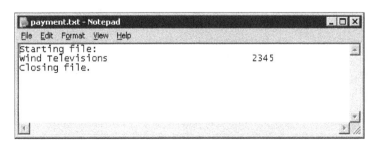

## How it works...

In this recipe we created two new classes, which are required for generating vendor payments, which are normally presented as text files to be sent to the bank. The first one is **VendOutPaymRecord_Test**, which is responsible for formatting payment lines and the second one **VendOutPaym_Test**, which generates header and footer records and creates the payment file itself.

The **VendOutPaymRecord_Test** class extends **VendOutPaymRecord** and inherits all required methods. We only need to override its output() to define our own logic for formatting payment lines. The idea here is to format a string variable, which represents a single payment line. We use outRecord for this purpose, which we initially fill in with **50** spaces using strrep() function. For demonstration purposes, we will only have two values—company name and bank account number—in each line. The global custVendPaym already holds that information and we only need to use the relevant methods— recieversCompanyName() and recieversBankAccount()—to retrieve it. Let's assume here that a bank requirement is to have the company name starting from position 1 and its length should be 40 symbols, and the bank account number should start from position 43 and its length should be 8 symbols (normally a bank provides specifications of its format). So first, we need to make sure that our value does not exceed the required length by trimming it using the substr() function. Next, we use the strpoke() function to insert the prepared values into outRecord at the 1st and 43rd positions. And finally, we insert this into the file by calling write() on the global file variable.

**VendOutPaym_Test** extends **VendOutPaym** and also inherits most of the common member methods. We only need to override those that are either mandatory or specific to our custom format:

▶ interfaceName() returns a name of the payment format. Normally, this text is shown in that user interface.

▶ custVendOutPaymRecordRootClassId() returns a number of the class, which generates payment lines. In our case, it is **VendOutPaymRecord_Test**.

▶ dialog() is used only if we need to add something to the user dialog when generating payments. Our payment is a text file so we need to ask a user to specify its name. We do that by calling dialogAddFileName(), which is a member method of the parent class. It will automatically add a file selection control and we do not have to worry about things like a label or how to get its user input. There are a number of other standard controls, which can be added to the dialog by calling various dialogAdd...() member methods. Additional controls can also be added here by using addField() or similar methods of the dialog object.

▶ validate() is one of the mandatory methods. Normally, user input validation should go here. Our example does not have any validation, so we simply return true.

▶ In `open()`, we are responsible for preparing a `file` object for further processing. Here we use `newFile()` on the **CustVendOutPaym** class to create a new `file` instance. After standard validations we set field and row delimiters by calling its `outFieldDelimiter()` and `outRecordDelimiter()` respectively. In this example, the values in each line should not be separated by any symbol, so we call `outFieldDelimiter()` with an empty `string`. We call `outRecordDelimiter()` with `\r\n` to define that every line ends with a line break. Note that the last line of this method writes some text to the file header. This probably will not make any sense to the bank, but it will definitely make sense to us. We will see that text later in the generated file.

▶ And the last one is `close()`, which is used to perform additional actions before the file is closed. Here we specify some text for simple tracking of what goes where in the generated file.

Now this new payment format is ready to be used. After some setup we can start creating vendor payment journals with this type of payment. Note the file generated in the example before. We can clearly see all texts and variables defined in the classes. These places should be replaced with your own code to build custom electronic payment formats for Dynamics AX.

# Building a "Display dimensions" dialog

People who use the Dynamics AX application often, probably must have already noticed the **Display dimensions** button on some forms. Normally it is displayed on its own or under the **Inventory** button. This button always comes on the forms that have an inventory item and its dimensions, for example Sales order or Purchase order forms. Normally, item dimensions are **Configuration**, **Size**, **Color**, **Warehouse**, and so on depending on the license and system configuration. The button invokes a dialog that allows controlling the number of displayed inventory dimensions in the overview grid.

In this recipe, we will learn how to create such a button and all the associated functionality. This is very useful when creating custom forms with inventory controls.

For this recipe, we will define our requirement to have a default item for each item group. So we are going to add an item number and inventory dimension controls to the **Item group** form.

## How to do it...

1. Open the **InventItemGroup** table in AOT and add a new field:

| Property | Value |
| --- | --- |
| Type | String |
| Name | ItemId |
| ExtendedDataType | ItemId |

2. Add another field to the same table:

| Property | Value |
|---|---|
| Type | String |
| Name | InventDimId |
| ExtendedDataType | InventDimId |

3. In AOT create a new job with the following code:

```
static void InventItemGroupPopulateDim(Args _args)
{
    InventItemGroup  inventItemGroup;
    InventDimId      inventDimIdBlank;
    ;

    inventDimIdBlank =
        InventDim::findOrCreateBlank(false).inventDimId;
    ttsbegin;
    while select forupdate inventItemGroup
    {
        inventItemGroup.InventDimId = inventDimIdBlank;
        inventItemGroup.doUpdate();
    }
    ttscommit;
}
```

4. Run the job to populate the empty **InventDimId** field in the **InventItemGroup** table:

5. In AOT, create a new class named **InventDimCtrl_Frm_ItemGroup** with the following code:

```
class InventDimCtrl_Frm_ItemGroup extends InventDimCtrl_Frm
{
}
public static InventDimCtrl_Frm_ItemGroup construct()
{
    return new InventDimCtrl_Frm_ItemGroup();
}
public static InventDimCtrl_Frm_ItemGroup newFromForm(
    FormRun _formRun)
{
    InventDimAxFormAdapter        adapter;
    InventDimCtrl_Frm_ItemGroup inventDimCtrl;
    ;

    adapter = InventDimAxFormAdapter::newFromForm(_formRun);
    inventDimCtrl = InventDimCtrl_Frm_ItemGroup::construct();
    inventDimCtrl.parmCallingElement(adapter);
```

```
        inventDimCtrl.init();
        return inventDimCtrl;
    }
    NoYes mustEnableField(FieldId _dimFieldId)
    {
        boolean ret;
        ;

        ret = this.dimSearch().find(
            inventDimGroupId,
            _dimFieldId);
        ret = ret && this.dimSearch().dimActive();
        return ret;
    }
    NoYes mustMarkFieldAsMandatory(FieldId _dimFieldId)
    {
        boolean ret;
        ;

        ret = this.mustEnableField(_dimFieldId);
        ret = ret && this.dimSearch().dimMandatory();

        return ret;
    }
```

6. Open the **InventItemGroup** form in AOT and add the following line of code to its class declaration:

```
InventDimCtrl_Frm_ItemGroup inventDimFormSetup;
```

7. Create the following methods on the same form:

```
void updateDesign(InventDimFormDesignUpdate _update)
{
    InventDimParm    inventDimParmVisibleGrid;
    InventTable      inventTable;
    ;

    switch (_update)
    {
        case InventDimFormDesignUpdate::Init:
            if (!inventDimFormSetup)
                inventDimFormSetup =
                    InventDimCtrl_Frm_ItemGroup::newFromForm(
                        element);
            inventDimParmVisibleGrid.ConfigIdFlag     = true;
            inventDimParmVisibleGrid.InventSizeIdFlag = true;
            inventDimParmVisibleGrid.InventColorIdFlag = true;
            inventDimFormSetup.parmDimParmVisibleGrid(
```

```
                inventDimParmVisibleGrid);
        case InventDimFormDesignUpdate::Active:
        case InventDimFormDesignUpdate::FieldChange:
            inventTable = InventTable::find(
                InventItemGroup.ItemId);
            inventDimFormSetup.formActiveSetup(
                inventTable.DimGroupId);
            inventDimFormSetup.formSetControls(true);
            break;
        default:
            throw error(Error::missingParameter(null));
    }
}
public void init()
{;
    super();
    element.updateDesign(InventDimFormDesignUpdate::Init);
}
Object inventDimSetupObject()
{
    return inventDimFormSetup;
}
```

8. Add a new data source to the form:

| Property | Value |
|---|---|
| Name | InventDim |
| Table | InventDim |
| JoinSource | InventItemGroup |
| LinkType | InnerJoin |
| DelayActive | No |

9. Override the `active()` and `validateWrite()` methods of the **InventItemGroup** data source with the following code:

```
public int active()
{
    int ret;
    ;

    ret = super();
    element.updateDesign(InventDimFormDesignUpdate::Active);
    return ret;
}
public boolean validateWrite()
{
```

```
        boolean ret;
        ;

        InventItemGroup.InventDimId =
            InventDim::findOrCreate(InventDim).InventDimId;
        ret = super();
        return ret;
    }
```

10. Override `modified()` on the **ItemId** field on the same data source:

```
public void modified()
{;
    super();
    element.updateDesign(
        InventDimFormDesignUpdate::FieldChange);
    inventDim.clearNotSelectedDim(
        element.inventDimSetupObject().parmDimParmEnabled());
}
```

11. Add a new **StringEdit** control to the form's grid:

| Property | Value |
|---|---|
| Name | InventItemGroup_ItemId |
| DataSource | InventItemGroup |
| DataField | ItemId |

12. Also add a new **Group** control to the form's grid:

| Property | Value |
|---|---|
| Name | InventoryDimensionsGrid |
| DataSource | InventDim |
| DataGroup | InventoryDimensions |
| AutoDataGroup | Yes |

13. Add a new **TabPage** control to the form's **Tab**:

| Property | Value |
|---|---|
| Name | Dimension |
| Caption | Dimension |

14. Add a new **Group** control to the created tab page:

| Property | Value |
| --- | --- |
| Name | InventoryDimensions |
| DataSource | InventDim |
| DataGroup | InventoryDimensions |
| AutoDataGroup | Yes |

15. And finally, add a new **MenuItemButton** control to the form's **ButtonGroup**:

| Property | Value |
| --- | --- |
| Name | InventDimParmFixed |
| MenuItemType | Display |
| MenuItemName | InventDimParmFixed |
| SaveRecord | No |

16. As a result, the form should look like following in AOT:

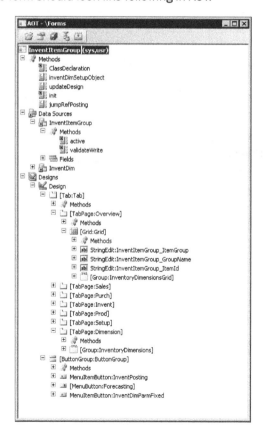

17. Now open **Inventory management | Setup | Item group** and notice the new inventory dimensions controls:

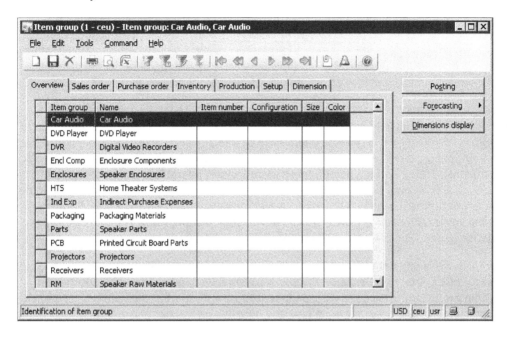

18. Use the **Dimensions display** button to control which dimension fields should be visible on the form:

## How it works...

In Dynamics AX each unique combination of inventory dimensions (**Configuration**, **Size**, **Color**, **Warehouse**, etc.) is stored in the **InventDim** table and has a unique identification number. This prevents us from having redundant information in every table where we need to store inventory dimensions. By using this principle instead of having a number of fields for each dimension separately, we have only one field referring to the **InventDim** table.

In this demonstration, the first step is to add two new fields to the **InventItemGroup** table. One field will store inventory item number and the other one, the number of the inventory dimension combination. In order to maintain data integrity of the existing item group, it is also important to populate the **InventDimId** field with the value of empty dimension combination. We create and run a new job named **InventItemGroupPopulateDim**, which does exactly that. Such a task is not necessary when creating new tables, which obviously initially do not have any data. The job loops through all item group records and fills the **InventDimId** field with the value representing the empty dimension combination, which is found by calling `findOrCreateBlank()` on the **InventDim** table.

Now when fields and data are ready, we need to create a helper class called **InventDimCtrl_Frm_ItemGroup** and design it to correctly handle dimension controls on the **Item group** form. This class extends **InventDimCtrl_Frm**, which contains all the generic functionality. We only need to create new and override several existing member methods in order to implement custom behavior:

> ▶ `construct()` is used to return a new instance of this class.

> ▶ `newFromForm()` creates a new instance of this class and additionally ensures correct integration with the form.

> ▶ `mustEnableField()` is used to determine whether dimension control is enabled. It accepts a dimension field number as an argument. Here we check if a particular dimension is active for the current dimension group, which is assigned to the current item. This method is automatically called every time the item number changes or the user selects a new line to make sure that the correct dimension controls are enabled or disabled.

> ▶ `mustMarkFieldAsMandatory()` is used to determine whether the dimension control requires mandatory user input. In this method, first we check if the current dimension is enabled and if it is then it is defined as mandatory in settings. The method returns `true` if both checks are positive.

And finally, we modify the **InventItemGroup** form. We start with its methods:

- In its class declaration we declare the **InventDimCtrl_Frm_ItemGroup** object..

- A new `updateDesign()` is called from a number of other places. The method is split into two parts—one for initialization and another one for updating form design when something changes. The initialization section uses `newFromForm()` of the **InventDimCtrl_Frm_ItemGroup** class to create a new instance, if it is not created yet. Here we can also specify which dimension controls are visible initially by calling `parmDimParmVisibleGrid()` on the `inventDimFormSetup` object. In this recipe, we chose to show **Configuration**, **Size**, and **Color** controls by default. The second section updates `inventDimFormSetup` with a new item dimension group if the user changes an item or selects another line. As we have seen before, the item dimension group is used to determine which dimension controls should be enabled and be mandatory.

- Form's `init()` calls `updateDesign()` to make sure that the `inventDimFormSetup` object is initialized properly.

- `inventDimSetupObject()` is used to get the reference to the `inventDimFormSetup` instance from the **Inventory dimensions** dialog.

A new data source **InventDim** has to be added to the form and it will be a source for dimension controls. It is connected to **InventItemGroup** using an inner join.

We also need to override several **InventItemGroup** data source methods to make sure everything works correctly:

- `active()` calls the form's `updateDesign()`, which updates dimension controls. `active()` is called every time the user selects another record.

- In `validateWrite()` we use `findOrCreate()` of the **InventDim** table to search for an existing inventory dimension combination. This method accepts a **InventDim** data source as a buffer for retrieving user input values. `findOrCreate()` creates a new dimension combination and its number if no existing dimension is found.

- `modified()` on the **ItemId** field behaves the same way as `active()` does, plus it clears non relevant dimension controls once the user selects a new item.

The final step is to add the item and its dimensions to the overview grid. We also add an additional tab page where all dimensions are listed. This ensures that the user has access to the required dimension even if it is hidden on the overview page. And of course, we add a new **MenuItemButton** button, which calls the **InventDimParmFixed** menu item upon user selection, to open dimension setup form.

# 6
# Integration with Microsoft Office

In this chapter, we will cover:

- ▶ Creating Excel files
- ▶ Reading Excel files
- ▶ Creating Word document from templates
- ▶ Creating configuration documents using Word
- ▶ Exporting data to Microsoft Project
- ▶ Sending email using Outlook

## Introduction

In most of the companies where Dynamics AX is implemented, people use **Microsoft Office** too. The new **Dynamics AX 2009** is now even closer—similar navigation, look and feel, out-of-the-box integration, etc.

In this chapter, we will pay special attention to **Microsoft Office** applications like **Excel**, **Word**, **Project**, and **Outlook**. We will learn how to create and read various Office documents, which could be used for exporting/importing business data for further distribution or analysis. We will also see how personalized documents could be created within Dynamics AX from predefined templates.

# Creating Excel files

**Microsoft Office Excel** format is one of the formats that have been supported by Dynamics AX since its early versions. For example, the **Document handling** feature allows producing **Excel** files using the data from the system. In the new version of Dynamics AX, i.e. Dynamics AX **2009**, this feature is extended even more. Now almost every form has a button called **Export to Excel**, which quickly allows loading form data into **Excel** for further analysis using powerful **Excel** tools.

**Microsoft Office Excel** format handling is done with the help of standard Dynamics AX application classes prefixed with **SysExcel**. Basically, those classes are **Excel** COM wrappers plus they contain additional helper methods to ease the developer's tasks.

To demonstrate the principle in this recipe, we will create a new **Excel** file and fill it with a customer list. This technique could be used to export any business data in a similar way.

## How to do it...

1. Open AOT, and create a new class named **CreateExcelFile** with the following code:

```
class CreateExcelFile
{
}
public static void main(Args args)
{
    CustTable            custTable;
    SysExcelApplication  application;
    SysExcelWorkbooks    workbooks;
    SysExcelWorkbook     workbook;
    SysExcelWorksheets   worksheets;
    SysExcelWorksheet    worksheet;
    SysExcelCells        cells;
    SysExcelCell         cell;
    int                  row;
    ;

    application = SysExcelApplication::construct();
    workbooks   = application.workbooks();
    workbook    = workbooks.add();
    worksheets  = workbook.worksheets();
    worksheet   = worksheets.itemFromNum(1);
    cells       = worksheet.cells();
    cells.range('A:A').numberFormat('@');
    while select custTable
    {
        row++;
```

```
            cell = cells.item(row, 1);
            cell.value(custTable.AccountNum);
            cell = cells.item(row, 2);
            cell.value(custTable.Name);
        }
        application.visible(true);
    }
```

2. Run the class, and check the exported list of customers on the screen:

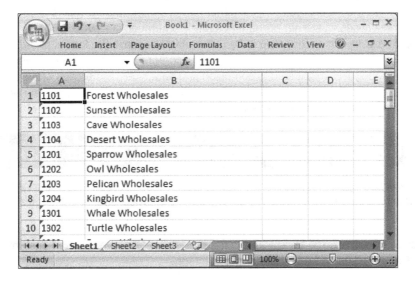

3. Save the list as a file to the documents folder or somewhere on your filesystem for further use in the Reading Excel files recipe.

## How it works...

We start the code by creating the `application` object, which represents **Excel** using one of the already mentioned **SysExcel** classes—**SysExcelApplication**. This is the very top of the **Excel** object hierarchy. The next object is a collection of **Excel** `workbooks`, which we get by calling `workbooks()` on the `application` object. We have to create a new `workbook` by calling `add()` on the `workbooks` object. Each workbook contains a collection of worksheets, which consists of three default worksheets. We get the `worksheets` object by calling `worksheets()` on the workbook, and we get the first sheet by calling `itemFromNum()` with the argument, 1, of the first sheet object. And finally, we get a collection of cells by calling `cells()` on the `worksheet`.

Once we have reached the `cells` object, we set the format of the first column to @. The range of `A:A` is the first column and format @ means text format. This will force the first column to be nothing else but text.

Next, we start looping through the **CustTable** table and fill customer account into the first column and customer name into the second column in each row. In this way, we populate as many rows as we have customers in the system.

Finally, we set the **Excel** `application` to show up on the screen by calling its `visible()` with a `true` argument. It is a good practice to show the **Excel** after all operations are completed, otherwise the user might start changing something while data is still being populated.

As you have noticed, we forced the first column of the sheet, customer account, to be formatted as text, but we left the second column, customer name, as per default. This is because in my data and in most cases, customer account actually is a number like **1000**, **1001**, and so on even though it is stored in a string field in Dynamics AX. If we leave the format of the first column intact, then **Excel** would automatically detect that customer account is a number and would store it as a number. This might lead to confusion and data type mismatches when processing this file later. This is a very common issue when dealing with **Excel** files. Customer name normally cannot have only numbers so it is always automatically detected by **Excel** as text.

# Reading Excel files

Reading **Excel** files is another side of **Excel** file manipulation. It is equally important as file creation. Usage could vary from importing simple data to processing user-filled files like timesheets, purchase orders, etc.

In this recipe, we will use the file created in the previous recipe. We will read customer data using **SysExcel** classes and will show it on the screen.

## How to do it...

1. In AOT, create a new class called **ReadExcelFile** with the following code:

```
class ReadExcelFile
{
}

public static void main(Args args)
{
    SysExcelApplication  application;
    SysExcelWorkbooks    workbooks;
    SysExcelWorkbook     workbook;
    SysExcelWorksheets   worksheets;
    SysExcelWorksheet    worksheet;
    SysExcelCells        cells;
    COMVariantType       type;
```

```
int                 row;
CustAccount         account;
CustName            name;
#define.Filename('<documents>\\customers.xlsx')
;

application = SysExcelApplication::construct();

workbooks   = application.workbooks();

try
{
    workbooks.open(#Filename);
}
catch (Exception::Error)
{
    throw error("File cannot be opened.");
}
workbook    = workbooks.item(1);

worksheets = workbook.worksheets();

worksheet   = worksheets.itemFromNum(1);

cells       = worksheet.cells();

do
{
    row++;
    account = cells.item(row, 1).value().bStr();
    name    = cells.item(row, 2).value().bStr();
    info(strfmt('%1 - %2', account, name));
    type = cells.item(row+1, 1).value().variantType();
}
while (type != COMVariantType::VT_EMPTY);

application.quit();
}
```

2. Run the class and check the results displayed in the **Infolog**:

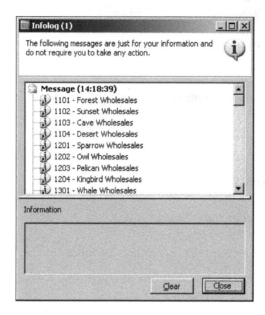

## How it works...

In the variable declaration section in `main()`, replace `<documents>` with your own directory path and `customers.xlsx` with your file saved in the previous recipe. Do not forget to use double backslashes for folder separation, i.e. `\\`.

The first few lines of code in the `main()` method creates a new **Excel** application object `application`, opens first workbook, and gets a reference to the cell collection object `cells`. This is done very much in the same way as in the previous recipe.

Next, we use a do...while loop until the first cell of the next row is empty. Inside the loop, we read the customer account from the first and customer name from the second cell of each row and output them on the screen using the `info()` function. The `value()` method of `cells` returns an object of type **COMVariant**. We know that both columns are formatted as text, so we use `bStr()` to get cell content.

Speaking about cell formats, the **COMVariant** class is used for storing various types of data when dealing with external objects. It could be of any type like string, integer, decimal, etc. In most cases when we do not know what type of data to expect for each cell, we may call `variantType()`, which returns a **COMVariantType** enumeration. This enumeration shows what kind of data is stored in the cell, and depending on the result, we may use `bStr()`, `int()`, `float()`, or other relevant methods of **COMVariant**. Normally, a whole range of checks has to be performed to determine the correct data type. A good example of such checks could be `convertVariant2Str()` of **COSExcelImport** or `variant2Str()` of **GanttVcDataTableField** in the standard application.

# Creating Word documents from templates

Even though **Microsoft Office Word** does not have standard helper classes in Dynamics AX like **Excel** does, **Word** documents can be created using very similar procedures by calling COM objects directly. A good example of how to create **Word** (also **PowerPoint** and **Visio**) documents from scratch is the **Task Records** tool, which is a part of the **Dynamics AX 2009** application (for older versions of Dynamics AX, it can be installed separately). The tool can be started from the **Tools** menu, and it can record a list of user actions to a **Word** document. The main document creation code is located in the **SysTaskRecorderDocStandardWord** class, and it is worth looking at the class to understand how **Word** documents can be created.

Another good place to start with **Word** documents in Dynamics AX is the standard **Document handling** feature. It allows building documents like a letter or fax from attached templates for any record in the system. But the usage of standard **Document handling** is somewhat limited, as, for example, it does not support table **display** methods and data with complex relations might not be displayed correctly. In such cases, customization is required.

To learn the principle in this recipe, we will add a function to the **Contact Details** form, which allows creating a personalized letter for a selected contact. Instead of creating a **Word** document from scratch, we will use a prepared template very similar way the **Document handling** does.

## Getting ready

Before we start with the code, we create a new **Microsoft Word** template, and save it as `Letter.dotx`. Add some text and four bookmarks (**Insert | Links | Bookmark** menu) as per the list below:

- **ContactPerson_Name** one space after **Dear**.
- **DirPartyTable_Name** next line after **Kind Regards,**.
- **CompanyInfo_Name** next line after **DirPartyTable_Name**.
- **CompanyInfo_Phone** one space after **Tel.:**.

The letter should look like the following:

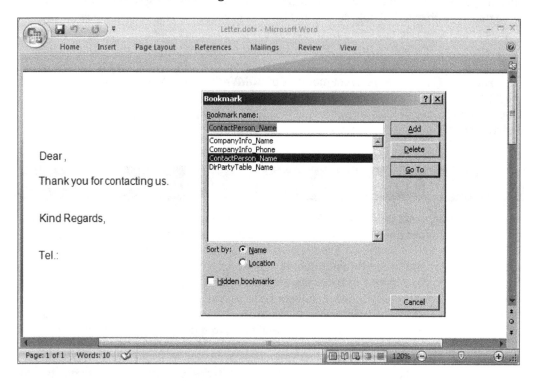

## How to do it...

1. In AOT, create a new class called **CreateWordLetter** with the following code:

```
class CreateWordLetter extends RunBase
{
    DialogField dlgTemplate;
    Filename    template;
    Common      common;
    COM         word;
    COM         document;
    COM         bookmarks;

    #define.Word('Word.Application')

    #define.CurrentVersion(1)
    #localmacro.CurrentList
        template
    #endmacro
}
```

```
public Common parmCommon(Common _common = common)
{;
    common = _common;
    return common;
}

public static CreateWordLetter construct(Common _common)
{
    CreateWordLetter createWordLetter;
    ;

    createWordLetter = new CreateWordLetter();
    createWordLetter.parmCommon(_common);

    return createWordLetter;
}

public container pack()
{
    return [#CurrentVersion, #CurrentList];
}

public boolean unpack(container packedClass)
{
    int version = RunBase::getVersion(packedClass);
    ;

    switch (version)
    {
        case #CurrentVersion:
            [version, #CurrentList] = packedClass;
            return true;
        default :
            return false;
    }

    return false;
}

protected Object dialog()
{
    Dialog          dialog;
    ;
```

```
        dialog = super();

        dialog.caption("Select letter template");

        dlgTemplate = dialog.addFieldValue(
            typeid(FilenameOpen), template, "Template");

        return dialog;
    }

public boolean getFromDialog()
{;
        template = dlgTemplate.value();

        return true;
    }

void openWord()
{
    COM documents;
    ;

    try
    {
        word = new COM(#Word);
    }
    catch (Exception::Internal)
    {
        if (word == null)
        {
            throw error("Microsoft Word is not installed.");
        }
    }

    documents = word.documents();
    document  = documents.add(template);
    }

void processBookmark(str _name, anytype _value)
{
    COM bookmark;
    COM range;
    ;

    if (!bookmarks.exists(_name))
    {
```

```
        return;
    }

    bookmark = bookmarks.item(_name);
    range    = bookmark.range();

    range.insertAfter(_value);
}

void processTable(Common _common)
{
    DictTable dictTable;
    FieldId   fieldId;
    DictField dictField;
    ;

    dictTable = new DictTable(_common.TableId);

    for (fieldId = dictTable.fieldNext(0);
         fieldId;
         fieldId = dictTable.fieldNext(fieldId))
    {
        dictField = dictTable.fieldObject(fieldId);
        this.processBookmark(
            dictTable.name()+'_'+dictField.name(),
            _common.(dictField.id())));
    }
}

public boolean validate()
{;
    if (!common)
    {
        return false;
    }

    return true;
}

public void run()
{
```

```
        EmplTable emplTable;
        ;

        this.openWord();

        bookmarks = document.bookmarks();

        emplTable = EmplTable::find(
            SysCompanyUserInfo::current().EmplId);

        this.processBookmark('Date', systemdateget());
        this.processTable(common);
        this.processTable(CompanyInfo::find());
        this.processTable(emplTable.dirPartyTable());

        word.visible(true);
    }

public static void main(Args _args)
{
    CreateWordLetter createWordLetter;
    ;

    if (!_args || !_args.record())
    {
        throw error(Error::missingRecord(funcname()));
    }

    createWordLetter = CreateWordLetter::construct(
        _args.record());

    if (createWordLetter.prompt())
    {
        createWordLetter.run();
    }
}
```

2. In AOT, create a new **Action** menu item with the following properties:

| Property | Value |
| --- | --- |
| Name | CreateWordLetter |
| ObjectType | Class |
| Object | CreateWordLetter |
| Label | Create letter |

3. Add the created menu item to the bottom of the **smmContactPerson** form's **ButtonGroup** by creating a new MenuItemButton control with the following properties:

| Property | Value |
| --- | --- |
| Name | CreateWordLetter |
| MenuItemType | Action |
| MenuItemName | CreateWordLetter |
| DataSource | ContactPerson |

4. In AOT, the form should look like the following screenshot:

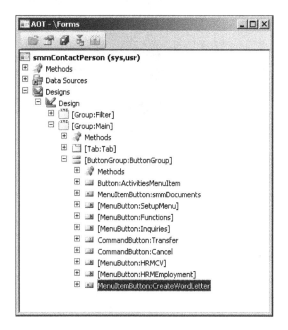

5.   Open **Basic | Setup | Addresses | Contact Details** or **CRM | Contact Details** and select any record:

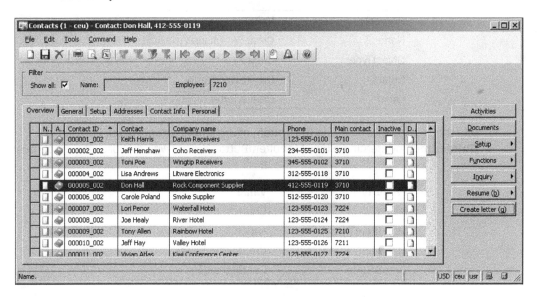

6.   Click the **Create letter** button, and choose the previously created **Word** template in the following dialog:

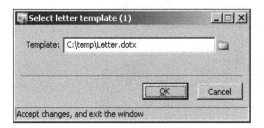

7. Click **OK** to view prepared letter. Note the data taken from the contact record, company information table, and details of the currently logged user:

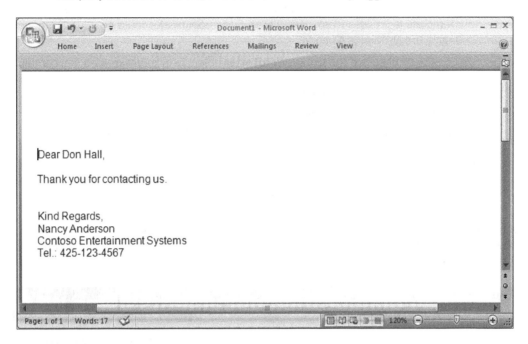

# How it works...

For the purpose of this recipe we created a new class, which extends the **RunBase** framework. This allows us to utilize its automatic features like last value or displaying dialog in our custom class. The following member methods were added:

- `parmCommon()` sets or gets the `common` parameter.
- `construct()` creates a new instance of this class.
- `pack()` prepares user data to be stored for the next time.
- `unpack()` retrieves stored data (if any).
- `dialog()` changes the default dialog caption and adds a new file selection field.
- `getFromDialog()` stores the user file selection into the `template` variable upon dialog closure.
- `openWord()` creates a new instance of **Word** and initializes the `document` object for further use. We create this object by calling `add()` on the document collection object `documents` with the template name as an argument.
- `processBookmark()` searches the collection of **Word** bookmarks for an existing one and inserts the given value if the bookmark is found.

- ▶ `ProcessTable()` accepts any record as an argument and loops through all its fields and values trying to find an existing bookmark formatted as **<table>_<field>** in our **Word** template and insert the field value. The given format will ensure that our template is processed successfully and new bookmarks could be added without changing the Dynamics AX code.

- ▶ `validate()` checks if the **CreateWordLetter** object is properly created, i.e. contains a value to be processed in the `common` variable. In our case, this is **ContactPerson** table records, but in theory could be any other table.

- ▶ `run()` is where the major code is located. In here, we first initialize the **Word** application and `bookmarks`. The next step is to find the **EmplTable** table record of the currently logged user and then start inserting values into bookmarks—contact person record, company information, and employee information. And finally, we display the results.

- ▶ `main()` simply puts everything together.

Once the class is ready, we create an **Action** menu item pointing to this class and add it to the **Contact Details** form as a button. This allows us to use the button to create and display a personalized letter for the selected contact person.

# Creating configuration documents using Word

When a Dynamics AX project comes to an end it is time to create a system configuration document and present it to the customer. Normally, it is a time-consuming task to manually go though all the parameter tables used and transfer their content to a document, in most of the cases, **Word** document.

Just recently, I created a small Dynamics AX job for myself, which helps me with this task, and I think it is worth sharing. The job reads the data from a defined list of parameter tables and dumps all the data into a **Word** document along with field labels. The only manual thing to do is to tidy up the document and send it to the customer.

In this recipe, we will explore the principle behind this. To make this example more interesting, we will integrate this function into Dynamics AX by means of the right-click context menu.

## Getting ready

Again, prepare a new **Microsoft Word** template, and save it as `table.dotx`. The template should contain one bookmark named **TableName** at the top and one table with a single row and two columns, as shown next:

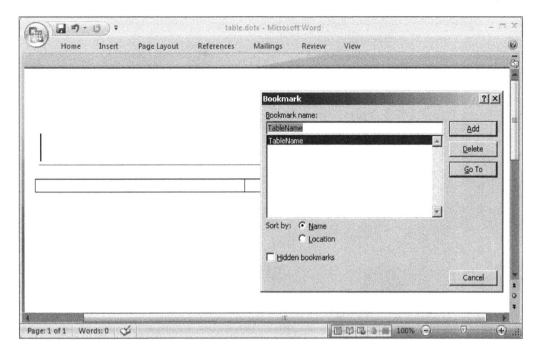

## How to do it...

1. In AOT, create a new class called **CreateWordTable** with the following code:

```
class CreateWordTable extends CreateWordLetter
{
    TableId tableId;
}

protected Object dialog()
{
    Dialog dialog;
    ;

    dialog = super();
    dialog.caption("Select table template");
    return dialog;
}

TableId parmTableId(TableId _tableId = tableId)
{;
```

```
            tableId = _tableId;
            return tableId;
        }

    void initCommon()
    {
        Query    query;
        QueryRun queryRun;
        ;

        query = new Query();
        query.addDataSource(tableId);

        queryRun = new QueryRun(query);
        queryRun.next();

        common = queryRun.get(tableId);
    }

    public boolean validate()
    {;
        if (!tableId)
        {
            return false;
        }
        return true;
    }

    public void run()
    {
        TmpSysTableField tmpSysTableField;
        DictField        dictField;
        int              i;
        COM              tables;
        COM              table;
        COM              rows;
        COM              row;
        COM              cells;
        COM              cell;
        COM              range;
```

```
;

this.openWord();

tables = document.tables();
table  = tables.Item(1);
rows   = table.rows();

bookmarks = document.bookmarks();
this.processBookmark('TableName', tableid2pname(tableId));

this.initCommon();

tmpSysTableField = TmpSysTableField::findTableFields(
    null, tableId);

while select tmpSysTableField
{
    dictField = new DictField(
        tableId,
        tmpSysTableField.FieldId);

    if (dictField.isSystem())
    {
        continue;
    }

    i++;

    row   = rows.item(i);
    cells = row.cells();

    cell  = cells.item(1);
    range = cell.range();
    range.insertAfter(tmpSysTableField.FieldLabel);

    cell  = cells.item(2);
    range = cell.range();
    range.insertAfter(
        strfmt('%1', common.(tmpSysTableField.FieldId)));

    row = rows.add();
```

```
        }

        row.delete();

        word.visible(true);

    }

    public static CreateWordTable construct(TableId _tableId)
    {
        CreateWordTable createWordTable;
        ;

        createWordTable = new CreateWordTable();
        createWordTable.parmTableId(_tableId);

        return createWordTable;
    }

    public client static void main(Args _args)
    {
        tableId         tableId;
        SysContextMenu  sysContextMenu;
        TreeNode        treeNode;
        CreateWordTable createWordTable;
        ;

        if (SysContextMenu::startedFrom(_args))
        {
            sysContextMenu  = _args.parmObject();
            treeNode        = sysContextMenu.first();
            if (treeNode.applObjectType() ==
                UtilElementType::Table)
            {
                tableId = treeNode.applObjectId();
            }
        }
        else
        {
            tableId = pickTable();
        }
```

```
createWordTable = CreateWordTable::construct(tableId);

if (createWordTable.prompt())
{
    createWordTable.run();
}
}
```

2. In AOT, create a new **Action** menu item with the following properties:

| Property | Value |
| --- | --- |
| Name | CreateWordTable |
| ObjectType | Class |
| Object | CreateWordTable |
| Label | Export to Word |

3. Open the **SysContextMenu** menu in AOT, and add the created menu item to the top:

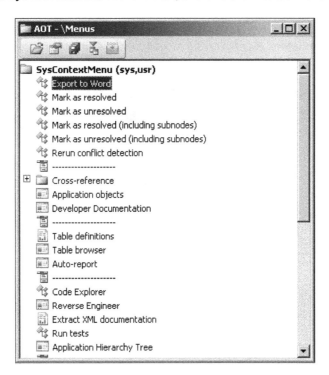

4. Locate the **SysContextMenu** class in AOT, and add the following code to the `verifyItem()` method:

```
case menuitemactionstr(CreateWordTable):
    if (this.selectionCount() != 1 ||
        firstNode.AOTIsOld())
    {
        return 0;
    }
    if (!docNode &&
        _firstType == UtilElementType::Table &&
        SysDictTable::newTreeNode(
            firstNode).tableGroup() == TableGroup::Parameter)
    {
        return 1;
    }
    return 0;
```

The code has to be added to this method right after the following lines:

```
case MenuItemType::Action:
    switch (menuItemName)
    {
```

5. To test the results, open **AOT** and find one of the parameters tables, for example, **LedgerParameters**. Right-click the mouse, select **Add-Ins**, and then choose the newly created option **Export to Word**:

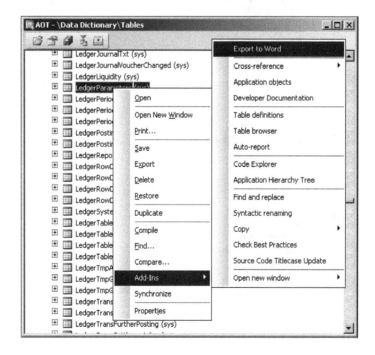

7. The template selection dialog should appear. Choose the previously created **Word** template as follows:

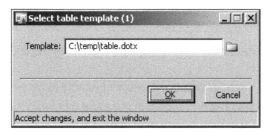

8. Click the **OK** button, and view the results:

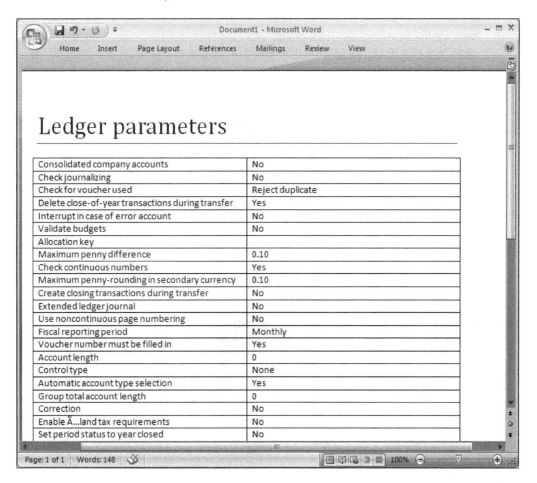

## How it works...

To save our time and to reuse existing code, we are creating a new class that extends **CreateWordLetter** from the previous recipe. The new class contains the following methods:

- `dialog()` only changes the dialog caption. The rest of the code comes from the parent class.
- `parmTableId()` sets or gets the number of a table to be processed.
- `initCommon()` sets the first record of the input table into the `common` variable.
- `validate()` checks if the input table number is present.
- `run()` does the job. We start it by opening the **Word** application and drilling down its object hierarchy, and we get a reference to the table row collection object `rows`. We are going to use it later for adding new rows to it.

  Next, we initialize a `bookmarks` object, and insert the input table name as the document title. Then, we find the first record of the input table to be dumped into the document. Our modification will only be working with parameter tables, which have only a single record, so which is we are not expecting and not processing other records.

  `findTableFields()` of the **TmpSysTableField** table is a useful utility, which returns all given table field properties inserted into a temporary table, which leads us to a following step to loop through this table and insert its data into the document.

  Inside the loop, first we exclude system fields like **RecId**, **dataAreaId**, **modifiedBy**, and so on. Then, we get a reference to a cell collection object `cells` and insert a field label as a first cell and the field value as a second. To insert the data into the cell, we use COM range object `range`, which is a part of the **Word** COM model. We finish each loop by adding a new empty row to the end of the table for the next loop.

  At the end of the `run()`, we delete the last empty table row and show the **Word** application to the user.
- `construct()` creates a new instance of this class.
- `main()` puts everything together.

Next, we create a new **Action** menu item pointing to the new class, and we add that item to the **SysContextMenu** menu. This menu is actually the **Add-Ins** section of the right-click AOT context menu. In this way, we ensure that the user will see an option **Export to Word** once they right-click on some object in AOT.

The last step is to make sure that this option is only visible for parameter tables. We can achieve this by adding a new `case` to the `switch` statement of `verifyItem()` in the **SysContextMenu** class. This method along with the `switch` statement is executed every time a user right-clicks the mouse button on some object in AOT. The method is responsible for checking whether each item of the **SysContextMenu** menu is relevant to the current AOT object. It returns 1 if yes and 0 if no. Our code checks the **CreateWordTable** menu item and returns a positive result if the selected object is not in the old layer (tables in old layer do not have any data) and is a parameter table. This simply means that **Export to Word** will be available only for parameter tables.

# Exporting data to Microsoft Project

Probably, everybody knows that new **Dynamics AX 2009** supports two-way synchronization with **Microsoft Project Server**. Sounds good, but in reality it takes a lot of effort to install and configure all the required components. This feature is also not available for older versions of Dynamics AX. But, what if one wants to simply display Dynamics AX project data as nice chart without installing and configuring additional features? Of course, you could use the integrated **Gantt** chart **ActiveX**, but this again cannot be used that smoothly in practice, especially when it is not possible to save it as a file and share it with other people.

Another approach, which I successfully implemented in one of my projects, could be to use **Microsoft Project** for displaying Dynamics AX project data. In this case, the data is displayed in a well known format and what is very important is that it can be stored as a **Microsoft Project** file for further usage.

In this recipe, we will use **Microsoft Project** to display Dynamics AX hours forecast data in the **Project** module. Here we are going to use COM objects to access **Microsoft Project** in a similar way in which we accessed **Excel** and **Word**.

## Getting ready

We again need to set up some demonstration data. Open the **Project Details** form from the **Project** module. Create a new or select an existing open project. In my case, I selected project No. **10001**. Click on the **Forecast | Hour** button to open the **Hours forecast** form, and create several forecast lines. I created the following records:

| Field | Value |
| --- | --- |
| Forecast model | P-2008 |
| Category | Service |
| Transaction text | Inspection 1 |
| Hours | 20 |
| Work center | 00201 |

| Field | Value |
| --- | --- |
| Forecast model | P-2008 |
| Category | Service |
| Transaction text | Inspection 2 |
| Hours | 12 |
| Work center | 00201 |

The data entered in the **Overview** tab page should look as shown in the following screenshot:

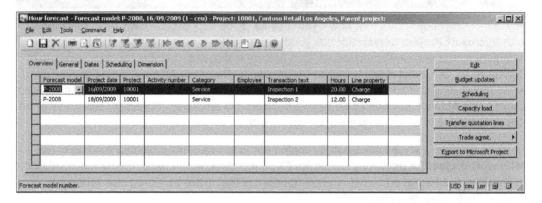

To update scheduling, click **Schedule** and click **OK** to accept the default parameters.

Now, the information on the **Scheduling** tab page should look like the following:

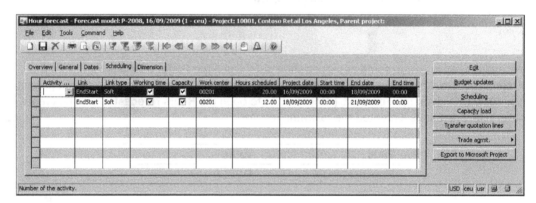

## How to do it...

1. In AOT, create a new class called **CreateProjectFile** with the following code:

```
class CreateProjectFile
{
}

public client static void main(Args _args)
{
    ProjTable          projTable;
    ProjForecastEmpl   forecastEmpl;
    ProjForecastEmpl   parmForecastEmpl;
```

```
COM             msproject;
COM             projects;
COM             project;
COM             tasks;
COM             task;
int             n;
#define.MSProject('MSProject.Application')
;

if (!_args ||
    _args.dataset() != tablenum(projForecastEmpl))
{
    throw error(Error::missingRecord(funcname()));
}

parmForecastEmpl = _args.record();

projTable = ProjTable::find(parmForecastEmpl.ProjId);

try
{
    msproject = new COM(#MSProject);
}
catch (Exception::Internal)
{
    if (msproject == null)
    {
        throw error(
            "Microsoft Project is not installed.");
    }
}

projects = msproject.Projects();
project  = projects.Add();

tasks = project.Tasks();

task = tasks.Add();
task.Name(ProjTable.Name);
task.OutlineLevel(1);
```

```
      while select forecastEmpl
          where forecastEmpl.ProjId  == projTable.ProjId
            && forecastEmpl.ModelId == parmForecastEmpl.ModelId
      {
          task = tasks.Add();
          task.OutlineLevel(2);
          task.Name(forecastEmpl.Txt);
          task.Start(forecastEmpl.SchedFromDate);
          task.Duration(forecastEmpl.SchedTimeHours*60);
          if (n)
          {
              task.LinkPredecessors(tasks.UniqueID(n));
          }
          n = task.UniqueID();
      }

      msproject.visible(true);
  }
```

2.  In AOT, create a new **Action** menu item with the following properties:

| Property | Value |
|----------|-------|
| Name | CreateProjectFile |
| ObjectType | Class |
| Object | CreateProjectFile |
| Label | Export to Microsoft Project |

3.  Add the created menu item to the bottom of the **ProjForecastEmpl** form's **ButtonGroup** group. Set its properties to:

| Property | Value |
|----------|-------|
| Name | CreateProjectFile |
| MenuItemType | Action |
| MenuItemName | CreateProjectFile |
| DataSource | ProjForecastEmpl |

4. In AOT, the form should look like the following:

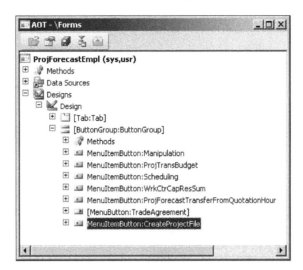

5. To test the export file, open **Project | Project Details**, select the project mentioned earlier, go to **Forecast | Hour**, and click the **Export to Microsoft Project** button to view the forecasted hours as a **Microsoft Project** plan:

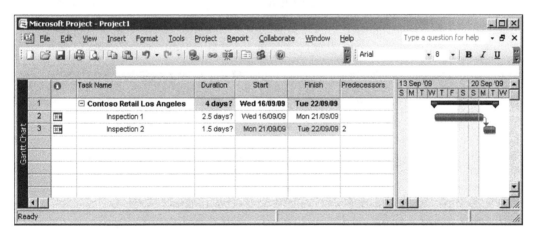

## How it works...

For the purpose of this recipe, we created a new class and placed all code in its `main()` method. The code starts with checking the input record, initializing the `projTable` record, and starting the **Microsoft Project** application.

Using the Microsoft Project model hierarchy, we first get a reference to the project collection object `projects`. Then, we create a new project by calling `Add()`. Each project contains a task collection, where we could add new tasks by calling its `Add()`. We do exactly that for the first level in the project plan, i.e. we create a task whose name is a project name and set its level to `1`.

Next, we loop through all Dynamics AX project hour forecast records and start inserting tasks into the **Microsoft Project** chart into the next level, i.e. `2`. Here, we call `Add()` on the task collection again to create a new task object called `task`. We set its properties like name, start date, and duration. We also define every task to be dependent on the previous one by calling `LinkPredecessors()` with the number of the previous task as an argument.

Once the code is executed, we make Microsoft Project along with the diagram visible to the user.

Finally, we create a new **Action** menu item pointing to our class and add this item to the **Hours forecast** form to make sure the user is able to run it for a selected Dynamics AX project.

Depending on the requirements, this technique could be used to control other aspects like resources, custom properties, and other objects provided by the **Microsoft Project** COM model.

# Sending email using Outlook

In most projects it is required to send emails using Dynamics AX. It might be business alerts, monthly reports, customer statements, and so on. Dynamics AX has a number of ways to send emails. One of them is to use **Microsoft Office Outlook**. Although Dynamics AX supports tight integration with Outlook contacts, calendar, and tasks as a part of the **CRM** module, emailing using **Outlook** is still very basic across the application. Normally, required emailing functions have to be implemented as additional application customizations.

In this recipe, we will see how emails can be sent from Dynamics AX using Outlook. Dynamics AX provides an **API** to access the **Outlook** application. We will use it to create a function that allows sending template-based personalized emails to customers.

## Getting ready

Before we start with this recipe, we need to create an email template. This is standard Dynamics AX functionality. Open **Basic | Setup | E-mail templates**, and create the following record:

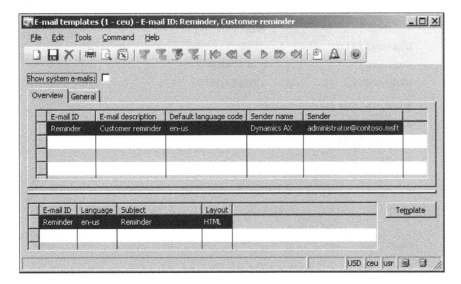

Next click on the **Template** button, and enter the email body:

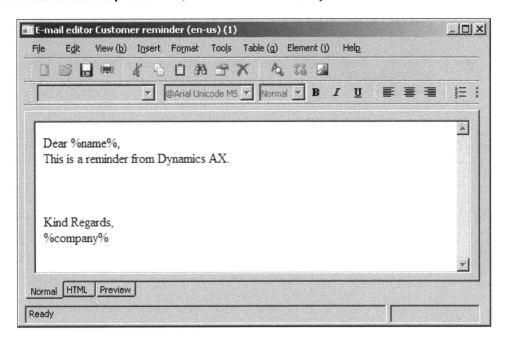

## How to do it...

1.  In AOT, create a new class called **SendEmail** with the following code:

```
class SendEmail extends RunBase
{
    SysEmailId          emailId;
    DialogField         dlgEmailId;
    CustTable           custTable;
    LanguageId          languageId;

    #define.CurrentVersion(1)
    #localmacro.CurrentList
        emailId
    #endmacro
}

void new()
{;
    super();

    languageId = infolog.language();
}

public CustTable parmCustTable(
    CustTable _custTable = custTable)
{;
    custTable = _custTable;
    return custTable;
}

public container pack()
{
    return [#CurrentVersion, #CurrentList];
}

public boolean unpack(container packedClass)
{
```

```
        int version = RunBase::getVersion(packedClass);
        ;

        switch (version)
        {
            case #CurrentVersion:
                [version, #CurrentList] = packedClass;
                return true;
            default :
                return false;
        }

        return false;
    }

    public static SendEmail construct(CustTable _custTable)
    {
        SendEmail sendEmail;
        ;

        sendEmail = new SendEmail();
        sendEmail.parmCustTable(_custTable);

        return sendEmail;
    }

    protected Object dialog()
    {
        Dialog          dialog;
        ;

        dialog = super();

        dialog.caption("Select email template");

        dlgEmailid = dialog.addFieldValue(
            typeid(SysEmailId), emailId);

        return dialog;
    }

    public boolean getFromDialog()
    {;
```

```
            emailId = dlgEmailId.value();

            return true;
        }
    str subject()
        {
            return SysEmailMessageTable::find(
                emailId, languageId).Subject;
        }
    str processMappings(str _message)
        {
            Map mappings;
            ;

            mappings = new Map(Types::String, Types::String);
            mappings.insert('name', custTable.Name);
            mappings.insert('company', CompanyInfo::name());

            return SysEmailMessage::stringExpand(_message, mappings);
        }
    str message()
        {
            COM                 document;
            COM                 body;
            str                 ret;
            SysEmailMessageTable message;
            #help
            ;

            message = SysEmailMessageTable::find(emailId, languageId);

            ret = this.processMappings(message.Mail);

            ret = WebLet::weblets2Html4Help(ret, '');

            document = new COM(#HTMLDocumentClassName);

            SysEmailTable::insertHTML2Document(document, ret);

            body = document.body();

            if (!body)
            {
                return '';
            }
            return body.outerText();
        }
    public boolean validate()
```

```
{;
    if (!custTable)
    {
        return false;
    }

    return true;
}
public void run()
{
    SysInetMail mail;
    ;

    mail = new SysInetMail();
    mail.parmForceSendDialog(true);
    mail.sendMail(
        custTable.Email,
        this.subject(),
        this.message(),
        true);
}

public static void main(Args _args)
{
    SendEmail sendEmail;
    ;

    if (!_args || !_args.record())
    {
        throw error(Error::missingRecord(funcname()));
    }
    sendEmail = SendEmail::construct(
        _args.record());

    if (sendEmail.prompt())
    {
        sendEmail.run();
    }
}
```

2. In AOT, create a new **Action** menu item with the following properties

| Property | Value |
|----------|-------|
| Name | SendEmail |
| ObjectType | Class |
| Object | SendEmail |
| Label | Send email |

3. Add the newly created menu item to the bottom of the **CustTable** form's **ButtonGroup** group by creating a new **MenuItemButton** with the following properties:

| Property | Value |
|----------|-------|
| Name | SendEmail |
| MenuItemType | Action |
| MenuItemName | SendEmail |
| DataSource | CustTable |

4. In AOT, form should look like the following screenshot:

5. Open **Accounts receivable | Customer Details**, and select any customer:

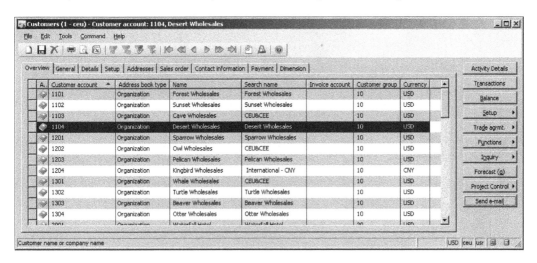

6. Click the **Send e-mail** button, and choose the previously created email template:

7. Click **OK**. If **Outlook** displays a security warning, then click **Allow**:

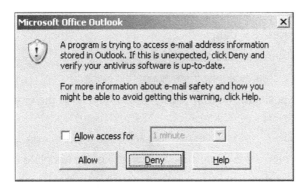

8. And finally, an **Outlook** message editing form is displayed allowing us to change its content before actually sending it:

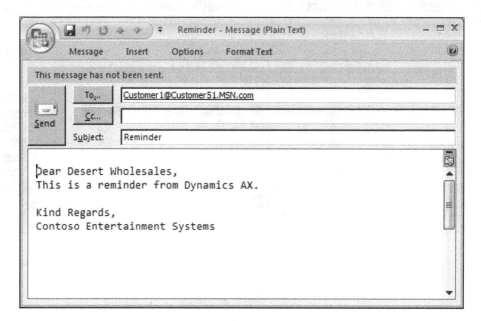

## How it works...

For this recipe we created a new **RunBase**-based class. It contains the following member methods:

- ▸ `new()` is the class constructor, and here we initialize the language variable.
- ▸ `parmCustTable()` sets or gets the `custTable` parameter.
- ▸ `pack()` prepares user data to be stored for the next time.
- ▸ `unpack()` retrieves stored data (if any).
- ▸ `construct()` creates a new instance of this class.
- ▸ `dialog()` changes the default dialog caption and adds the email template selection field.
- ▸ `getFromDialog()` stores the user file selection into the `emailId` variable.
- ▸ `subject()` returns the email subject from the email template table.
- ▸ `processMappings()` replaces the template placeholders with the actual values. Here we use `stringExpand()` of the **SysEmailMessage** class for this purpose.

- ▶ `message()` returns the email body from the email template set up with the processed placeholders. Because the body text is stored as a Dynamics AX weblet, we need to convert it into text format.

  First, we get rid of the weblet tags by using `weblets2Html4Help()` method of **WebLet** application class.

  Next, we convert HTML to text by using a COM class to create an HTML document object and get its content as text by calling `outerText()` on its body element.

- ▶ `validate()` checks if a valid buffer is passed.

- ▶ `run()` creates a new instance of **SysInetMail** and uses its `sendMail()` to send the email. This method takes customer email address, message subject, and message body as arguments.

  Here we also call `parmForceSendDialog()` with `true` right before `sendMail()`. This stops email from being sent automatically and allows the user to modify the message. This parameter overrides the last parameter of `sendMail()`, which does exactly the same but only if there is no email body text.

- ▶ `main()` puts everything together.

Lastly, we create an **Action** menu item pointing to this class, and add it to the **Customers** form as a button. This allows us to use the button to send an email to the selected customer.

# Index

**Thank you for buying**
# Microsoft Dynamics AX 2009 Development Cookbook

# Writing for Packt

We welcome all inquiries from people who are interested in authoring. Book proposals should be sent to author@packtpub.com. If your book idea is still at an early stage and you would like to discuss it first before writing a formal book proposal, contact us; one of our commissioning editors will get in touch with you.

We're not just looking for published authors; if you have strong technical skills but no writing experience, our experienced editors can help you develop a writing career, or simply get some additional reward for your expertise.

# About Packt Publishing

Packt, pronounced 'packed', published its first book "Mastering phpMyAdmin for Effective MySQL Management" in April 2004 and subsequently continued to specialize in publishing highly focused books on specific technologies and solutions.

Our books and publications share the experiences of your fellow IT professionals in adapting and customizing today's systems, applications, and frameworks. Our solution-based books give you the knowledge and power to customize the software and technologies you're using to get the job done. Packt books are more specific and less general than the IT books you have seen in the past. Our unique business model allows us to bring you more focused information, giving you more of what you need to know, and less of what you don't.

Packt is a modern, yet unique publishing company, which focuses on producing quality, cutting-edge books for communities of developers, administrators, and newbies alike. For more information, please visit our website: www.PacktPub.com.

# Microsoft Dynamics AX 2009 Programming: Getting Started

ISBN: 978-1-847197-30-6          Paperback: 320 pages

Get to grips with Dynamics AX 2009 development quickly to build reliable and robust business applications

1. Develop and maintain high performance applications with Microsoft Dynamics AX 2009

2. Create comprehensive management solutions to meet your customer's needs

3. Best-practices for customizing and extending your own high-performance solutions

# Programming Microsoft Dynamics NAV 2009

ISBN: 978-1-847196-52-1          Paperback: 620 pages

Develop and maintain high performance NAV applications to meet changing business needs with improved agility and enhanced flexibility

1. Create, modify, and maintain smart NAV applications to meet your client's business needs

2. Thoroughly covers the new features of NAV 2009, including Service Pack 1

3. Focused on development for the three-tier environment and the Role Tailored Client

Please check **www.PacktPub.com** for information on our titles